CLARENDON LIBRARY OF LOGIC
AND PHILOSOPHY

General Editor: L. Jonathan Cohen, The Queen's College, Oxford

CHANCE AND STRUCTURE

The Clarendon Library of Logic and Philosophy brings together books, by new as well as by established authors, that combine originality of theme with rigour of statement. Its aim is to encourage new research of a professional standard into problems that are of current or perennial interest.

General Editor: L. Jonathan Cohen, The Queen's College, Oxford

Oxford University Press, Walton Street, Oxford OX2 6DP

Oxford New York Toronto
Delhi Bombay Calcutta Madras Karachi
Petaling Jaya Singapore Hong Kong Tokyo
Nairobi Dar es Salaam Cape Town
Melbourne Auckland

and associated companies in
Berlin Ibadan

Oxford is a trade mark of Oxford University Press

Published in the United States
by Oxford University Press, New York

British Library Cataloguing in Publication Data
Vickers, John M.
Chance and structure : an essay on the
logical foundations of probability.—
(Clarendon library of logic and philosophy).
1. Probabilities—Philosophical perspectives
I. Title 121'.63
ISBN 0-19-824988-8

Library of Congress Cataloging in Publication Data
Vickers, John M.
Chance and structure : an essay on the logical
foundations of probability/John M. Vickers.
p. cm.—(Clarendon library of logic and
philosophy)
Bibliography: p. Includes index.
1. Probabilities. I. Title. II. Series
BC141.V53 1988 160—dc19 88-8652 CIP
ISBN 0-19-824988-8

Typeset in 10/12 pt Times by Colset Private Limited, Singapore
Printed in Great Britain by
Biddles Ltd., Guildford and King's Lynn

Chance and Structure

An Essay on
the Logical Foundations of Probability

JOHN M. VICKERS

CLARENDON PRESS · OXFORD
1988

Acknowledgements

Earlier versions of parts of chapters one, two, and three were given as talks in colloquia at the University of Southern California in 1977, at the University of California, Berkeley, in 1981, at the *Journées internationales sur le cercle de Vienne* in Paris in 1984, and at the 1984 meetings of the Pacific Division of the American Philosophical Association. Much of the material of chapters four and five was discussed in colloquia at the University of Paris (Sorbonne and Val de Marne) in 1979 and 1980 and again in 1982. I am grateful to these audiences and participants for their inspiration and assistance.

Chapters one, two, and three were much improved by Peter Payne's careful and thorough reading and commentary. Donald Davidson read an earlier draft and chapters one and two, in particular, have benefited substantially from his thorough and sympathetic criticism. The advisor to the Oxford University Press read the entire work with comprehensive care. His or her comments motivated revisions, notably in the exposition of chapters four and five, which have improved the work as a whole and those chapters in some detail.

I thank the University of Paris (Val de Marne) for a generous research grant in 1979, and its Institut de recherche universitaire d'histoire de la connaissance, des idées et des mentalités for welcoming me and my work in 1982. I thank above all the Claremont Graduate School and my colleagues there for providing the time and encouragement that made the work possible.

J.M.V.

Paris
March 1986

Table of Contents

Introduction

LAPLACE said that probability depends on our ignorance. Nothing could, for him, be probable in itself; he insisted that "all events, even those which on account of their insignificance do not seem to follow the great laws of nature, are a result of it just as necessarily as the revolutions of the sun".[1] Laplace held a roughly Leibnizean view of knowledge, truth, and probability: all possible worlds, of which just one is actual, consist of different arrangements of the same atoms. An infinite intelligence, capable of knowing these worlds in their entirety, could have no doubt about which of them is actual. Such an intelligence would have no need for probability. It is only the finite capacity of the human mind that supports the central role of probability in our thought. We know some features of the actual world, enough to say that it is one of a certain class W of worlds, though we cannot say precisely which world in W it is. The probability of a judgement is the ratio of the number of worlds in W in which the judgement holds to the total number of worlds in W. As we gain knowledge about the actual world, we exclude worlds from W and hence arrive at probabilities which reflect a greater preponderance of knowledge than ignorance. In some cases and for some judgements we may even be able to exclude from W all worlds in which the judgement fails to hold or all those in which it holds. The probability of the judgement will then be one or zero, and the judgement, or its denial, will be an instance of knowledge. Ignorance will play no role in it.

On this classical view of probability, probabilistic judgement is a way station in the progress to real knowledge. It makes little sense to speak of the real or correct probability of a judgement, since what the probability is depends always upon what we know, upon what worlds can be excluded from the relevant class W.

Kant's view of probability was much like this. He did not take worlds to be arrangements of atoms; not that he took them to be anything else, for he thought that the very notion of a world, as a totality of all that exists, was a confusion. He took possibility to be

---

[1] *A Philosophical Essay on Probabilities*, 3, 6.

an epistemic concept, to be defined in terms of judgement and evidence, not in terms of alternative non-actual entities. Further, Kant took Leibnizean atomism, as well as the contrary view that substance is continuous, to be unverifiable metaphysical conjectures. He did, however, hold that probability depends upon ignorance: "[T]he cognition of the probable", he writes in the *Logic*, ". . . is to be regarded as an approximation to certainty". He took probability to be a ratio, not of numbers of cases or worlds, but of *reasons*; "the proportion of insufficient reasons to the sufficient reason",[2] by which he apparently meant something like the proportion of disjuncts in a necessary disjunctive judgement, each of which entails the statement in question. The disjunction would of course have to consist of equipossible disjuncts, and the non-circular characterization of this seems not to have concerned Kant.

Although he did not think in terms of arrangements of atoms, Kant did hold that "every *thing*, as regards its possibility, is likewise subject to the principle of *complete* determination, according to which if *all the possible* predicates of *things* be taken together with their contradictory opposites, then one of each pair of opposites must belong to it".[3] He also held that, as we might put it today, whatever is known has a consistent and complete extension; that there is one all-inclusive consistent and complete theory that includes all and only the truths about phenomena. Leibniz's mistake, Kant would have said, was to presume that the principle of complete determination entailed that this theory constituted knowledge of things in themselves. He shared Leibniz's progressivism and intellectual optimism; the view that knowledge is cumulative, that we know more than our ancestors did and less than our descendants will, and his view that genuine knowledge could not be probabilistic goes along with this: "Probability", as Laplace would put it, "is relative, in part to [our] ignorance, in part to our knowledge".[4] As science progresses, probability gives way to certainty.

Atomism returned in the present century in the thought of Wittgenstein and Russell. *Logical atomism* is the view that reality consists of simple or atomic *facts* which are compounded in various ways to make up the ordinary objects and situations we take to be real. Logical atomism must thus be distinguished from the physical atomism of Laplace and Democritus, and again from the meta-

---

2 *Logic*, 89, 90.
3 First *Critique*, A571 = B599.
4 *A Philosophical Essay*, 6.

physical atomism of Leibniz. Leibnizean monads are not in space or time, which are just ways in which a monad organizes its apprehensions of other monads. The atomic facts of logical atomism on the other hand can come into being and pass away: "The things that are really real", writes Russell, "last a very short time".[5] A person may, on one form of the view, consist of a spatially and temporally extended series of atomic facts. To say that Socrates is mortal is to say that a certain personal series of atomic facts is arranged in a certain way. To put our language in proper form to describe and discuss reality is to eliminate from it such terms as "Socrates" and "mortal" in favour of more complex and accurate descriptions of the atomic facts and their relations and characters. Indeed, the example just given presumes too much. We cannot even be sure that whatever complex fact corresponds to "Socrates is mortal" will have constituent facts corresponding to "Socrates" and "mortal". The ultimate sectioning of the world may not follow the grammatical lines of that sentence. We must thus treat "Socrates" and "mortal" as what Russell called *incomplete symbols*; grammatical substantives which are not logical substantives, which do not refer to complexes of atomic facts.

Kant's principle of complete determination, formulated by Frege as the requirement that "concepts have sharp boundaries"[6] is as much a part of logical atomism as it was of Laplace's physical atomism. It is an article of intellectual and scientific faith that knowledge rests upon the presumption of its own completability, at least as an ideal.

The account of probability that goes with logical atomism and the theory of incomplete symbols prohibits knowledge from being probabilistic. This account is structurally quite like Laplace's view, though it is less sophisticated and not so carefully worked out. Its outlines are given in section 5.1 of Wittgenstein's *Tractatus Logico-Philosophicus*. The probability of a proposition B, conditional upon a proposition A, is the ratio of the number of *truth-grounds* of A and B together to the number of truth-grounds of A. A truth-ground of a proposition is, roughly, a row in the truth table of the proposition taken as a truth function of atomic facts, in which the proposition receives the value *true*. Wittgenstein says that no proposition in itself can be either probable or improbable. "Only in

---

[5] "The Philosophy of Logical Atomism", 274.

[6] See "Function and Concept" in *Translations from the Philosophical Writings of Gottlob Frege*.

default of certainty do we need probability".[7] Again, as in the classical account, as science progresses and knowledge accumulates, probability gives way to certainty.

More recent accounts of probability along generally atomistic lines have exploited the combined resources of measure theory and metalogic. Tarski showed how sets of theories on a given vocabulary (each theory is a deductively closed set of sentences on the given vocabulary) formed Boolean algebras:[8] the set of all complete and consistent theories including the negation of a sentence A is the complement of the set of all those including the sentence itself; set-theoretical union and intersection correspond similarly to sentential disjunction and conjunction, and so on. It is natural to define probabilities on these sets in accordance with the usual laws of probability interpreted as a definition of normal measures on Boolean algebras.[9] Each theory describes a possible world, and the probability of a sentence is just the probability of the set of all theories that include it; of the set of possible worlds in which the sentence is true. Carnap followed and elaborated the general lines of this development. An exposition and continued elaboration of it is the subject of chapter 2 below. The quite general philosophical setting for this view of probability remains the principle of complete determination according to which probability is an incomplete or imperfect form of knowledge: one of those complete and consistent theories is the whole truth and nothing but the truth. Probabilistic judgement is an admission that we don't know enough to say which one it is.

Atomism, in logical as well as physical and metaphysical forms, is now a pretty tenuous position. The principle of complete determination is also questionable if not discredited. That principle is part of progressivism, the view that knowledge is cumulative, and it is entailed by the denial of discontinuities or cuts between the conceptual schemes of different epochs. It is also tied to the unity and univocity of truth, the presumption of one ideal complete and consistent theory of the world. These quite classical views may not be

[7] *Tractatus Logico-Philosophicus*, 5.156.
[8] See "Foundations of the Calculus of Systems" in *Logic, Semantics, and Metamathematics*.
[9] Stefan Mazurkiewicz seems to have been the first to build on Tarski's work in this way: see "Über die Grundlagen der Wahrscheinlichkeitsrechnung". Tarski refers to this at the end of the article cited above.

obviously wrong, but they should clearly not be taken as philosophical axioms, and to the extent that the classical account of probabilistic knowledge depends upon and nourishes them, that account should be called into question and revised.

These matters are not treated in this book, but they are a part of its motivation. It is at least a great lack, if not a scandal, in epistemology that probabilistic knowledge is still discussed within a generally positivistic framework. It is certainly a scandal that philosophers today should try to address issues in the theories of knowledge, action, value, and mind without serious attention to the function of probabilistic judgement and deliberation in these. We understand how Kant and Husserl could attempt this, but the presumptions that allowed that cannot today go unquestioned.

Rejecting the classical picture of probability and its role in judgement raises new questions and puts old questions in a different light. One old question, much debated by the positivists, was that of the nature or essence of probability. They gave answers of three sorts: probability judgements are either (i) analytic, or (ii) synthetic, or (iii) not judgements at all, not true or false, but expressions of feeling or attitude. To these should be added normative views, according to which probability denotes rational or prudent belief. The first two of these, at least, proposed reductions of probability; definitions of probability in non-probabilistic terms which would adequately account for its function in ordinary and scientific judgement. The third—subjectivism—was often confused about what it proposed, but its temper was in general reductionistic, and it worked to characterize probability in generally psychologistic ways. Normative views raise slightly different questions, but they may nevertheless be considered in the same general framework, roughly as a blend of logical and psychologistic accounts. Contemporary philosophy suspects the analytic–synthetic distinction, and is equally mistrustful of the cluster of concepts that make up the classical account of subjectivity; the distinction of inner from outer, the presumption that the subject's awareness of his own inner states has an evidential privilege all its own, the principle that the honest expression of feelings and attitudes reveals them to the world. None of the above sorts of answer can thus be accepted in its own terms today. Indeed, even the question to which they respond should change. The quest for essences or natures is predicated upon the same scheme of eidetic structure and conceptual composition as the classical notion of analyticity. The question of the definition of probability remains, but in a quite different form; it refers now to the power of certain axiomatic theories of probability measures or functions, and little remains of the epistemological debate of a half-century ago over the nature of probability judgements.

If the question of the nature of probability no longer seems answerable in an interesting way, the task of the characterization of probabilistic knowledge takes on new depth and needs to be faced in the light of probability's changed situation. The important question here is that of *consistency* of probabilistic judgement: under what conditions are sets of probabilistic judgements consistent? A good answer to that question will go a long way toward supplying a good characterization of probabilistic knowledge. Not only will it tell us what probabilistic judgements are valid, but it will also let us know in what ways probabilistic judgements are constrained by other probabilistic judgements about logically related subject matter. Further, an inventory of the terms needed to give adequate consistency criteria will be of great philosophical significance, for it will let us see to what extent probability depends upon other sorts of knowledge. This leads back to something very much like the positivistic question about the nature of probability, but with an important difference, for no reduction or analysis is proposed or looked for. It also lets us see a part of what was deep and appealing about logicism in probability; namely the requirement that probability, in order to be universally applicable, should not depend upon the principles of any special science. For if it does, if the criteria of probabilistic consistency are in part psychological, for example, then its application to psychology will presume what it seeks to adjudicate, namely the status of psychological knowledge.

The criteria of consistency of probabilistic judgement are, it might be said, obvious. They are just the laws of probability, the laws that require that probability is (finitely) additive and that the probability of what is necessary is unity. That is so, but when we think of probability in logical terms, as the consistency question invites us to do, and from a philosophical point of view, two issues move to the foreground. First is that of the status of the laws of probability themselves. That is just the old question of justification, of what Kant called a *deduction* of those laws which justifies their application as a priori principles. Some idea of the import of this can be gained by referring to a question put some years ago in a talk by

C. G. Hempel: a child writes a sum in an arithmetic lesson. What is the function of the laws of arithmetic in our understanding of this action? That is a serious question for the foundations of arithmetic; not that the foundations of arithmetic should provide an answer to the question, but one must always take great care not to render a good answer impossible. The corresponding question about the laws of probability is equally serious: what is the function of the laws of probability in our understanding of probabilistic judgement? Hempel's question is a forceful and elegant reminder of the inadequacies of psychologism as a response to this question.

The second issue is an almost inevitable consequence of thinking of probability in logical (as distinct from metalogical) terms. It is that the laws of probability make no explicit provision for the treatment of embedded or iterated probabilities. Probabilities of probabilities figure essentially in the theory of probability, yet neither frequentism nor logicism develops good consistency criteria for them. De Finetti thought about the problem, though not quite in these terms. Indeed, he usually characterizes his position (subjectivism) as a sort of pre-Kantian empirical idealism and psychologism which looks to "sensations of probability" or prudential imperatives governing the dedicated pursuit of gain to found criteria of consistency.[10] That did not, however, prevent him from conceiving and proving a remarkable reduction of embedded probabilities (discussed in section 2.4, below) in a wide and important class of cases. It is pretty clear that the philosophical and conceptual importance of this result is frequently overlooked or misstated not only by his readers, but also by de Finetti himself.

The question of embedded probabilities is a major topic of this book. The system of probability quantifiers of chapters 4 and 5 is aimed precisely at providing smooth and general consistency criteria for them, section 3.8 treats them in a Carnapian, metalinguistic, framework, and the discussion of chapters 1 and 2 keeps them always in view. Chapters 1 and 2 are an attempt to understand the roots of Carnapian logical probability in a classical (mostly Humean) theory of ideas and judgements. The point of that is to underscore the central role of probability in the classical and contemporary theory of knowledge. Chapter 3 collects in one place the

---

[10] Kant, he says, was a "narrow minded spirit who mortified [thought] and tried to mummify it": *Theory of Probability* vol. 1, p. 22.

basic principles on which Carnapian logical probability depends. The point of that is to give a self-contained and naïve development of enough of that theory to let the general philosophical reader grasp its outlines and relevance.

The subtitle of the book honours Carnap's work of that name and should also make clear the aim of continuing his project. Some justification of that project, suitably transformed, grows out of the discussion of the first two chapters. The fourth and fifth chapters develop a form of logicism in probability which, though quite different from Carnapian logical probability in principles and details, is nevertheless sympathetic with its motivation.

1

Classical Thought and its Transformations

1.1 *The classical theory of ideas*

HUME'S discussion of probability in the *Treatise*[1] is a convenient reference point for an exposition of the philosophy of probability of the time. The distinction that he makes between the probability of chances and the probability of causes is well rooted in the contemporary conceptual structure, and it has significant consequences in the thought of his successors. There is little or no question here of looking for the historical origins of the twentieth-century distinction. The point is rather to see first how an earlier form of that distinction functions in its environment, and secondly, how this earlier form is transformed to become what we know today, in large part through the work of the positivists, as the distinction between logical and empirical probability.

Hume's distinction between two kinds of probability is based on a distinction, which is both evidential and structural, between *relations of ideas* and *matters of fact*. Let us start with an exposition of this.

The classical logicians had nothing like set theory as we know it, and there is thus some anachronism in developing the theory of ideas, as is done here, in terms of set theory. The reasons that justify the anachronism are, first, that the exposition is, for a modern reader, greatly simplified. Secondly, it would be difficult for us to read an historically pure exposition, supposing there to be such, without translating it into set-theoretical form. The great simplification effected in our thought by set theory is practically impossible for us to ignore. Thirdly, the set theory in question is pretty rudimentary, and there is little danger of falling into the trap of attributing set-theoretical views to thinkers of the seventeenth century. For these reasons the exposition that follows makes free use of simple

---

[1] *A Treatise of Human Nature* book 1, part 3, sections 11 and 12.

set-theoretical vocabulary and ideas. What anachronism results is arguably ineliminable in indirect discourse when the object discourse is at this remove from that in which it is discussed.

The classical theory of ideas[2] begins with the distinction of a particular individual substance from its properties or qualities. The properties of a substance are divided into those that are essential to it—those such that any change in them would entail a change in the identity of the substance—and those that the substance possesses contingently.

A property may be simple or complex. In what follows (the source texts respect no such convention) the term *attribute* is reserved always for simple properties. There are thus no complex attributes.

The *idea* of a substance comprehends it in terms of the set of attributes each of which is essential to it. Without trying to say what an idea is, the *comprehension* of an idea may be defined as the set of those attributes each of which is essential to any substance of which it is the idea. So, let us presume, the comprehension of the idea *human* is the set {animal, rational}; whatever is (or is essentially) human must be animal and rational. The *extension* of an idea is the set of individual substances to each of which it applies. The theory is not clear whether an idea must be an idea *of* every substance to which it applies. That is to say, whether an idea has in its extension substances to which some attribute in the comprehension of the idea is not essential. Such a substance would have that attribute, but the attribute would not be essential to it. So, for example, a parrot or a chimpanzee may learn to speak or to write (let us assume) though these skills are not essential to such beasts as they are to men. The theory is not always clear whether or not the beasts are in the extension of the idea of a thing that speaks or writes. Most of the present discussion, the exceptions are noted, applies in either case.

Given a set S of (simple) attributes, the *comprehension space* C(S) is the collection of all non-empty subsets of S. A member of the comprehension space—a set of attributes—is a complex property, made up of the attributes in the set. The *finite* comprehension space with respect to S is the collection $C_f(S)$ of all the finite subsets of the set S of attributes in question. So $C_f(S)$ may be a finite comprehension space even when S is infinite. Clearly a comprehension space is

---

[2] This exposition is based largely on Arnauld, *The Art of Thinking* and on Locke, *An Essay Concerning Human Understanding*. I have also made use of Auroux's *La sémiotique des encyclopédistes*.

closed under unions (finite unions in the case of a finite comprehension space). Of course if the basic set S of attributes is finite then there is no distinction between the two sorts of comprehension space. Comprehension spaces are not in general closed under intersection or relative difference.

A comprehension space may be associated with a collection of ideas and a set W of objects or individual substances. The extension of an idea is the set of objects in W to each of which the idea applies, or, in the strict version, to each of which the idea necessarily applies. In the latter case the comprehension of (i.e., associated with) an idea is the set of attributes each of which is essential to each object in the extension. An idea is simple if its comprehension consists of just one attribute, otherwise complex. An idea is finite or infinite accordingly as its comprehension has these features. One idea is said to be a *logical part* of another if the comprehension of the first is a subset of the comprehension of the second. The decomposition of an idea into logical parts is not unique, though the decomposition into simple logical parts is unique.

It should be remarked that the relation of containment or subset between comprehensions does not quite represent entailment between properties as we think of it today. The simplest counter-instance to this representation is provided by the assumption of *necessary* attributes; if two comprehensions differ only in that one includes some necessary attribute that the other lacks, then the second comprehension should—in contemporary terms at least—be said to imply the first, since nothing in the extension of the smaller comprehension could fail to be in that of the larger comprehension. This example shows that containment is not necessary for implication or entailment of comprehensions. It may not be quite an honest rendering of the classical theory to allow necessary attributes, but the same point can be made without this assumption in a more general way: if implication is the same as containment, then all attributes are logically independent; there can be no distinct attributes $A_1, A_2 \ldots, B$ such that the comprehension $\{A_1, A_2 \ldots\}$ entails B. For were there such this would be a case of entailment without containment. The classical thinkers themselves seem often to presume the logical independence of simple attributes. It is not clear, however, how on this assumption there could be inconsistent ideas or comprehensions.

Given a set W of individual substances, the comprehension of an idea determines its extension. This is true for both senses (contingent and strict) of extensions. For, given a collection of attributes and a collection of substances, the set of substances to each of which every attribute in the collection belongs is uniquely determined, as is the set of substances to each of which every attribute in the collection applies essentially.

The classical thinkers may not have had a separable idea of negation—either of propositions or of properties; they seem most of the time to consider not what we should today call negation, but rather a form of judgement that we might call *denial*, the polar opposite of assertion. Our modern notion is hard to separate from the general Fregean theory of judgement, propositions, and truth functions, and we should thus not presume, for example, that the negation of a property is, within the theory of ideas, a property. Though negation may not be precisely defined for properties and attributes, there is nonetheless a classical notion of impossibility or inconsistency. There are inconsistent comprehensions, and inconsistency behaves in fairly regular ways that may be summarized in four principles:

A1. There are inconsistent comprehensions.
A2. Every simple comprehension is consistent.
A3. Every non-null subset of a consistent comprehension is consistent.
A4. The extension of an inconsistent comprehension is always null.

Each idea has a comprehension and an extension, and we may think of them as associated even without the mediation of the idea. So we may speak (in both the strict and contingent senses) of the extension of a comprehension. The following principle then holds for both senses of extension.

1.1 The extension of the union of comprehensions is the intersection of their extensions.

As a corollary to principle 1.1 we have the well known classical principle relating comprehensions and extensions:

CP. If the comprehension A includes the comprehension B, then the extension of B includes the extension of A.

This principle is asserted and presumed in roughly this form in the classical period. It underlies Hume's notion of relations of ideas and

Leibniz's and Kant's notions of analyticity. That this is so provides at least indirect support for the above development of the theory.

The dual of principle 1.1 does not hold for either sense of extension; the extension of the intersection of comprehensions is not in general the union of their extensions. To see this, suppose the comprehension of the idea of *man* to be {rational, bipedal}, and the comprehension of the idea of *ape* to be {furry, bipedal}. Then the union of the extensions of these ideas is the class of men and apes, which excludes such bipeds as chickens. But the intersection of the two comprehensions is {bipedal}, and its extension is the class of bipeds, including chickens.

Indeed, the converse of the principle CP does not hold in general: if A and B are coextensive attributes (and it is quite in harmony with the theory that there be such) then the extension of {A} is a subset of the extension of {A, B}, but the latter comprehension is not a subset of the former.

Does every non-null collection of substances form the extension of some idea? Let us say that a collection of substances is *thinkable* if it is the extension of some idea. Suppose first that extensions are understood in essential terms (so talking parrots are not in the extension of the idea of a thing that speaks). Then the question whether every class of substances is thinkable has the simplest answer when every class of substances shares an essential attribute which no object outside the collection has essentially. If this were so, then the talking parrots would have some *simple* and essential property that marked them off from other substances. Even if not every collection of objects shares a peculiar simple attribute, essential to each of them, it may still be that every non-null collection of objects is thinkable by means of some comprehension. Every attribute in the comprehension would be essential to every substance in the collection, and any substance not in the collection would fail to have some of the attributes essentially. In this case every class of substances will be the extension (in the essential sense) of some idea. Again, we may apply the same reasoning to finite sets of attributes. These conditions are also necessary: if every non-null collection of objects is the extension of some (finite) idea, then every non-null collection of objects shares a (finite) set of attributes, each of which is essential to each of them, and not all of which are essential to any object not in the collection.

Without pretending to decide whether every class of objects is thinkable, we can in any event consider the collection of thinkable, or finitely thinkable, classes of objects. What is its structure? The collection of thinkable sets of objects is closed under intersections. That is a consequence of principle 1.1. The intersection of thinkable sets is the extension of the union of the comprehensions in terms of which the sets are thinkable. Similarly, the collection of finitely thinkable sets is closed under finite intersections—for the union of finitely many finite sets of attributes is finite. But the thinkable sets are not in general closed under the formation of unions, as the counterexample to the dual of principle 1.1 makes evident: the sets of rational bipeds and of furry bipeds may be thinkable, but it does not follow that the union of these sets is thinkable. If we could form disjunctive properties, such as *furry or rational*, it would then follow that the union of finitely many finitely thinkable sets is finitely thinkable; but such formation does not seem to be part of the theory. The epistemic principles at work seem to be these: as more attributes are thought, the extensions converge in regular ways. But as fewer attributes are thought, there is no assurance that the concomitant expansion of extensions has any particular sort of regularity.

If it is implausible that the set of talking parrots is the extension of a simple attribute, it is less implausible that it should be thinkable. For if the sets of parrots and of talking things are thinkable, then so is their intersection.

Though it is not essential to the classical theory of probability, and in particular not to Hume's theory of the probability of chances, it is of independent interest to treat briefly the theory of universal, particular, and singular ideas. Before Frege, quantification was defined in terms of intention or supposition; the intention or supposition of him who asserts the quantified judgement. So— the simplest case—a universal idea is intended in its full extension: whoever asserts that all men are mortal intends that the idea *man* be taken to have its full extension. The idea *man* is then universal, or, as it is sometimes put, the idea *man* has universal supposition. A particular idea is intended or supposed to have only some undetermined non-null part of its extension, and a singular idea purports to have just one individual in its extension.

Let us say that a *particularization* of a comprehension is any comprehension that contains it. Now instead of speaking of an idea intended or supposed to have some undetermined and non-null part of its extension, we may speak of undetermined and exemplified (that is, with non-null extensions) particularizations of an idea. In general, not every subset of an extension is thinkable, hence we cannot presume that particularization of a comprehension can determine every subset of its extension. In these terms, then, the universal idea *all S*, has as its comprehension just the comprehension of S. A particular idea *some S*, has the comprehension of some exemplified particularization of S, it being always presumed, in the employment of a particular idea, that it is exemplified.

The logic of comprehensions permits a brief and intuitive development of an intensional logic of the classical form of judgement. One further simple and contestable principle is required here:

Principle of plenitude. Every consistent idea is exemplified. That is to say, if A is consistent, then the extension of A is not null.

Corollary. Every simple attribute is exemplified.

The principle of plenitude can be supported on roughly Leibnizean grounds: a world in which every consistent idea is exemplified would contain more reality than one in which some of what is possible did not exist. What is perhaps of more interest is that the principle of plenitude relates the abstract notion of consistency employed in the principles of the theory of comprehensions with consistency in terms of extension or exemplification. The general technique is just that of model building in the standard and modern sense.

Perhaps the most fundamental principle of the classical logic of judgement is this: every judgement has a subject and a predicate. The classical logicians tried to analyse every judgement in this form, accommodating apparent counterexamples by complicating the subject or predicate (or sometimes the verb). They would sometimes even change the semantical level, to make of what appeared to be a judgement about things a judgement about judgements. Kant thus took the hypothetical to be a judgement about the connection between two judgements. The classical judgement may be of any of four types, depending upon whether the subject idea is universal (All S) or particular (Some S) and whether the judgement asserts or denies the predicate of it. The result is the well known four-part taxonomy:

A: All S is P. (Universal affirmative)
E: No S is P. (Universal negative)

I: Some S is P. (Particular affirmative)
O: Some S is not P. (Particular negative)

These basic types are governed by the following four semantical rules:

All S is P is necessary if and only if the comprehension of P is a subset of the comprehension of S.

No S is P is necessary if and only if the union of the comprehensions of S and P is inconsistent.

Some S is P is possible if and only if the union of the comprehensions of S and P is consistent.

Some S is not P is possible if and only if the comprehension of P is not a subset of the comprehension of S.

1.2 *Conception and judgement*

One of the most profound and respected distinctions in the classical period was that of conception from judgement. Conception, the act of the mind in which an idea is grasped or comprehended, was presupposed in judging, the act of the mind in which an idea is predicated of a substance or of another idea. The algebra of ideas and their comprehensions developed above provides the structure upon which the logical relations among ideas, and consequently among judgements, are based, and the distinction of judgement from conception is fundamental to it. It is thus not the least revolutionary principle of Hume's thought that he denies, explicitly and completely, any distinction between conception and judgement, [I.3.7, n 1].[3] This denial has the consequence that the classical logic of judgement—for which the distinction is a primary presupposition—would require at least modification to apply to a Humean theory of ideas and judgements. One would need, for example, some way to distinguish *All As are Bs* from *All Bs are As*, for on Hume's account these both amount to having the ideas *A* and *B* before the mind. This is not to say that the needed modifications could not be carried out, but it is clear that Hume never took account of the need for them. Indeed, the discussion of ideas in the first part of the *Treatise* reads easily when the distinction is presumed, and with some difficulty when it is not. Thus, "[T]hose complex ideas which are the common

---

[3] *Treatise* book I, part 3, section 7.

subjects of our thought and reasoning . . . may be divided into *relations, modes* and *substances*"[I.1.4]. This is quite plausible in the context of the classical theory of ideas, but not at all plausible if the identification of judgement and conception is taken seriously. Again, Hume's account of knowledge and probability seems to presume, quite in the classical tradition, that the algebra of ideas is in place, and that the forms of judgement are just the different ways in which one idea may be predicated of another. Thus he begins his discussion of the probability of chances by accepting the classical definition of knowledge as "the assurance arising from the comparison of ideas"[I.3.11]. And the ensuing discussion of probability applies probability to judgement. In sum, Hume seems not to have appreciated the depth and extent of theoretical modification that would be needed to accommodate the identification of judgement and conception. Much of his discussion of ideas, as well as that of knowledge and probability, presumes the distinction. And the classical algebra of ideas, which Hume seems to accept and to use, depends heavily upon it. For these reasons, the logical bases of Hume's theory of probability need to be treated with care, and at some risk of incongruity.

A judgement based upon the relation of ideas is, in the simplest case, of the form "All S is P", where the idea of S includes that of P. This inclusion may be understood in terms of the algebra of comprehensions developed above; the comprehension of P is a logical part of the comprehension of S. Such a judgement is to be contrasted with judgements based upon causal or contingent connections, in which the extension of the predicate is asserted to include that of the subject, without entailing the converse relation between their comprehensions. The probability of chances generalizes judgements of the first sort; the probability of causes those of the second.

Judgements of the probability of chances may be conceived as mixtures of universal judgements based upon relations of ideas. A judgement of the relations of ideas, "All S is P", asserts that the comprehension of S includes that of P. "The chance of P given S is n/k" asserts that of k possible *cases* of S, the comprehensions of n of these include as logical part the comprehension of P. Now it must be said what a *case* of S is.

Given a comprehension space C(S) we say that the collection A_1 .. A_k of comprehensions is a *(logical) partition* of the comprehension B if,

(i) the A_i are individually consistent but inconsistent by pairs;
(ii) The intersection $A_1 \cap \ldots \cap A_k$ of the members of this collection is the comprehension B;

and a logical partition $\{A_1 \ldots A_k\}$ is *finest* if none of the A_i has a distinct logical partition.

Given a finest partition $\{A_1 \ldots A_k\}$ of the idea B, the *chance probability* of an idea C given B is $1/k$ times the number of A_i that include the comprehension of C.

The existence of finest partitions is by no means always guaranteed. Further, in many ordinary and relevant situations there will be no finest partition, so that in these situations the probability of chances, as here defined, will have no application. In an infinite comprehension space, no finite logical partition of a comprehension B will be finest if, for example, for every finite partition $\{A_1 \ldots A_k\}$ of B, there is some pair of contradictory properties, C and $\neg$C, such that each of $A_i \cup C$, $A_i \cup \neg C$ is consistent for each i. Then the resulting collection of unions is a logical partition, finer than the given partition $\{A_1 \ldots A_k\}$. Indeed, this seems to be the case in the world at large, where the properties in question cannot be limited in advance. So, if B is the throw of a die, then for any finite partition of B, and in particular for the favoured one giving the six possible outcomes of the throw, we can always find some property of the die—that money is bet on the outcome of its throw, for example— which is logically independent of each of the outcomes. In the world at large, considerations of *relevance* may enter here: it is acknowledged that finer partitions can always be found, but they are almost inevitably irrelevant to the outcome. The famous difficulty with this is that it is not at all easy to say what is meant by relevance here without reference to just those probabilities for which the logical partitions are supposed to provide a definition or foundation. One wants to say that the addition, in the case of the die, of the property that money is bet on the outcome, does not change the probability of the outcome. But that would be circular.

It is simplest to restrict consideration to finite comprehension spaces, based on collections of attributes given in advance. The definition of chance probability is then relativized to such a space, and it must be admitted that extensions or ramifications of the space to include new attributes, logically independent of those already in the space, may change chance probabilities. And that seems also in the spirit of the enterprise. There are two tasks here: one is to understand the logical bases of the classical theory of the probability of chances; the other is the construction of a complete and consistent theory of chance or logical probability on the basis of the classical theory. The first leads naturally to the consideration of certain questions that belong also to the second. It is however possible to make some progress on the first task without completing the second, and that is the option taken in this chapter. The main point of the chapter is to understand the relations between logic and probability, and to understand the modern form of these relations as a transformation of their classical form. To do that, the classical logic needs to be filled in somewhat—some of what was implicit presupposition for the thinkers of the period needs to be made explicit for us—but as much as possible the classical theory should be left intact, and it should be allowed to remain silent on questions which have little meaning in its own terms.

Perhaps the most significant characteristic that the classical theory of chance probability shares with its modern successors is that probability is defined in so far as it can be in purely logical terms. Given the logic, given, in the classical case, the algebra of ideas and the logic of comprehensions that results from it, chance or logical probability is, as far as possible, determined. As formulated here, that determination is relativized to a space of comprehensions built up from a finite set of attributes, and that seems the best way to come to terms with those difficulties of the classical principle of indifference that are not remarked by such classical thinkers as Hume.

1.3 *Hume and the probability of chances*

Chance probability as Hume defines it conforms to the laws of finite probability: If "All A is B" is a truth of the relations of ideas, then $P(B/A) = 1$, and if "No A is B" is such a truth, then $P(B/A) = 0$. These conditions are also necessary; it is only in cases of containment and exclusion respectively that the values of zero and one hold. There are evident problems consequent upon the incompleteness of the definition and also because of the failure or refusal of the classical theory to provide a theoretical treatment of negation. So, since negation is not clearly defined for ideas, no law can be precisely formulated relating $P(B/A)$ and $P(\neg B/A)$. Nor is any pronouncement made on the question of chance probabilities with inconsistent antecedents, and questions about denumerable additivity could not be well formulated without anachronism. There is, however, enough said, and with sufficient clarity, to support the claim that chance probabilities are, in Hume's theory, the general case of which non-probabilistic judgements of the relations of ideas are particular instances—the two primary forms of these being given above. The general nature of logical relations is probabilistic. About this three remarks:

1. Hume's theory of the probability of chances is thoroughly intensional. Whatever conclusions may follow from it about extensions are consequences of the classical principle governing intensions and extensions, and the fundamental concepts on which the definition of chance probability is based are formulated in terms of the comprehension or intension of ideas. In Hume's case, it should be remarked, the distinction between relations of ideas and matters of fact is not a distinction between extensional and intensional judgement. Leibniz wanted to read "All S is P" ambiguously; as an intensional assertion (the comprehension of S includes that of P) and also as an extensional assertion (the extension of P includes that of S).[4] For a perfect intelligence the two would correspond—all knowledge is analytic for God—but for finite reasoners a judgement of this sort might be extensionally true and intensionally false. So in this way judgements about extensions are what later thinkers would call synthetic, as opposed to the analytic or intensional judgements that depend only upon the relations of ideas. There are thus two distinctions that follow roughly the same lines: intension/extension, and necessary/contingent. For Hume this is not quite right. His thorough idealism makes him suspicious of talk of extensions, which threatens to turn metaphysical. Hence contingent judgements are also in a quite clear sense judgements of "relations of ideas", and they are marked off from necessary judgements by the contingency of the eidetic relations in question. The two definitions of cause [I.3.14] provide a good example. Both definitions, Hume says, define causality as a relation of ideas. The main mark of a causal or contingent judgement is that the eidetic connection does not follow from the structure of the ideas, but depends upon a habit of associating them.

---

[4] See, for example, "Elements of Calculus" in *Philosophical Papers*, 235–40, especially section 7, and Lewis's discussion of Leibniz's views in *A Survey of Symbolic Logic*, 5–18.

2. The unclarities introduced by Hume's identification of judgement and conception tend to obscure the structure given by his theory to judgements of the probability of chances. These judgements consist of two ideas put in probabilistic relation. The judgemental tie, or copula, is probabilistic or partial. This sounds much less radical than in fact it was, for we can think also, for example, of a universal affirmative judgement as a universalization of the copula. But at the time, as the above sketch of the theory of ideas shows, the characteristic of a universal judgement was the universal supposition of the subject idea. Logic left the copula pretty much alone, except for modalities.

3. Hume says, in his discussion of the probability of chances, that there are always "causes among the chances". This should be understood as a remarkable anticipation of difficulties to come in sustaining a sharp and clear distinction between the necessary and the contingent. Hume is of course counting on this distinction, and it is the basis of the difference between the two sorts of probability—chances and causes. But he is nevertheless clearly aware of the problem in separating causal and logical notions. The function of causes in determining chances is to limit possibilities. So, in his example of throwing the die, the field of possible outcomes excludes such eventualities as the die going out of existence: "Where nothing limits the chances, every notion that the most extravagant fancy can form is upon a footing of equality" [I.3.11]. In terms of the above development, this limitation represents a limitation of the comprehension space.

In sum, the characters of classical analytic or chance probability that are important for what follows are, first, that probability is a logical notion. It is defined as far as possible in terms of the algebra of ideas which is the foundation of the logic of the period. Secondly, chance judgements are in fact a generalization of necessary judgement—in particular of the necessary or intensional universal judgement. In this way probability (of this sort) is not a concept added on to pure logic, but is rather the general case of pure logic. It is not as if logic was applied to certain synthetic principles—the principles of probability—to develop the theory of probability. Rather the principles of probability are themselves logical principles that follow from pure and general logic.

1.4 *A general description of the transformation of chance probability to logical probability of the modern sort*

The modern theory of logical probability, and Carnap's theory in particular, can be understood as a transformation of the earlier, classical account of probability. Here is a very rough sketch of the transformation in question. The classical theory of chance probability was an important part of classical logic. In fact, as argued above, chance probability is the general case of logical relations among ideas and their comprehensions. Classical logic was in many ways conceptually unstable, and in the nineteenth century, approximately from the publication of Kant's first *Critique* in 1781 to that of Frege's *Begriffschrift* in 1879, that logic underwent a revolution that was in several respects radical and extensive. This modification of logic involved also a modification of logical probability, and in many ways the contemporary theory of logical probability is the outcome of the transformation in question.

The thesis here is at bottom not a historical one. That is to say, it is not a question of what authors or texts influenced whom. It is rather a thesis in what might be called the topology of thought; in the ways in which conceptual networks can be transformed. The two networks here in question—classical logical probability and post-Fregean, essentially positivistic, logical probability—enjoyed, and in the case of the latter still enjoy, wide currency at a deep level in the thought of the epochs in question. Much of the structure can be grasped only in retrospect, only in virtue of the contrast afforded by conceptual shifts that put certain unchanged features in relief. Retrospective description is also much aided by the availability of new descriptive techniques, such as the set theory used above to describe the classical theory of ideas.

Let us begin with a quite general description of contemporary logical probability, mainly to contrast it with the classical view. This description will be filled in and situated in more detail in the next chapter.

For ease of exposition—and no further significance attaches to these labels—the features of contemporary logical probability that distinguish it from its classical counterpart may be grouped under three heads: mathematical, epistemological, and logical. The present concern is with the last of these; the mathematical and epistemological features are considered below in rather more detail, so they receive only brief mention here.

From a mathematical point of view there are three striking differences: contemporary logical probability is normally developed *axiomatically*, which was not the case with the classical theory, the modern treatment of and dependence upon *infinities* is quite different, and modern probability is incorporated in the theory of *measure*. These are interdependent. Probability was comprehensively axiomatized by Kolmogorov in 1933[5] at a time when the spirit of axiomatization was at its height. This axiomatization facilitated the vision of probability as a special sort of measure, in the sense of the theory of measure, abstractly defined as a function on a Boolean algebra of sets of points. New questions about infinity could then assume more importance. So, for example, the distinction between denumerable and non-denumerable infinities, which is at the basis of the distinction between denumerable and perfect additivity, was not operative in the classical period. In classical probability infinity was always in the form of a limiting distribution, whereas the advent of Lebesgue measure opens new possibilities for additivity and completeness of definition. We return to this question in chapters 2 and 3.

As far as the epistemological differences are concerned, the most significant is the sharp distinction in contemporary theories between logical and psychological accounts of probability. In Hume's theory of chance probability, logic and psychology mix easily and thoroughly. It would not be easy, if indeed it were possible, to separate Hume's psychology of judgement from his logic of judgement, and this is not only because of the psychological nature of ideas on some versions of the classical theory. Even amongst thinkers of the period for whom ideas were treated on a Cartesian model—objects for thought not psychologically constituted—the classical notion of judgement as an act of the mind, even an abstract act, not essentially tied to any particular mind that performed it, made logic and psychology difficult to separate. The ideas might be abstract and non-mental objects, but they were joined in judgement only by a mind, and it was not possible to think of the proposition as pre-existing such juncture or its possibility.

As difficult as it might seem to separate the logical and psychological strains in Hume's theory of chance probability, his theory is nonetheless the ancestor of theories that differ among themselves precisely and thoroughly in this respect. Carnap's early (1950)

---

[5] In *Foundations of the Theory of Probability*.

theory of logical probability is as resolutely anti-psychologistic as are the Fregean and Husserlian theories with which he associates himself. And de Finetti's subjectivism is about as psychologistic, in at least one clear sense, as possible.[6] As far as Carnap's later views (1960 and later) are concerned, there are important nuances. His compromises with subjectivism led him to an account of probability based upon the psychology of partial belief. So an attribution of a partial belief to someone is an empirical and descriptive assertion, the testable content of which is, for example, betting behaviour.

Carnap's view of expressive and affective phenomena is that they are sufficiently ineffable to elude precise and metrical treatment.[7]

Finally, and of immediate concern here, are the logical differences between classical and contemporary logical probability. These are the subject of the following section.

1.5 *Logical transformations*

This section looks at five of the ways in which classical logic was transformed into modern logic and which have particular bearing on shifts in logical probability. These five ways are:

   (i) the creation of the proposition as an object of judgement, not dependent upon an act of judging;

  (ii) the description and treatment in logical terms of evidential relations;

 (iii) The shift to language, rather than thought or judgement, as the field of logical relations;

 (iv) The use of transcendental techniques, which, in the logical study of language, involves the distinction of metalanguage from object language;

  (v) Changes in the nature and effects of the analytic–synthetic distinction.

These transformations in logical theory are quite general, and their effects in the theory of logical probability should be understood as instances of more widespread changes. It may thus be

---

[6] See especially sections 11 and 12 of Carnap's *Logical Foundations of Probability*. On de Finetti's psychologism see section 2.3 below.

[7] See the last paragraph of section 12 of *Logical Foundations*. On expressive and affective phenomena, see "The Elimination of Metaphysics Through Logical Analysis of Language", especially section 7.

helpful to consider them first in a more general setting, before examining more closely the specific case of logical probability.

Frege's work is a convenient reference point for the situation of these changes. He was, in fact, responsible for them in considerable part, and they are in any event clearly marked in his work. The method of the present exposition is as follows: it is presumed that before Frege logic was based on the classical algebra of ideas and comprehensions. Frege destroyed most of that categorization to introduce a genuine discontinuity in thought. Logic since Frege is very different from what it was before he transformed it. The picture is thus one of two fairly static conceptual organizations, related by a discontinuous transformation. No great amount of research is required to reveal the historical inaccuracy of this scheme. Neither pre-Fregean nor post-Fregean logic has the stability here presumed, and there is little reason to suppose that Frege's thought is the route by which classical logic passed to arrive at modern logic. But the point is not a historical one. There is a pretty clear and coherent theory of ideas that underlies classical logic. Implausible as it is that any one thinker held the theory in the form given here, this form is nevertheless not implausible as an embodiment of certain shared principles in a coherent whole. A similar remark may be made about post-Fregean logic and the characteristics (i)–(v) listed above. No sooner are these formulated than disagreements about them come immediately to mind, but they are, and have been, since about 1900, the locus of these disagreements. And the disagreements in question were not even formulable within the classical framework.[8]

The creation of the proposition, what Frege called the *thought*, is one great modification for which he was responsible and which is the source of considerable conceptual change. From our present point of view the situation can be simply described: in the classical theory, a judgement was the act of putting ideas together predicatively. So a judgement could not exist except as an act of the mind, and even to describe a possible judgement was always to describe an act of the mind. Every judgement had a subject idea and predicate idea, and the verb both joined these and signified the assertion or making of the judgement. For us the problems with this are obvious; embedded verbs are just unmanageable, it not being clear how a proposition can be formulated without being asserted. Indeed, when

---

[8] This point is argued in more detail in my paper "Definability and Logical Structure in Frege".

Kant described the hypothetical he was forced to make it a judgement of second order, a judgement about possible judgements.[9] Further, the doctrine of subject–predicate structure renders impossible any account of relations or embedded generality—embedded quantifiers must be put into the predicate and are inaccessible to structural transformation. Frege's simple and radical solution of the problem was to separate the force of assertion from the copulative function of holding the parts of the judgement together. Assertion—assertive judgement—is then conceived as an act or operation performed upon an already structured object. This object is constructed without being asserted; in assertion the mind finds its object already made. What was the copulative power of the verb, the power to consolidate and unify the parts of a judgement, is taken over by the power of complete and incomplete parts of the thought to fit together into a structured whole. The first result of this structuration is precisely what Frege intended: propositional structure is freed from illocutionary force, and the proposition or thought may be constructed with no help from assertion or judgement. Once constructed it may be asserted, but it need not be; a thought can be grasped without being asserted.[10] So what Kant called the problematic form of judgement[11]—judgement without assertion—becomes rather the unjudged matter of all judgement. This independence of the thought enables the rejection of the dogma of subject and predicate, and thus opens the way to a varied and powerful structure of the thought. In particular, Frege's invention of the quantifiers and his account of relations as functions from pairs of objects to truth values together give the resolution of the great traditional problems of generality and relations.

The separate existence of the proposition also leads to the second of the changes mentioned above: the shift to language as the field of logical relations. The proposition or thought is the meaning of a declarative sentence. As long as the proposition depended upon the act of judgement for its existence, sentences could not be said to have meaning in the same sense as that could be said, for example, of nouns: the meaning of a (common) noun was just the idea it expressed. And one could thus move back and forth between the noun system, with the complex of relations introduced therein by

---

9 "Thus the two judgements, the relation of which constitutes the hypothetical judgement . . .": First *Critique*, A 75 = B 100.

10 See "The Thought", for example.   11 First *Critique*, A 70 = B 95.

ties of definition, and the algebra of ideas. In the most favourable case a complex noun expressed an idea the comprehension of which was the union of the comprehensions of its parts. That is a rudimentary semantical theory, and, though rudimentary, it has sufficient structure—the meaning of a complex noun is determined by the meanings of its parts—to give a fair account of nominal sense and reference, at least in an envisioned perfect language freed from the embarrassing counterinstances of ordinary discourse. But no eidetic object can serve as the meaning of the sentence so long as what the sentence expresses is an act of the mind. Once freed from this constraint, however, the relation between a sentence and the thought it expresses is sufficiently like that between a noun and the idea that is its meaning that it is easy to think of the thought as the meaning of a sentence. This done, one can move back and forth between sentences and the thoughts they express. And it is now possible to introduce logical relations among sentences, even if these relations are at first derivative of logical relations among the thoughts they express. The project of a perfect language, the structures of which are isomorphic to those of its meanings, is a great help in this progression. Logical relations are above all structured, and this primacy is even reinforced by Frege's anti-psychologism, which rejects on strong principle a logic based on conceivability or psychic possibility. Thus eventually it is possible and fruitful to define logical relations among sentences. This is not yet formalism in any important sense, for one may still maintain that sentences are significant and that their logic just reflects the more fundamental logic of the thoughts that are their meanings. Something like this, in fact, is Frege's view after 1891.[12]

Just as the constitution of the proposition opened the field of language for the imposition of logical relations among sentences, so did it also, and for the same reasons, make possible the question of *evidential* relations among propositions or among sentences. One could now ask to what extent one proposition or sentence supported or provided evidence for another. As recently as Kant, that question had been possible only as a question about a given hypothetical judgement, and then only in absolute, non-probabilistic terms. The relation of ground to consequent had to be formulated as a question

---

[12] After "Function and Concept", that is. See also "Sense and Reference". Both are in *Translations from the Philosophical Writings*.

about judgement. With the advent of a semantics of propositions, however, for which a sentence becomes a separate meaningful unit in its own right, one sentence can be thought of as evidence for another with no reference, explicit or implicit, to any judgement. It is then natural to subsume evidential relations of this sort under general logical relations, and, just as Hume was led to think of the probability of chances as a generalization of eidetic inclusion, one is easily led to think of evidential relations of varying degrees as the general case of which implication is a particular instance: degree one.

The distinction of analytic from synthetic judgements, propositions, or sentences has been both a central topic and an important tool in philosophy since the classical period. Here again Frege's work is a crucial point at which the distinction undergoes quite fundamental changes. Indeed, these shifts in the foundations of analyticity provide a good point of reference for mapping the general transformation which is here in question.

To begin, we should note two sorts of distinctions about judgements (in the pre-Fregean sense) that may be made independently of each other. Judgements may be distinguished in terms of their *structure* or, again, in terms of *evidence* or support. The Humean category of relations of ideas is structural: if the comprehension of the subject idea includes that of the predicate idea, then the judgement may be said to express a relation of ideas. Other structural relations of judgements will give other relations of ideas, as shown in section 1.2 above. Hume's concept of *matters of fact*, however, is not structural but evidential or epistemic. A judgement expresses a matter of fact if it is supported by experience, if its truth value depends upon experience. One important thesis of Hume's empiricism is the exhaustiveness of these two classes of judgement— any judgement not supported or refuted by experience expresses a relation of ideas. A judgement that purports to be neither can be only senseless metaphysics. From this point of view the two oppositions—analytic/synthetic and a priori/a posteriori—come into being when the two original categories are negated. Hume's judgements of relations of ideas become analytic judgements. Synthetic judgements are just judgements that are not analytic. The distinction is still a structural one, based upon the algebra of ideas, and depends not at all upon any particular notion of experience. Judgements of matters of fact become a posteriori judgements,

judgements that depend upon and are supported or refuted by experience. A priori judgements are those that are not a posteriori. Synthetic a priori judgements are those that neither express relations of ideas nor depend upon experience.

The pair of oppositions, and the disagreement about the possibility of synthetic a priori judgements, depend upon and nourish certain concepts of experience—that experience has inner and outer sides, that it is of objects and a subject, for example—as well as the algebra of ideas and the theses that surround it. The second of these in particular is severely undermined by Frege. Two related features of this undermining bear mention here: the most far-reaching of these is Frege's creation of the proposition and the concomitant restructuration of the realm of significations or ideas. The classical algebra of ideas had nothing corresponding to the meaning or comprehension of a sentence. The algebra, as we have seen, was a collection of sets of attributes, closed under intersections. It provided a subtle and surprisingly powerful semantics of the noun system, but the account it could give of the semantics of sentences gives no meaning or comprehension to the sentence; nothing that stood to the sentence as an idea stood to the common noun. That in itself threatens the structure of the algebra. There are, for example, in the absence of extensive ramification, no structural laws relating propositions and ideas. And the creation of the proposition is only the beginning of it. Frege introduced an articulated system of differently structured senses—complete senses of proper nouns, incomplete senses of predicates and other function-names, senses of higher-order functions and concepts, and so on. The simple structure of the classical algebra could hardly be modified to accommodate this.

The second way in which Frege undermined the classical algebra of ideas was by his direct criticism of the classical and Kantian notion of analyticity, together with the new way of thinking of analyticity that he proposed and enforced. Frege criticized the Kantian definition on the grounds that it applied only to universal affirmative judgements.[13] We have seen that the classical algebra, admittedly in company with such strong principles as that of plenitude, gave intensional readings of judgements of the four classical types, and these may plausibly be taken as defining the analyticity of those forms, but in Fregean logic these forms are

---

[13] *The Foundations of Arithmetic*, section 88.

derivative and are far from comprehending all propositional structures. So, for example, propositions with embedded quantifiers are
simply not treatable in any way within the classical structure. Thus
to rest within the Kantian definition, even when that definition is
enriched and modified to its limits, would entail a drastically incomplete concept of analyticity, inapplicable to propositions of certain
important structures. Frege thus proposed a radically different concept of analyticity, one that, at least on the surface, depends not at
all upon eidetic structure and which applies to propositions or
thoughts of any form whatever. The passage is justly famous and
worth quoting.

Now these distinctions between a priori and a posteriori, synthetic and
analytic, concern, as I see it,[14] not the content of the judgement but the
justification for making the judgement. Where there is no such justification, the possibility of drawing the distinctions vanishes. An a priori error is
thus as complete a nonsense as, say, a blue concept. When a proposition is
called a posteriori or analytic in my sense, this is not a judgement about the
conditions, psychological, physiological and physical, which have made it
possible to form the content of the proposition in our consciousness; nor is
it a judgement about the way in which some other man has come, perhaps
erroneously, to believe it true; rather, it is a judgement about the ultimate
ground upon which rests the justification for holding it to be true.
   This means that the question is removed from the sphere of psychology,
and assigned, if the truth concerned is a mathematical one, to the sphere of
mathematics. The problem becomes, in fact, that of finding the proof of the
proposition, and of following it up right back to the primitive truths. If, in
carrying out this process, we come only on general logical laws and on
definitions, then the truth is an analytic one, bearing in mind that we must
take account also of all propositions upon which the admissibility of any of
the definitions depends. If, however, it is impossible to give the proof
without making use of truths which are not of a general logical nature, but
belong to the sphere of some special science, then the proposition is a
synthetic one. For a truth to be a posteriori, it must be impossible to construct a proof of it without including an appeal to facts, i.e., to truths which
cannot be proved and are not general, since they contain assertions about
particular objects. But if, on the contrary, its proof can be derived exclusively from general laws, which themselves neither need nor admit of proof,
then the truth is a priori.[15]

---

[14] Frege adds a note: "By this I do not, of course, mean to assign a new sense to
these terms, but only to state accurately what earlier writers, Kant in particular, have
meant by them."
[15] *Foundations*, section 3.

And then, in a note:

If we recognize the existence of general truths at all, we must also admit the existence of such primitive laws, since from mere individual facts nothing follows, unless it be on the strength of a law. Induction itself depends upon the general proposition that the inductive method can establish the truth of a law, or at least some probability for it. If we deny this, induction becomes nothing more than a psychological phenomenon, a procedure which induces men to believe the truth of a proposition, without affording the slightest justification for so believing.

The classical notion of an a posteriori proposition is thus left roughly intact—what cannot be demonstrated without an appeal to facts is a posteriori. An a priori proposition may be established without appeal to particular objects. The important change is in the formulation of the analytic/synthetic distinction. That formulation has two components: *definition* and *general logical law.* Frege's logical theory gives a comprehensive account of the second of these; in fact the account that we should give today of the nature of logic, though it might differ from Frege's on certain important points, is nevertheless still quite within the general theoretical lines that he laid down. As far as definition is concerned, Frege had much to say. Whether he had an adequate theory of definition or not, and the merit of his arguments against implicit definition, are questions that need not be considered here.[16] Two consequences of the modified definition of analyticity will be important in the sequel: one is the shifts it induces in the relations between logic and logical probability; that is discussed below in chapter 3, section 7. The second consequence is that the algebra of ideas is further undermined, since it no longer has any function in structuring judgements or in deciding their analyticity.

Frege's definition of analyticity is the one upon which the positivists' use of the distinction depends. Their general position differs from his, and represents in this respect a return to something like Hume's empiricism, since they deny the possibility of synthetic a priori propositions. Or, to put this as a positive claim in Fregean terms, they insist that every general law must "belong to the sphere of some special science", and that whatever is not analytic, in the sense of the above quoted passage, cannot be proved "without including an appeal to the facts", i.e., to truths which cannot be

---

[16] See Vickers, "Definability and Logical Structure in Frege".

proved and are not general, since they contain assertions about particular objects. The difficulties of this position are well known and may safely go unrehearsed here. The present project, it may be recalled, is to chart the conceptual shifts which underlay the transformation of classical logical probability—Hume's probability of chances is the instance given—into the modern and Carnapian theory of logical probability. The present section has mentioned some differences between classical and modern logic. In the next section the effects of positivism upon probabilistic concepts are considered.

2

Positivism and Subjectivism

2.1 *Positivism and other forces*

THE recent and contemporary philosophy of probability is positivistic; it stays pretty well within the general lines of the positivistic problematic. The precision of this claim, its support, and its meaning for probability are the concerns of this section.

The analytic/synthetic distinction in Fregean terms is central to positivistic thought. It is presumed, as remarked above, in the positivistic formulation of empiricism—the denial of the synthetic a priori. One of the important functions of the distinction, in these terms, was to invalidate an orthogonal distinction: that between the natural and the human sciences. This latter distinction divided German and Austrian academic and intellectual circles.[1] It enforced a strong prohibition against the use of scientific and experimental methods in the human sciences; a prohibition which, evidently, had quite general moral and political features as well as specific methodological bases and implications. The analytic/synthetic distinction and its powerful use in the hands of the positivists can be seen as a response to this situation and as an offensive move against the methodological prohibitions that it enforced. A response, for it divided scientific labour along different lines, following the distinction between the formal and experimental sciences; and an offensive move since it enabled the unification of physical scientists and those workers in the human sciences of an experimental spirit who were hindered and excluded by the traditional distinction and the inapplicability of experimental methods in the study of life and mind. The unification of science meant, above all, for the positivists, the application of empirical and experimental methods in the human sciences. This was sometimes, particularly in the early

---

[1] See the manifesto of the Vienna Circle, *The Scientific Conception of the World: The Vienna Circle*, in R. S. Cohen and M. Neurath (eds.), *Empiricism and Sociology*, and the discussions in Janik and Toulmin, *Wittgenstein's Vienna*, and in Carnap's intellectual autobiography in *The Philosophy of Rudolf Carnap*.

days of the movement, complemented by various kinds of reductionism, metaphysical or epistemological. But in retrospect, the heart of the offensive, and that feature of it which endured, was methodological.

The power and depth of the division of all cognitive discourse into formal and experimental, the principle that whatever is not analytic cannot be proved "without including an appeal to the facts", which is to say, to experiment, may distract attention from another distinction, equally important, and the source of some disagreement among the positivists themselves. This is the distinction between what is cognitive and what is not cognitive. It has far-reaching implications in moral and aesthetic theory and, as we shall see, in the philosophy of probability.

At the base of the cognitive/non-cognitive distinction is the difference between what has and what lacks truth value. The quite different methodologies of the formal and empirical sciences are nevertheless the same in this respect; they both have to do with demonstration, with the support or establishment of what is true. Purely expressive discourse, and non-discursive activities, thus fall outside the applicability of these methodologies, and a vast field of human experience, of which the positivists would never minimize the importance, thus required conceptual tools of a different order. This is evident in the ethical theories of the positivists.

In considering positivistic theories of morality and value it is helpful to distinguish at the outset certain views about moral and evaluative discourse. While these are not independent of their accounts of morality and value, there are at least a few positivistic claims that are linguistic rather than ethical.

Perhaps the best known positivistic account of ethical discourse is emotivism, developed and defended notably by Charles L. Stevenson in his book *Ethics and Language*. For the emotivists, what looks to be a statement of value—"X is good"—is really an expression of approval and an exhortation that others should share this approval. Thus the grammatical mood of such sentences—the indicative—is misleading. "X is good" can be neither true nor false. Such utterances may be deceptive, as in hypocrisy, for example, and certain sorts of mistakes and disagreements are possible with respect to them. But these are mistakes and disagreements in attitude, not about matters of fact, and they are often irresoluble even in the presence of agreement on all the relevant facts. Theoretical work in moral and evaluative theory will thus be directed toward the description of these non-cognitive errors and disagreements, and towards the development of criteria of evidence or support for these attitudes, which criteria do not depend upon truth conditions or matters of empirical fact.

In the simplest case, that of sentences of the form "X is good", the object of approval is typically an individual substance, perhaps, where the subject of the sentence is a definite description, an individual substance viewed or envisioned under a certain aspect. Extending the theory to evaluations and moral discourse of other and more complex structure will present considerable technical difficulties, which should not be minimized, but the extended theory will follow roughly the same conceptual lines. So, expressions of individual obligation, "X ought to do A", might be explained along the lines of "X ought to make it the case that A", which would be understood again in terms of approval and exhortation.

In opposition to emotivism is what might be called *descriptivism*, the view that ethical discourse is assertive, and that evaluations such as "X is good" are true or false accordingly as X has or lacks the property of goodness.

It is worth mentioning that descriptivism eases treatment of a problem that is difficult for emotivism, namely the account of logical relations between ethical and scientific language. It is not clear how the logic of assertion and truth applies to what is expressive and without truth value.[2] Emotivism does not entail that there can be no scientific discourse about values, and its disagreements with descriptivism should thus not be overemphasized. This is clear in the light of what the positivists say about morality and value.

One positivistic view, or rather cluster of views, relevant here is *naturalism*. Naturalism takes moral and evaluative properties to be natural properties, usually properties of human attitudes and situations.[3] Evaluative propositions are then either true or false, cognitive, and are a fit subject for scientific inquiry. So no new forms of disagreement or error are called into play, and the criteria for settling moral disagreements and errors are, as in other sorts of cognitive discourse, based upon truth conditions and verification. Among the different forms of naturalism, two will be of interest in

---

[2] Stevenson's book, *Ethics and Language*, takes this problem seriously. See in particular the chapter on "Validity".

[3] Schlick's *Problems of Ethics* is an excellent example of this approach.

the discussion of probability. In one of these, human attitudes—desires and preferences—are the foundation of value and obligation, and in the other, human conditions—happiness or satisfaction—are fundamental. In the first case goodness is defined in terms of what people want, independently of whether or not what they want will or would satisfy them. And in the second case it is defined in terms of what would or will satisfy them, independently of whether they want it or not. In both cases the consequence is to open the way for a science of value, either by way of the psychology of preference and desire, or by way of the study of satisfaction. These two forms of naturalism are sharply distinguished by the evident existence of "false desires"—desires such that their satisfaction leaves the agent unsatisfied.

Emotivism and naturalism are, as they are formulated here, not contraries. It may be that the main function of evaluative discourse is expressive, and that, in this function, evaluative sentences lack truth value, while at the same time the preferences and desires expressed in these sentences are the proper subject matter of the science of value. Two uses of evaluative expressions, perhaps two different classes of expressions, would thus be needed: one use or class for the expression of desire, and the other for values defined in terms of desire or happiness. The compatibility of the two positions is clearest when naturalism defines value in terms of happiness or welfare. Then the science of value is concerned primarily with the conditions under which people are happy or satisfied. It is evidently consistent with this account of value that evaluations are primarily expressive of what people desire. There the compatibility is pretty obvious. But though less obviously so, the form of naturalism that defines value in terms of preference or desire is also consistent with the emotivistic view that evaluative language is primarily expressive: people express their desires in evaluative language. This language is non-cognitive and has no truth conditions. The desires expressed are nonetheless natural phenomena, the subject matter of a natural science of value, for which values are defined in terms of those desires.

The compatibility of emotivism and naturalism, both formulated here in a general positivistic setting, invites the question of the relation between them. Since most of the discussion between emotivists and naturalists is critical and argumentative, the question seems not to have been considered explicitly. It has, however, a worthy answer in clear positivistic terms. The formulation of this answer is interesting here for the light it will shed on similar questions in the theory of probability.

The question may be put as follows: suppose that evaluative language expresses desires, that values are defined in terms of desires or satisfactions. Then an evaluative sentence "X is good" may be read in two ways: as expressing a desire for X, and as the assertion that X is in fact valuable. There are, in fact, two questions here, since there are two forms of naturalism. Consider first naturalism that defines value in terms of satisfaction or welfare. What then is the relation between the two readings of "X is good"? One response, quite within the general lines of positivism, is in terms of *rationality*: an expression of desire is rational just in case what is desired will in fact satisfy or be good for the agent. Desire thus aims not at truth but at rationality in this sense, and it is this component of rationality that gives to desire its normative component. The science of value—the study of welfare and satisfaction—plays an obvious and crucial role in the development of rationality of desire, for one who is informed about what will satisfy him will come to have desires that are rational.

This is the first question and answer. It depends upon the gap between desire and satisfaction, indicated by the existence of false desires mentioned above. The second question asks about the relation between expressed desire and what is valuable when value is defined in terms of desire. One way of responding to this question is by giving the relevant definition, again depending characteristically upon such normative concepts as rationality. This may be done by taking value to be determined by rational desire, thought of as a limiting case of empirical desire, where the approach to this limit is achieved by purifying empirical desire of personal and contextual aspects. So what is valuable is what would be desired under certain ideal conditions, conditions in which, for example, particular advantages of the agent are bracketed or put out of play.

The concern here is not to criticize these theories, but to expose their structures. These structures are compared below with those of certain theories of probability.

One characteristic difficulty of emotivistic theories needs to be mentioned before turning to other matters. These theories take evaluative language to be expressive, neither true nor false. This gives rise to a peculiar and deep logical problem. It is, namely, not possible to give on this basis a uniform reading of all evaluative discourse. If "This apple is good" expresses approval of the indicated apple, no approval is expressed by,

  (i) If John came, then he took all the good apples.

The difficulty is a general one: expressions of attitude do not accept embedding within the scopes of logical operators. If "good" is understandable in this context, then it must not be purely expressive. The plausible response of emotivism is to make "good" in (i) descriptive of the attitudes that would be held under conditions given or inferrable from the rest of the sentence in the context. So (i) makes an assertion: it says that if John came then he took all the apples of which the speaker would approve. If this, or something like it, is an adequate analysis of (i), then clearly not all evaluative language is expressive. Further, some theoretical means need to be given for associating expressions and descriptions.

Similar considerations apply in other cases. So, one great obstacle in the development of the modern theory of the proposition was the double function of the verb—both copula and expression of assertion. Frege's separation of these two roles allowed him to put the assertive force completely outside what was expressed, and thus to eliminate a crucial expressive element from the interior of the proposition, where it hindered the construction of complex semantical structures. That is a sort of eliminative or reductive technique: assertive force is vested in a single act, external to the proposition.

2.2 Metalinguistic techniques

Among the most obvious and powerful of logical techniques of the present century is the distinction between object language and metalanguage, and the semantical theories based upon this distinction. Carnap and Tarski were pioneers of this development, and the consequent theories of reference, meaning, and truth have been given wider application—to natural languages in particular—by Montague and Davidson.[4]

---

[4] See Carnap's *The Logical Syntax of Language* and *Introduction to Semantics*; Tarski's "Concept of Truth" in *Logic, Semantics, Metamathematics*; Davidson's "Truth and Meaning" in *Inquiries into Truth and Interpretation*; and Montague's "English as a Formal Language" in *Formal Philosophy*.

One chooses as an object language typically a formal language with a clearly given syntactic structure, or some fragment of a natural language, the structure of which is known or conjectured. In the simplest case this language or fragment is written, not merely spoken. If spoken language is in question then it may be represented in some notation that gives only its acoustical properties. In any case, the object language, whether as spatial forms or sequences of sounds, is conceptualized in independence of signification. This is not to say that the language lacks signification, only that, for example, one may know what its expressions are without knowing what they mean. Indeed, it is usually a presumption of this approach that the object language in question should be significant, and that the metalanguage include not only a name for each object language expression but also a translation of each of its meaningful expressions. The metalanguage will include, in addition to these names and translations, means of referring to various syntactical and semantical relations and properties, and perhaps other significant expressions as well. The metalanguage will typically and in the most useful cases be sufficient to formulate first the definition of well-formed or grammatical expression of the object language, as well as the definitions of certain appropriate categories of those expressions; and secondly, whatever theoretical principles are relevant to the task at hand—a theory of reference or truth, for example.

It is clear that the possibility of a clear distinction between object and metalanguage presumes what was referred to above as the creation of the proposition and the corresponding shift to language as the bearer of meaning. Of course philosophers have long exploited the possibility of writing about language as a structured object, but the aims and powers of the modern approach are much more extensive than this: the language (or fragment) is defined as a structured class of expressions, closed under the repeated application of precise rules of formation, and the semantical characteristics (reference and truth, or logical relations, for example) of these expressions are defined so as to apply throughout this structured class. In view of this totalizing power, the metalanguage itself may become the object language of a second-level metalanguage, which may in turn become the object of a third-level metalanguage, and so on. Structures of this sort have been the support of many of the most revealing results and insights about reference, truth, and logical relations.

It should be remarked that the path of metalinguistic technique lies in general outside the Fregean problematic.[5] It is not so much that these techniques are more advanced than Frege's, though that is in many respects so, but rather that they go in different directions. Frege thought, for example, of definitions as expressions *within* rather than *about* a language, and he resisted relativization of truth, reference, meaning, and logical relations such as is entailed in the metalinguistic development of these concepts. Again, Frege would guarantee the objectivity of logic and logical structure by the existence of logical objects. If the classical theory of suppositions accounted for generality by a mixture of intention and idea, for Frege, even if ideas are non-psychological, this was still an invidious pollution of logic by psychology. One of his main and enduring aims was to give logic the means to mark itself off from all psychological influences. In considerable part he accomplished this by introducing non-psychological logical objects. Thus, to continue with the example of generality, the universal quantifier, "For all . . .", refers to a concept of second order, under which fall just those concepts of first order that are true of every object. The theory of truth functions, description operators, and logic in general follows this same line: logical objectivity rests upon the existence of logical objects. Carnap's metalinguistic work follows Frege's in this respect, and it is rather Tarski's semantics that marks off the metaphysical differences of the metalinguistic approach. In that approach the objectivity of logic depends not upon logical objects but upon the definition of truth. The universal quantifier does not refer, and its meaning cannot be grasped outside the definition of truth that applies to expressions of the object language in virtue of their structures. Thus the universal quantifier has no meaning that can be separated from that of the other logical operators and connectives. The logic of the language is to be grasped as a whole through the complex definition of truth. This radical holism may in certain important respects—the question is touched on below—permit logical and philosophical advances over Frege's logic, but it must also be remarked that Frege would have resisted it, and that in fact he did resist such of its harbingers as came within his ken. Nor was this resistance inessential. It marks a fundamental incompatibility, issuing from such principles as his rejection of implicit definition, for example. The

---

[5] In spite of some suggestive remarks in the fragment "On Logical Generality" in Frege's *Posthumous Writings*.

details of this are beside the immediate point, which is just to draw the lines of difference between the two sorts of forces, two vectors, that forced certain changes in the classical theory of logical probability. For these purposes there are two significant features of the metalinguistic approach, in addition to those that it shares with Fregean logic, already discussed above. The first of these is that just remarked on: its holism. The second is the precise distinction and treatment of transcendental conditions that it makes possible.

There are many different understandings of the notion of transcendental conditions. Perhaps the weakest is just this: transcendental conditions for knowledge or understanding are conditions upon which that knowledge or understanding depends but which are not included in what is known or understood. This is pretty vague, and it will allow as transcendental conditions much of what should plausibly be excluded. So, for example, the presence of a breathable atmosphere is clearly a condition of mathematical knowledge, since without it there would be no people. And such presence is not itself mathematical knowledge. But it is not a transcendental precondition of mathematical knowledge. In spite of such, and less frivolous, counter instances, this characterization of transcendental conditions may nevertheless serve to point the way to employment of the concept, and in that way it gives, as remarked above, a weakest notion. At the other limit, that of strong notions of transcendental, are such precise and detailed accounts as those of Kant and Husserl, which follow for the most part from equally detailed accounts of understanding, evidence, and experience. In the present work some understanding of this tradition is presumed. The notion of the transcendental is usually understood in as weak a sense as possible for the task at hand, and when stronger senses are required, they are introduced explicitly.

It is in any event clear that the framework of metalinguistic theory provides an ideal situation for the description and study of transcendental conditions in most good understandings of that term. This is not to say that every feature of language and its understanding, that every kind of language, or language in all its uses, lends itself to this sort of study. It is only to insist that certain important sorts and parts of language, the language of truth, reference, and logical relations—that, approximately, of written cognitive discourse—are well treated by these methods, and that they make many of the transcendental conditions of such discourse explicit and available to theory. The outstanding example of this is Tarskian truth definition. The clauses of such a definition are precisely transcendental conditions of understanding the language in question. Of course, they are not part of what is understood, nor part of what is expressed, but understanding and expression depend upon them for their objectivity. Here is an advantage over Fregean accounts, according to which, for example, the understanding of generality requires the grasp of a concept or sense that is or refers to a second-level concept. It is not easy on that view to see how one who is ignorant of Frege's theory could understand generality. There is no good criterion for separating principle from content. And on just this point Tarskian theory allows a precise and satisfying description.

2.3 What is subjectivism?

It was some help in discussing positivistic moral theory to distinguish views on morality from views about the semantics and functions of moral and evaluative language and discourse. The distinction between discourse and its subject matter should also be respected in discussing positivistic theories of probability, and subjectivism in particular. Subjectivists and their critics sometimes succumb to the temptation to slip back and forth between claims of the two sorts: claims about probability, and claims about probabilistic language. These are clearly not independent, but they should be approached separately.

As concerns probability itself, subjectivists agree in identifying probability, or one important species of it,[6] with partial belief. Different varieties of subjectivism then result from differing views about the nature of partial belief. One simple and time-honoured view about this is Hume's. He held that belief is a feeling, and that partial belief is the complex form of this feeling which occurs when one holds several alternatives simultaneously before the mind, seeing them to be exclusive, exhaustive, and atomic. The cognitive force, which in the case of non-probabilistic belief is just the way in which the object occurs in or before the mind, is in the partial case "divided and split in pieces by the intermingled chances".[7] This

[6] See, for example, David Lewis, "A Subjectivist's Guide to Objective Chance", in R. Jeffrey (ed.), Studies in Inductive Logic and Probability vol. II.
[7] Hume, Treatise, 129.

view is typical of subjectivism in several ways which bear brief mention before turning to some of its modern heirs. It is, first, ineliminably subjective. My partial belief is my feeling, and you can no more share it than you can my horror or joy. What intersubjectivity is possible for partial belief is consequent upon intersubjectivity in eidetic simplicity, exclusiveness, and completeness. To the extent that the identification of finest logical partitions is a formal logical matter, the partial beliefs will follow categorically when the same partition is contemplated by different subjects; but this will be so only in the probability of chances. When it is a question of causes, variations in the experience of different subjects will induce variations in what is exclusive, atomic, and exhaustive, with consequent variations in partial belief. Indeed, even as concerns the probability of chances, it is only in artificial and extreme cases that the eidetic structure will not depend upon "causes among the chances", so here, too, there will be little intersubjective uniformity of partial belief. The dependence of partial belief upon general rules will introduce even more variation.

A second mark of Hume's account also common among subjectivistic views is its holism. Belief of degree p in A is defined not in isolation, but only in so far as A belongs to a logical structure. Different structures, amounting to different partitions of the logical space, may result in different probabilities for the same object.

The third shared feature is treated more extensively below. It is that on Hume's and other subjectivistic accounts *embedded* partial beliefs are not easily accounted for. That is because belief is a feeling with which ideas occur in the mind, a way of intending and not a part or feature of what is intended. The feeling of belief thus adds nothing to the idea felt or believed. Hence accounting for belief that one believes something will require a distinction between feeling an idea (in the believing way) and feeling the feeling of that idea. Since feeling the idea adds nothing to the idea, it is not easy to see in what this distinction could consist. One option is to hold that believing always entails having the certain belief that one believes,[8] and that there is hence no need to distinguish feeling the idea from feeling the

---

[8] Hume seems most of the time not to question the principle that one always knows his own beliefs, but he begins his discussion of scepticism with regard to reason by arguing that "we must . . . in every reasoning form a new judgment, as a check or controul on our first judgment or belief; and must enlarge our view to comprehend a kind of history of all the instances, wherein our understanding has deceiv'd us, compar'd with those, wherein its testimony was just and true": *Treatise*, 180.

feeling of the idea. But in cases in which the first belief is partial and offered as an account of probability, this puts a great obstacle in the way of a plausible account of dispersion: if probability is partial belief and partial belief is a feeling, then probabilities of probabilities—where a proposition has different probabilities with different probabilities—will be beliefs about beliefs and hence feelings about feelings. Consider a case in which prolonged experimentation with a coin strengthens what was my initial tenuous belief of degree 1/2 that the coin will land heads, without changing that degree. One wants to say that the mean has not changed, but that the distribution is less dispersed (that the variance has decreased) as a result of the experimentation. But if I could not have this partial belief without being certain that I have it then it is not clear that this is possible.[9]

The infallibility of reflection has its roots in the certainty of Cartesian inner sense. It is an integral part of the modern view of subjectivity, of the accompanying distinction between internal states, to which the subject has privileged and immediate access, and external facts and conditions, which are known only through the mediation of internal states. This view has been amply criticized in recent decades. Little more will be said about it here or elsewhere in this book. One consequence of the recent discussion is this: to the extent that one has infallible access to his feelings, feelings are not intentional. This is hard to reconcile with the intentional and systematic nature of belief. Further, as Ramsey argues,

[I]t is not easy to ascribe numbers to the intensities of feelings; but apart from this it seems to me observably false [that by the degree of a belief we mean the intensity of the feeling that accompanies it], for the beliefs which we hold most strongly are often accompanied by practically no feeling at all; no one feels strongly about things he takes for granted.[10]

Phenomenology has often tried to make good sense of beliefs about beliefs, but the end of this has been to give the beliefs about beliefs a kind of certainty that beliefs about the world could never enjoy, typically on the basis of a distinction of kinds of evidence. The phenomenological distinction may thus succeed in distinguishing

---

[9] The example is Peirce's; see *The Collected Works of Charles Saunders Peirce* vol. II, p. 677.

[10] Ramsey, "Truth and Probability", in R. B. Braithwaite (ed.), *The Foundations of Mathematics and Other Essays*.

the two sorts of belief, but to no profit as concerns partial beliefs about partial beliefs.

De Finetti, perhaps the central figure of modern subjectivism, often follows Hume in taking belief to be a feeling. He identifies probability with partial belief and writes of "one's own sensations of probability".[11] Earlier in the same work he insists that "The subjective opinion is something known by the individual", and he stresses that probability evaluations are "subjective and therefore arbitrary", after insisting that "You are completely free in this respect".[12] One is thus led to think of probability evaluations as like protocol judgements or expressions of attitude: irrefutable and without truth value. De Finetti is not quite consistent in this course, however: in the fifth chapter of *Theory of Probability* the evaluation of probabilities is presented as a *task* which may be performed more or less well and in the performance of which one may solicit and make use of expert advice. Probabilities are now "realities in the minds of people", but there may be difficulties in gaining access to them. Further, probabilities have propositional content or objects, and the possibility of comparing probability evaluations across subjects is possible only because they share a common content.[13]

The shift in logical form—from the nominal or substantive form of Hume's ideas to propositional or assertoric forms—is not without significance. The objects of Humean belief could not be true or false. Though, as remarked above, Hume himself often did not take seriously the strictures of his own theory in this regard, the absence of predicative or assertoric structures meant that at a very fundamental level Hume could not accommodate what his later critics, most notably Kant and Frege, insist is the very essence of belief, namely its claim to truth. The introduction of the proposition as object gives a certain measure of objectivity to the theory of partial belief, at least at the level of its logic, since propositions may be identified as the same structures in or before the minds of different subjects. If I believe to degree 1/2 and you believe to degree 1/3 that it will rain, then our beliefs share the common structured object "it will rain". The Lockean problem about the objective reference of ideas is thus diminished if not avoided by shifting the burden of

---

[11] De Finetti, *Theory of Probability*, vol. I, p. 72.
[12] Ibid., 6, 179.   [13] Ibid., 84, 197.

objectivity to truth. Locke could find no empiricistically acceptable way to identify the objects of thought of different subjects.[14] The proposition or thought makes such identification a possibility, at least for belief and assertion, precisely because these aim at the truth by way of the thought. There is thus at least a certain sense that can be given to commonality of the object of partial belief, understood as a feeling directed towards a proposition. On the other hand, however, the intersubjectivity of Humean partial belief consequent upon the presumption of a structure within which the probability is determined by symmetry and equipossibility disappears when that presumption is relaxed. A feeling is, as Hume puts it in describing the passions, "an original existence",[15] it has no intentionality of its own, and can become significant only by incorporation into a structured system. Hume saw this quite clearly, and he invented the indirect passions and his theory of probability to give intentionality to the passions and belief, which can have no objective reference in themselves.[16] When those feelings are considered apart from such a structured setting they can mean no more than what they are. The consequence is that feelings of partial belief, as such, can neither imply nor be incompatible with each other. That I feel belief of strength 1/3 when the thought that the coin lands heads is present can have no essential connection with whatever I might feel when the thought that the coin does not land heads is present. These feelings have no more connection among themselves—each being an original existence—than do my sadness in the evening and my wonder at sunrise. Hume could explain the logical relations among partial beliefs by making them part of the same system, as we explain apodeictic logical relations today by interpreting their objects in a common model. Since each atom of a finest logical partition contains either heads or tails and not both, he could say that their probabilities, or the forces with which they are believed, cannot but sum to one. The power of this account is clear in the example of the die. The later propositional theory lacks the resources to reach this conclusion.

[14] *Essay* book 3, chapter 6, section 26, for example.

[15] "A passion is an original existence, or, if you will, modification of existence, and contains not any representative quality, which renders it a copy of any other existence or modification": *Treatise*, 415.

[16] *Treatise* book 2, parts 1 and 2. See also Davidson, "Hume's Cognitive Theory of Pride" in *Essays on Actions and Events*.

The consequence of this lack, in the presence of an obvious need to give some structure to partial belief, has been to shift the focus from the feelings themselves to the actions or dispositions with which those feelings are correlated or to which they give rise. The feeling of probability 1/3 in the presence of the thought that the coin lands heads is taken to entail a willingness to wager at odds of 1 : 2 that the coin will land heads. Subjectivism thus adapts a roughly Humean (or lately Davidsonian)[17] account of action according to which dispositions to act are the consequences of certain feelings and attitudes. This claim is generalized to allow the feelings to be partial, and further elaborated to associate partiality of feeling with a factor in the calculation of expected gain. The structure that disappeared when Hume's systematic assumptions were dropped is reintroduced when the betting or belief system, defined for a Boolean algebra of propositions, is put in place. Now it is assumed that the subject has quantitative feelings towards truth functions of propositions for which he has such feelings. This system of feelings gives rise to a system of betting dispositions. There are here at least the seeds of relations of incompatibility and implication: a man who will bet at odds of 1 : 2 on a proposition will, it is presumed, bet at odds of 2 : 1 against that proposition. There is some understandable tendency to make of this an a priori principle governing dispositions, but when one looks hard at the complete independence of the original and primitive belief feelings, this tendency wavers. If a belief feeling places no constraint on any other belief feeling, how can their associated dispositions acquire a power to constrain each other? The response to this is to introduce a normative and prudential element into the theory. The subject has not only belief feelings, but also desires or preferences for goods or states of affairs. Presuming a certain consistency in these desires, some systems of betting dispositions can be shown to be necessarily imprudent,[18] one who is unfortunately disposed to act in such ways will necessarily frustrate his own acknowledged desires. The theory is not always clear about the line between what governs dispositions as such, and what requires the additional prudential condition. One consequence of the move to behavioural dispositions in place of feelings is however both evident and expected. Since the original belief feelings

17 See Davidson, "Actions, Reasons and Causes" in *Essays on Actions and Events*.
18 See the coherence theorem in section 2.4.

perform no important function in the developed theory, further reference to them is inessential. The behavioural dispositions now move to the centre of the stage. It is worth pointing out in passing that the shift from feelings to behaviour is at least greatly facilitated by, if it does not require, the shift in objects from ideas to propositions. Wagers require objects that have truth values.

Hume had a fair idea how partial belief interacted with non-partial belief. Partial belief is the general case, non-partial belief is the limit in which cognitive force is concentrated on one object. Here again he was greatly helped by the failure of his theory to insist upon the claim of belief to truth. In both cases, partial and non-partial belief, there is just the feeling, here divided and there concentrated. The modern theory loses this advantage however. For non-partial belief in propositions does aim at the truth, and it is not clear, on subjectivistic grounds, how partial belief—a partial feeling or disposition to act—can do this. This means that an issue that Hume's theory could sidestep becomes critical and central for its successor: how does partial and probabilistic belief relate to the truths of science?

To the extent that subjectivism involves a non-cognitive view of partial belief the relation of probability to truth is an important problem for it. This problem is much less critical for logical and empirical views of probability: for these accounts probability judgements are cognitively meaningful, either true or false, on logical or empirical grounds. Empirical accounts, and frequentism in particular, count probability statements as hypotheses about the relative frequencies of empirical properties. These relative frequencies are themselves the subject of synthetic judgements, which judgements mix easily with other empirical claims. The relations among probability judgements may be complex and hard to characterize, but this difficulty is not different in kind from those that arise in considering ordinary, non-probabilistic, empirical judgements. Again, logical accounts of probability take probability relations to be necessary deductive relations. These relations are not essentially different from other logical relations and these involve no new conceptual questions beyond those treated in logic and mathematics, though here, too, the issues may be quite complex and difficult.

Subjectivism, on the other hand, raises conceptual and philosophical difficulties quite like those mentioned in the discussion of ethical emotivism in section 2.2 above: how do attitudes which do not aim at the truth relate to assertion, truth, and belief?

Assertion and belief are cognitive: who asserts A cannot consistently assert not-A. At least since Frege such structured principles are taken to be based in the nature and laws of truth. But feelings have no such basis in or relation to truth, and subjectivism thus looks to put probability judgements in the non-cognitive sector of human experience. They would then be like expressions of taste or aesthetic experience, exempt from the rules of consistency, evidence, and truth. The relation between probability feelings or sensations and scientific judgements would be like that of the expression of emotion or passion to scientific judgement.

There is one obvious way in which probability judgements can have objective truth values on a subjectivistic interpretation. This is to take partial belief (which is to say, probability) of a given strength in a given proposition to be a psychological property of individual people (and perhaps of beasts as well). Then the full form of a probability judgement is "X believes A to degree p", or "the probability of A for X is p". (These forms might also be relativized to a time, but that is inessential here.) "For the subjectivist", writes de Finetti in *The Theory of Probability*, "everything is clear and rigorous when he is expressing something about somebody's evaluation of probabilities: evaluation which is, simply, what it is."[19] Let me call this view *descriptive psychologism*. Subjectivism becomes in this way a sort of relativism: that probability judgements— judgements of the form "the probability of A is p"—not relativized to a subject lack truth value is due to their incompleteness. This view is independent of relativism about truth. Relativism about probability is compatible with holding truth to be a relation between a proposition or sentence and a subject or culture, and it is also compatible with taking truth to be a property or character of propositions or sentences. The first of these options, the relativistic view of truth, resolves the question of the relation between probability judgements and the truths of science, though this resolution might be thought to be Draconian: it makes truth itself subjective or relative. No problem remains then about relating probabilistic and non-probabilistic judgements, for these latter are also subjective, in the sense of being relative to a subject or culture. De Finetti at least flirts with such a view. In treating the question of the relations between probabilistic connections and causal laws he writes,

---

[19] *Theory of Probability* vol. I, p. 8.

Rigid laws are formulated and accepted by our minds for the same reasons that lead us to formulate and accept any judgement of probability whatever; the only difference consists in the very high probability that we attribute, in the case of rigid laws, to their exact agreement with experimental facts. The probability is so high that we call it "practically absolute certainty", or, simply, "certainty", understanding all the while the qualification that is essential from the philosophical and logical point of view.

The notion of "cause" thus depends upon the notion of probability, and it follows also from the same subjective source as do all judgements of probability.[20]

In other places, though, de Finetti seems to want to avoid this view. Thus in the introduction to *Theory of Probability* he writes that "statements have *objective* meaning if one can say, on the basis of a well determined observation . . . whether they are true or false" and a few lines later that "statements of this nature [i.e., with objective meaning] . . . are the objects *to which* judgements of probability apply (as long as one does not know whether they are true or false) and are called either *propositions*, if one is thinking more in terms of the expressions in which they are formulated, or *events*, if one is thinking more in terms of the circumstances to which their being true or false corresponds". Again in the appendix to the same work we find, "By definition, an event must be either *true* or *false*". And in a curious note on the following page:

At this point, in order to avoid confusion and misunderstandings, we should clarify the relationship between subjectivism in the field of probability, and subjectivism in relation to knowledge in general.

It is sometimes said that "yes, of course probability is subjective . . . because *everything* is subjective." Put this way, however, the statement is not in accordance with the subjectivistic conception of probability, and is, in fact, at odds with it.[21]

The latter view, that is the denial that truth is subjective or relative in company with the assertion that probability is subjective and relative to a believer, will then claim that probability (or partial belief), like belief *simpliciter*, is a relation between a subject and a proposition, which proposition is either true or false. De Finetti seems clearly to announce such a view in the above passages. The problem

[20] "Foresight, its Logical Laws, its Subjective Sources", in H.E. Kyburg and H. Smokler (eds.), *Studies in Subjective Probability*, 154 ff. "[I]n place of extending the character of reality of the classical laws to the probability laws, we can try on the contrary to make even the classical laws participate in the subjective character of the statistical laws". Idem.

[21] De Finetti, *Theory of Probability* vol. I, p. 6; vol. II, pp. 264, 265 n.

of the scientific function of probability judgements, of the relation between them and scientific truth, thus remains. Both forms of subjectivism hold that there are no criteria of correctness for non-relativized probability judgements. They are distinguished by their views about non-partial belief. On one view there are no objective criteria for the correctness of such beliefs not relativized to a subject. On the other, truth of the believed proposition provides a criterion for correctness of belief.

One traditional way of dealing with this question of the relation of truth to probability, while remaining faithful at least in principle to subjectivism in probability, is to eliminate the relativistic reference to a subject who believes or with respect to whom the probability is determined, by introducing an ideal subject. Neither probability nor truth will then be relative, and the conceptual difficulties of their relation which arise on the mixed form of subjectivism are thus calmed. On such an account to say that the probability of A is p just means that the ideal subject does or would believe A to degree p. Without going into any detail, two forms of this method may be briefly described. Both involve the introduction of normative concepts. One form is due to Carnap, the other is a variation on Peirce's view of scientific truth.

Carnap conceived the project of *The Logical Foundations of Probability* as the task of giving a complete axiomatic definition of degree of confirmation or logical probability for an appropriate (first-order) language. Degree of confirmation is conceived as a metrical generalization of the metalinguistic relation of logical implication. The laws of probability—that degree of confirmation is a conditional probability on sentences of the language in question, invariant for replacements of logical equivalents—are an essential part of this axiomatization, but these laws are not sufficient to complete the axiomatization, since in standard cases they admit infinitely many instances. Carnap thus proposed augmenting the probability axioms with the principle of regularity (that the values of zero and one are reserved for cases of inconsistency and implication respectively) and by various symmetry constraints; for example, that probability should be invariant for sentences which differ only by permuting the proper names of individuals. When the proposed symmetry principles were seen to entail difficulties—typically that they prevented or impeded changes of degree of confirmation on the basis of evidence—the original goal of a complete axiomatic definition was replaced by the goal of describing appropriate functions with more and more precision. By 1960 Carnap envisioned the task of logical foundations to be the definition of rational degree of belief. This degree of belief was conceived in a roughly behaviouristic fashion, in terms of expected gain, and of the principle of prudence mentioned above. Again, this imperative and plausible extensions of it fall short of completely specifying degree of confirmation. Carnap seems then to have come to view the task of logic in general, not just that of the logic of probability, to be to make precise the concept of rational belief as a limit case of the belief of an empirical subject, an existing person.[22] The logical concepts are to be arrived at by the progressive refinement of psychological concepts under the force of principles of prudence and rationality. This represents at least a *rapprochement* with subjectivism, certainly compared with the resolute anti-psychologism of *The Logical Foundations of Probability*: probability is identified as a form of belief, and subjective and psychological forms of belief are taken as the starting-points for the refining and limiting process that will eventually give the definition of rational (partial) belief. This view might be called *normative psychologism*, since it strives to define logical concepts by mixing psychological and normative concepts. It would, if successful, provide an answer to the question of the relations between probability and truth. These relations would pass by way of the logical concepts, and in particular the logical concept of probability.[23]

Peirce's idea is structurally similar to this. It too depends upon

[22] See "The Aim of Inductive Logic" in E. Nagel, P. Suppes, and A. Tarski (eds.), *Logic, Methodology and Philosophy of Science*. A later and modified version appears in R. Carnap and R. Jeffrey (eds.), *Studies in Inductive Logic and Probability*, vol. II. A more recent and quite different normative theory is proposed and elaborated by Kyburg in *The Logical Foundations of Statistical Inference*. Kyburg relativizes probability to a *rational corpus* which, since it is logically closed, functions a bit like the theories in the account of chapter 3 below, with the important differences, first that probability is an interval rather than a quantity, and secondly that the languages for which it is defined are much richer than first-order.

[23] De Finetti also seems sometimes to favour such a view. Thus in the appendix to *Theory of Probability* he mentions "a formulation which is subjectivistic in a purely psychological sense, and in which no axioms would be acceptable. This is the approach in which one simply thinks of evaluations of probability—in general, incoherent—being made by some, arbitrary, individual. It is clear that without sufficient preparation and thought everyone would give incoherent answers in every field (e.g. by estimating distances, areas, speeds, etc., in an incoherent manner)": (vol. II, 340). Here, it is clear, he is slipping back and forth between thinking of probability as a feeling to which no structural constraints apply, and thinking of it as a prudent disposition to place and accept wagers. Hume's theory, too, has a certain normative cast, as the section of the *Treatise* on unphilosophical probabilities makes clear.

notions of rationality and the progression to a limit. In contrast to Carnap's synchronic passage to the limit, in which temporality plays no essential role, Peirce based the pragmatic notion of scientific truth upon the presumption that scientific investigation, if continued by a community of investigators using the scientific method, would result, in the limit, in agreement among them. The scientifically true propositions are just those upon which all reasonable scientific investigators will or would come eventually to agree.

There are two components to this famous pragmatic definition of scientific truth, which Peirce himself does not separate. There is first the question of *consensus*; of agreement among all reasonable investigators. Consensus does not however entail that the beliefs of reasonable investigators do not fluctuate: we might all believe A on odd days and not-A on even days. Consensus would then be complete, but neither A nor not-A could be said to be (pragmatically) true. We should thus distinguish consensus from *convergence*—that beliefs settle and do not change. Nor is convergence sufficient for consensus—half of us might believe A and the rest believe not-A now and forever. Beliefs would then be stable, but we should not agree. Pragmatic truth requires both that our beliefs tend to settle or converge and that we tend to reach consensus. The major presumption of Peirce's account is that the scientific method assures convergence and consensus in the beliefs of a community of scientific investigators.

The pragmatic definition of scientific truth is easily applied to partial beliefs or subjective probabilities. Suppose that partial beliefs satisfy the laws of probability. The mean or average value for a group of investigators of their partial beliefs in A will then be a probability.[24] Given a proposition A, *convergence* can then be inversely correlated with the variance of partial beliefs in the proposition (the average of the squares of their distances from the mean). And a group of partial beliefs in a proposition may be said to *converge* if their mean tends to stabilize in time. If, then, Peirce's powerful and vague presumptions about the nature of scientific method are in force, the result is a non-relativistic notion of truth or correctness of partial belief, which then conforms to the laws of probability. We have then a clear meaning to the probability of a proposition. This definition is different from Carnap's, for it

---

[24] This is shown, and the application of the pragmatic definition to partial belief is worked out, in my paper "Truth, Consensus and Probability".

depends upon presumptions about the operation of a method through time. It also differs from Carnap's resolution in redefining truth. This redefinition is accomplished in such a way that the relation of probability to scientific truth is no longer problematical. The account is not without its philosophical difficulties, however. It is in particular not clear how truth is the end of inquiry; how it is that science seeks the truth. To see this just ask what the individual investigator is trying to do. If he wants to reach the truth his best strategy is to ask not how the world is, but rather what his colleagues think about it, and to adopt as his belief measure the mean of their belief measures. If every investigator does this, they are sure quickly to arrive at the truth, pragmatically conceived. Peirce's account will not easily be able to say what is wrong with this strategy.

The issue of embedded probabilities is best considered in the context of the meaning and use of probabilistic discourse. The different views of the nature of probability discussed above suggest and accommodate, if they do not imply, corresponding views of probabilistic language. Neither logical nor empirical views of probability raise any special problems in this regard, at least at the outset, for by incorporating probability statements in the bodies of logical and empirical statements they bring them under the authority of general theories of logical and empirical assertoric discourse. Probability assertions are true or false, and to understand their meaning we work at understanding their truth conditions.

The semantics of Hume's expressive theory of probability is almost this simple, at least in its first formulation: what appear to be probability assertions are not really assertions at all; they are the expressions of probability feelings. As such they may be deceptive or misleading, but they cannot be true or false, since what they express is without truth value. It is important to keep in mind, however, that probability expressions are not *pure* expressions of feeling, they are expressions of feelings directed toward certain structured objects. If all the expressions were pure, then there would be no difference between expressing that the probability of heads is 1/2 and expressing that the probability of rain is 1/2. The difference between these is not in the expression, but in the object towards which the expressed attitude is directed. So, in the original and Humean form of the theory, the expression must be situated in a context of equipossible alternatives. The difference is like that between the direct and indirect passions on Hume's view: the direct passions (joy and sadness, for example) are not intentional. The cause of my joy is not its object. Hume saw that certain passions (pride and humility; love and hate) have objects which are constitutive of them; pride in my house is constituted differently from pride in my fencing skill, whereas the joy that one of these brings about is not in itself to be distinguished from that brought about by the other. Hume called these four intentional passions, those that take objects, the *indirect* passions. The indirect passions, we might say today, have a logic, which the direct passions lack. One who is proud of his house cannot at the same time be ashamed of it in the same respect, and this impossibility is based upon the structure given by Hume's theory to the indirect passions. This structure is not part of the feeling itself, the feeling that makes pride in my house and pride in my fencing skill both cases of pride, it is determined by the situation of and beliefs regarding the objects of the passion. Thus when I say that I am proud of my house, I am, first, identifying the object and my situation with respect to it, and, secondly, expressing my feeling about this object. The moral to be drawn in the present context is that expressions of probability feelings must, like expressions of indirect passion, have a logic. Hume's account of the probability of chances provides such a logic. In the later propositional form of the theory, expressions of probability are expressions of feelings towards propositions. The proposition itself, however, cannot be an expressed feeling. It must be the same neutral object towards which other feelings of probability might be expressed. To put it in phenomenological terms, the proposition is the noematic object of the noetic intending which is the probability feeling. The linguistic expression of this feeling, in order clearly to express *this* feeling, must identify the proposition which is its object and also reveal the feeling that it expresses. If probability is to be understood as a feeling, or in terms of probability sensations, then the subject who expresses such a feeling or reveals such a sensation must understand what object it is directed towards. Probability feelings are in this way like pride in my house, not like the joy caused by my house. I may mistake the source of that joy, believing it to be brought about by my car. This does not change the joy felt or expressed. But I cannot be wrong about the object of my pride without changing that pride itself. In quite the same way, if my feeling of probability 1/2 is really directed towards rain, then I must know this, and that it is not directed towards heads, to express it.

At least some of these subtleties are avoided in the straight-forward assertoric account of probabilistic language which goes naturally with descriptive psychologism. If probability is just partial belief, then a sentence like "The probability of A for X is p" just asserts a certain psychological matter of fact. This may be a fact about X's feelings, or it may concern his behavioural dispositions. That will depend upon the particular psychological theory in force. The statement will be true if X has those feelings or dispositions, false otherwise. Probability statements lacking reference to a subject may be presumed to have implicit first-person reference. When I say that the probability of A is p, then what I say is true or false accordingly as I have or lack the feelings or dispositions which constitute partial belief of degree p in A. I may, of course, be wrong about this; that will depend upon how well I know myself and my beliefs. Of course in both the third- and first-person cases it is essential that the proposition believed be correctly identified. So, if partial belief is disposition to wager, then the believer must understand the object, at least well enough to enter into contracts that depend upon whether or not it obtains or comes about. Hence a simple and pure behaviouristic theory is ruled out on much the same grounds that rule out a purely expressive account of the expressions of probability feelings. Just as the probability feeling must be directed towards the correct object, so the behaviour in question must be behaviour towards or concerning the correct proposition or sentence, and in the case of the sentence, it must be the sentence as understood, not simply the written words or spoken sounds.

Normative psychologism raises no essentially different linguistic or semantical questions here. Although probability is a normative or prudential concept, probability assertions involve no different semantics than those required for understanding other assertions about rationality or prudence.

Descriptive psychologism also invites what might be called a *performative* account of at least some probabilistic discourse.[25] Certain first-person, present-tense probability statements may be understood not as descriptions of beliefs, but as engagements or commitments to enter into wagers at the given odds: when I say that the probability of rain is 1/2, I commit myself to accept bets at those

---

[25] See Bas van Fraassen, "Belief and the Will". De Finetti sometimes seems to favour this interpretation as well: see, for example, his remarks in *Theory of Probability* vol. I, p. 74 about what "one must be prepared to buy".

odds, presumably within my means, on either side of the proposition. There may or may not be probability feelings behind such performatives. I may or may not have the long term disposition to bet in this way (so I may commit myself to bet against my beliefs, carried away at the moment). Here again, as in the general case of performatives, the proposition in question enters into the act itself, and it must be understood as such by the agent. Performative subjectivism is hence incompatible with a subjectivistic or relativistic view of truth, for the reasons pointed out earlier: wagers require objects with truth value.

Let us now turn to embedded probabilities, and first to the question of their importance. We may begin by comparing probability with the modal operators—necessity and possibility. This comparison will be useful because it will invite an examination of analogues to Quine's well-known arguments about embedded modalities: arguments that possibility and necessity are not properly speaking logical operators.[26] It is also natural, at least at the outset, to follow Carnap in thinking of probability as a metrical generalization of the contrast between necessity and impossibility.

Quine distinguished three grades of modal involvement or embedding, according to whether the modal operator is unembedded:

1. $\Box A$;

embedded only within the scopes of truth functions:

2. $\neg \Box A$, $[A \rightarrow \Box B]$;

or embedded within the scopes of quantifiers as well:

3. $(\forall x)\Box A$.

To these we may add a "fourth grade", the embedding of modal operators within the scopes of modal operators:

4. $\Box\Box A$.

Embedded probabilities can be classed in this way too. There are first unembedded probabilities:

1. $P(A) = p$

then probabilities embedded within the scopes of truth functions:

2. $\neg [P(A) = p]$, $[A \rightarrow (P(B) = p)]$

26 In Quine, "Three Grades of Modal Involvement".

and within the scopes of quantifiers. (It will be simplest to restrict the variables bound to occurrence within the argument of the probability function, ignoring quantification over the functions themselves and over their values.)

3. $(\exists x)[P(A(x)) = p]$

Here only "x" occurs as a variable, the other letters are schematic symbols to be filled in by open sentences, function-letters, and numerical constants. In addition to these three types there will also be self-embeddings, in which probability is applied to arguments including probability:

4. $P[P(A) = p] = q$.

It is important to notice that Quine's arguments concerning embedded modalities are not merely negative or sceptical, but include also a strong positive account of modal involvements of the first two grades as well as of some self-embeddings of the fourth type. This well-founded account is roughly that suggested by Frege.[27] It is to read "A is necessary" as asserting that A follows logically from general laws. In the case of the logical modalities, these laws are taken to be general logical laws. Since logical implication is a metalinguistic relation, this view interprets necessity as a metalinguistic property or operator. Necessity has thus a metalinguistic component, and this assures that the content it governs will be referentially opaque or intensional to at least some extent. This causes no difficulty, though there are structural complications, in second-grade embeddings, but third-grade embeddings, since they involve quantifying into referentially opaque contexts, encounter well-known obstacles. Self-embeddings, as Quine is careful to point out, can in some cases be adequately accounted for in the context of a metalinguistic interpretation of laws of a higher level. From an abstract and structural point of view, then, the Frege–Quine interpretation of embedded modalities is *hierarchical*. Each additional modal operator raises the linguistic level, and the logic of embedded modalities is just the logic of relations among these levels.

The analogy with Carnapian logical probability is striking. Carnapian probability is a metalinguistic operator, and embedded probabilities will call forth a precisely analogous hierarchy to that generated by embedded or iterated modalities. Each probability

[27] In the fourth section of Frege's *Begriffschrift*.

operator carries with it a set of quotation marks. As one would expect, third-grade probability embeddings are sources of complication here. This is examined in more detail in the next two chapters.

The hierarchical structure of embedded logical probabilities is not restricted to logical probabilities. If one thinks, as Hume did and Patrick Suppes does,[28] of probability as the general form of causality—invariable causal connection being a special case—then probabilities of probabilities will have the same layered structure as causes of causal relations: "that A caused B caused C". Though there are cases, in particular involving human reactions, where this makes sense, it frequently does not, and for very good reasons: causality is a habit of the mind (Hume) or a category (Kant). It is a categorial relation of phenomena. Since it is categorial and not itself phenomenal it can be referred to only at a transcendental level. So "That A caused B caused C" involves just the metaphysical confusion tracked by Hume and trapped by Kant. For Hume, as pointed out above, self-embedded belief causes problems as well, since it would require distinguishing the feeling from the feeling of that feeling. And it is easy to see that these problems extend to all embeddings of belief on a Humean account. Even embedded beliefs at the second grade are difficult. Failing to have a feeling is not itself a feeling, so "I don't believe it's raining" (as distinct from "I believe it's not raining") resists interpretation, as do compounds involving the other truth functions. The obvious move here is to switch to a descriptive account for embedded occurrences. Then simple expressions of belief express my belief feeling, and embedded ones are referential or descriptive of those feelings. When I say that I believe that it is raining, I *express* my feeling of belief towards that proposition. When I say that I don't believe that it is raining, I *assert* that I do not have the feeling of belief towards that proposition, and similarly for the other truth functions. Third-grade embeddings will bring on the usual difficulties. If the object of belief is a proposition, then what looks to be a propositional function ("x is a spy"), must somehow be accounted for as a proposition believed in "(∃x) Ralph believes that x is a spy". It must be said what object is the target of the feeling in this case.

The performative account of probability statements will require the same accommodations: if "The probability of A is p" is just my

---

[28] See Suppes, *A Probabilistic Theory of Causality*.

commitment to place and to accept bets, then truth-functionally embedded occurrences of this same sentence cannot also perform such a function. They will be best understood as assertions in which my dispositions to enter into commitments are described or referred to. So, "If B then P(A) = p" asserts that if B then I shall be disposed to place and to accept bets on A at odds given by p. I make no commitment by saying or writing this. Should B be the case, if I refuse such a bet then what I said will have been false, but I shall not have failed to live up to my engagements as I should if I refused a bet after a simple statement of probability.

Both the performative and expressive accounts thus require some form of descriptivism and some understanding of the assertive use of probability statements to complete them if they are to apply to embedded probabilities. And the account offered by descriptive psychologism of embedded probabilities will, like the metalinguistic Carnapian account, be hierarchical. From the point of view of intuitive psychology, this means that understanding embedded probabilities requires understanding the psychology of partial belief. So, I may assert that the chance of rain is 1/2, thereby committing myself to place bets on whether or not it rains, without knowing that in fact there are belief feelings or behavioural dispositions behind this. But should I assert that the chance of rain is not 1/2 I thereby make a psychological claim about my belief feelings or dispositions to place bets. And should I assert that it is more likely that the chance of rain is 1/2 than it is that this coin should land heads, I make a claim about my feelings about feelings, or, more plausibly, about my dispositions to place wagers on my dispositions to place wagers. As Brian Skyrms has shown in a careful series of papers, the details of this can be worked out, though they are far from trivial.[29] From a philosophical point of view the main question is to justify the constraints that relate probabilities of different levels. This question is discussed in more detail in the following chapters.

Embedded probabilities provide a good test case for logicism. If probability is a properly logical concept, then it should be comprehensible without reference to psychological or applied logical or epistemic concepts. Embedding is also, in our day, a salient mark of the logical, and thus a logical account of probability should find

29 See Skyrms, "Higher Order Degrees of Belief" and chapter 2 of *Pragmatics and Empiricism*.

embeddings natural. The theory proposed in chapters 4 and 5, below, is constructed on this premiss.

Something should also be said here about probability and intensionality. It is sometimes said that probability is an intensional operator, or, at least, that it is non-extensional.[30] By this is meant that probability is invariant only for intensionally equivalent propositions as arguments, or that the probabilities of extensionally equivalent propositions may differ. As far as Carnapian logical probability is concerned, in one quite clear and naïve sense probability is extensional. Carnapian probability is a function defined on sentences. It assigns values to sentences quite independently of how those sentences are named or intended, just as metalinguistic claims of logical consistency or implication depend not at all upon the ways in which the sentences concerned are named or intended. What is more to the point here is the specification of equivalence relations among sentences for which (Carnapian logical) probability is invariant. In this not quite straightforward sense, a logical probability is extensional if it always assigns the same value to sentences which differ only by replacement of coextensive terms. Similarly, probability applied to propositions is extensional if propositions that differ only in this way have always the same probability. Frege's famous argument that all true sentences have the same truth value can easily be applied to show that an extensional probability on propositions or sentences must assign one to all truths and zero to all falsehoods: that argument shows that equivalence under coextensive replacement cannot be restricted to a given position in a sentence.[31] Extensionalism is

---

[30] By me, for example: see "Truth, Consensus and Probability". I was there in distinguished company: see Reichenbach's discussion of "the problem of the reference class" in *The Theory of Probability*, 374; Carnap, *Logical Foundations of Probability*, section 52; and, more recently, Skyrms, "Higher Order Degrees of Belief".

[31] Here is a sketch of one case of the argument: suppose that a = b and that F and G are coextensive predicates. Suppose further that F(a) and G(a) are both true and that $P[F(a)] = 1$. Then (writing ιx for *the x):*

$$a = \iota x[x = a \& F(x)] = \iota x[x = b \& F(x)] = \iota x[x = b \& G(x)] = b$$

further, $F[\iota x(x = b \& G(x))]$ and $G[\iota x(x = b \& F(x))]$ are logically equivalent. If probability is extensional, then, since $P[F(a)] = 1$,

$$P[F(\iota x(x = b \& G(x)))] = 1$$

and by the above logical equivalence

$$P[G(\iota x(x = b \& F(x)))] = 1$$

thus incompatible not only with an interesting account of probability, but also with regularity, according to which zero and one are reserved for inconsistent and necessary arguments respectively. That is to say that if the bearers of probability are sentences or propositions, then probability cannot very well be an extensional operator.

From the point of view of expressive subjectivism, according to which probability is a feeling of partial belief directed towards a proposition, it is pretty clear, as argued above, that there can be few if any constraints on the invariance of probability for different arguments. For partial belief (which is to say probability) is not part of the object believed, but is constituted by the way in which the object is felt or intended. Even the strictest equivalence cannot assure invariance of feeling. Things are about the same with descriptive subjectivism of the behaviourist sort. If probability is partial belief, where this is understood as disposition to bet, it is determined not by the object but by my disposition towards it. This will obviously vary with how the proposition, event, or outcome is intended or understood. Indeed, if subjectivism includes the premiss that probability is partial belief, then, so long as belief is intensional or non-extensional, probability must be so too. The intensionality of probability is thus less a datum of subjectivism than it is a presupposition of its central principle.

The question of intensionality does not arise in quite the same form for frequentism. In the section cited above, Reichenbach identifies the *problem of the reference class* to be that of selecting the appropriate reference class to determine a probability. In some cases this is, as it seems, just the question of deciding which of the many classes an individual belongs to is to be used as antecedent in a conditional probability with a given consequent. This is just a probabilistic form of the problem of relevance or projectability, made famous by Nelson Goodman.[32] In other cases, however, it is

---

so, $P[G(b)] = 1$. This shows that extensionality cannot be restricted to subject positions, and that hence if any true sentence has probability one then every sentence with coextensive subject and predicate must have probability one. The result generalizes in pretty obvious ways. The argument was first given explicitly by Church in his review of Carnap's *Introduction to Semantics*. Frege states the principles on which it depends in "Sense and Reference". See Quine, *Word and Object*, section 31, for a striking application of it, and Vickers, *Belief and Probability*, 22 f. for an attempt at giving its general form.

[32] In Goodman, *Fact, Fiction, and Forecast*.

not so much the class itself that is in question as it is the order in which the class is conceived. If A is a denumerably infinite class, and if A ∩ B and A ∩ − B are also infinite, then the relative frequency of B in A can be anything from zero to one inclusive, depending upon the way in which A is ordered. Thus "the relative frequency of B in A" is not in general well defined. Reichenbach's theory applies to ordered classes or sequences, and the problem thus does not arise for it, at least not in this form. There is, however, an ensuing difficulty of application, since many, if not most, ordinary and scientific predicates do not impose any order on their extensions. The class of blue things, the class of valid formulas of predicate logic, each of these seems to be a class of objects that remains the same under different orderings. In the case of empirical classes Reichenbach shows an unfortunate tendency to identify the order of the class with the order in which its members are examined or observed. Goodman's discussion of this question, mentioned above, should by now have made us wary of this. We are thus led to a form of the problem of intensionality of probability, since the way in which an infinite class is ordered may naturally be regarded as a way of intending it. When things are considered in this light, Reichenbach's theory makes of probability an intensional operator on pairs of classes; the probability of B given A (where A and B are classes) is the limiting relative frequency of B in A under a certain presumed ordering of A. Here, as in the logical theory, the important question is that of invariance: which probability judgements are invariant under what sorts of changes in the orders of the classes under consideration? The theory of chapters 4 and 5 below gives the beginning of an answer to this question.

2.4 Two theorems for subjectivism

Subjectivism is a programme for interpreting and understanding probability and discourse about it, and it rests upon certain philosophically deep and pointed results. In this section, two of these results are informally described and briefly discussed. These descriptions and discussions are not proofs; the intent is to provide some background and motivation for those readers who know little or nothing about the matter.

The first result is known as the *dutch book* or *coherence* theorem.[33] It rests upon a simple fact about probabilities defined on the sentences of a formal language. Consider a formal language L, assumed for simplicity to be a first-order language, built up in the usual way from individual and predicate constants, individual variables, truth-functions, and quantifiers. A *consistent* set of sentences of L is one all the members of which are true in some model for L. A *closed* set of sentences of L is one that includes all of its logical consequences. A *probability on L* is a function P which assigns a value to each sentence of L in accordance with the following:

1. $0 \leq P(A) \leq 1$
2. If A is valid then $P(A) = 1$
3. If A is inconsistent with B then $P(A \lor B) = P(A) + P(B)$

If Γ is a set of sentences of L we write $N(\Gamma)$ for the cardinality of Γ; the number (perhaps infinite) of sentences in Γ. The simple fact upon which the coherence theorem rests is the following:

Sum condition. P is a probability on L if and only if for every set Γ of sentences of L there are Γ^- and Γ^+, subsets of Γ, such that

(i) Γ^- is closed;
(ii) Γ^+ is consistent;
(iii) $N(\Gamma^-) \leq \Sigma_{A \in \Gamma} P(A) \leq N(\Gamma^+)$.

Without proving the sum condition it may perhaps be made plausible by noticing first that if Γ_i is a consistent and closed set of sentences of L then a function that assigns one to every member of Γ_i and zero to every other sentence of L is a two-valued probability on sentences of L. The sum of the values of this probability on Γ_i is just $N(\Gamma_i)$. Any probability on L can be represented as a weighted average of these two-valued probabilities. It may also be remarked that the theorem and its proof make use of only quite general characteristics of logical necessity, consistency, and consequence. It thus holds for quite a large class of logics satisfying quite weak constraints.

Suppose now that probability is identified with partial belief, thought of as disposition to bet. Then if P gives your degree of

---

[33] First proved (independently) by Ramsey, in "Truth and Probability" and de Finetti in "Foresight: Its Logical Laws, its Subjective Sources". The present remarks ignore such important matters as the measurement of value. See Vickers, *Belief and Probability* for a more complete exposition including a proof of the sum condition.

belief, you will put up $P(A) on condition that you receive $1 if A and nothing if not-A. If Γ is a set of sentences of L, you will put up $\$\Sigma_{A \epsilon \Gamma}P(A)$ on condition that you receive just $1 for every A in Γ that turns out to be true. Let us say that your partial beliefs are *coherent* just in case for every subset Γ of L, should you bet on all sentences in Γ in accordance with P, it is neither necessary that you suffer a net loss nor necessary that you have a net gain. Then your partial beliefs are coherent just in case for every subset Γ of L, there is some closed subset Γ⁻ of Γ and some consistent subset Γ⁻ of Γ such that

$$N(\Gamma^-) \leq \Sigma_{A \epsilon \Gamma}P(A) \leq N(\Gamma^+).$$

By the sum condition we have:

Coherence theorem. P is coherent if and only if P is a probability.

The concept of coherence is relative to a concept of necessity. The relativity and generality of the sum condition are thus carried over to the coherence theorem. We have, in fact, not one but many theorems, one for each concept of necessity in quite a large class. The coherence theorem provides the rationale for that form of subjectivism referred to in the previous section as *normative psychologism*. Coherent, which is to say probabilistic, partial belief is said to be a minimal condition of prudence, for if one's beliefs violate its principles, then wagering in accordance with them may lead one into necessarily losing situations.

The second result depends upon the laws of probability and the ways in which they assign values to statements about frequencies. Readers with no previous background in probability may want to postpone reading the remainder of this section until after they have read section 3.2.[34]

The typical topic of probabilistic discourse is a *trial*, something within our control to bring about and which is followed by or results in certain *outcomes*. Some of these outcomes we class together, in any way we please, as *successful* outcomes of the trial. Any outcome not a success is counted as a *failure*. A sequence of trials of the same

---

[34] De Finetti first proved the theorem in "Foresight", proposition 19, 129. For later (and less laconic) proofs see Feller, *An Introduction to Probability Theory and its Applications*, vol. II, pp. 228 f. and Loève, *Probability Theory*, section 27.2. Diaconis, in "Finite Forms of de Finetti's Theorem", provides a clear exposition, and Jeffrey, in "Probability Integrals", puts the theorem in a general setting for inductive logic. For a general and elementary introduction to probability theory see Feller, *Introduction to Probability Theory* vol. I.

sort is known as an *experiment*. In applications experiments may include taking physical measurements, observing members of certain populations, operating mechanical devices, and, in fact, any act or observation that can be repeated in essentially the same way through time. One very common case is that of independent trials with constant probability of success. By *independent* is meant that the probability of success on any trial is unaffected by the outcomes of any other trials. Successive tosses of a coin provide a standard example, as do draws from an urn containing balls of two colours, the drawn ball being replaced and the urn remixed after each draw. If we write S_i for success on trial i, and $P(Y/X)$ for the probability of Y given X, then independence says that if i and j are distinct trials then:

$$P(S_j) = P(S_j/S_i) = P(S_j/\neg S_i)$$
$$P(\neg S_j) = P(\neg S_j/S_i) = P(\neg S_j/\neg S_i)$$

and further that these equalities hold when "S_i" is replaced by any conjunction of successes and failures on trials different from j. That probability of success is constant means just that for some fixed quantity p, for all i

$$P(S_i) = p; P(\neg S_i) = 1 - p$$

Given a kind of trials and outcomes, we represent the successive trials by the positive integers $1, 2, \ldots$. Assuming that the probability of success is constant, if t is a sequence of outcomes we write S_i^t for the outcome on trial i. So S_i^t is either S_i or $\neg S_i$. Thus

$$t = S_1^t, S_2^t, \ldots$$

and we write t_k for the segment consisting of the first k members of t:

$$t_k = S_1^t, \ldots, S_k^t.$$

With S and t as above, for each k the number of successes in t_k (i.e., the number of those places i at which S_i^t is S_i) is denoted by $F(t_k)$. Hence

$$0 \leq F(t_k) \leq k.$$

The *relative frequency* of success in t_k is defined

$$f(t_k) = (1/k)F(t_k)$$

so this latter quantity is always between zero and one, inclusive. In some cases as the index k increases without bound the relative frequencies $f(t_k)$ converge to a quantity r:

$$\lim_{k \to \infty} f(t_k) = r.$$

In such a case we define

$$f(t) = r.$$

The case of independent trials with constant probability of success will be referred to here, as it is in many places, as the case of *Bernoulli trials*. In Bernoulli trials with probability p of success we have that, where $n = F(t_k)$:

$$P(t_k) = [p^n][(1 - p)^{(k - n)}].$$

Consider an experiment involving two urns, one of which includes two red balls and one black ball, and the other of which includes one red ball and two black balls. Take a successful outcome to be drawing a red ball from one of the urns. Perceiving no relevant difference between the urns, a ball is to be drawn from one of them, its colour recorded, and it is to be replaced.

As far as a single draw is concerned, this experiment is indistinguishable from one in which all six balls are in one urn. In both cases $P(S_i) = 1/2$ for each i. We return to this view of the experiment later.

What are our beliefs before the experiment begins? The classical account is that we take the draws to constitute Bernoulli trials with constant but unknown (either 1/3 or 2/3) probability of success; that the experiment will lead us to adopt one or the other of these values for the probability of success with more or less conviction depending upon the number k of trials and the relative frequency $f(t_k)$ of success. Finally, that before the experiment begins the two possible values for probability of success are equally likely; it is equally likely that the probability of success is 2/3 or 1/3. This leads us to compute the constant probability of success before the experiment starts as the *expectation* of the probability P; the weighted average of those possible values:

$$E(P) = (1/2)(2/3) + (1/2)(1/3) = 1/2$$

Enough has already been said about subjectivism in the preceding section to make it clear that the classical account is, from a subjectivistic viewpoint, deeply confused.[35] The account depends essentially upon embedded probabilities, and, in fact, upon self-embedded probabilities. The probability of success is said to be *constant but unknown*. If probability is, as subjectivists claim, degree of belief, then this (classical) description requires that I be uncertain about my beliefs. We have seen that a Humean or psychological account of belief in terms of feelings or presence can make no good sense of this, and, at least in the present instance, a behaviouristic account in terms of disposition to bet can do little better: if the probability is constant but unknown, and if probability is degree of belief, then my degree of belief is constant but unknown. That is to say, I believe with equal strength (i) that I believe to degree 1/3 that the first ball drawn will be red, and (ii) that I believe to degree 2/3 that the first ball drawn will be red. Hence, if belief determines disposition to bet, I will bet at even odds that I will bet (now and in the future, since the belief is constant) at odds of 2 : 1 that the next draw will be red, and I will also bet at even odds (now and in the future) at odds of 1 : 2 that the next draw will be red. This is obviously inadequate. I know full well that I'll now give even odds that the first draw will be red, and I also think it likely that evidence will change this disposition.

One might try to modify this to an account in terms of my present beliefs about what my future beliefs will be: that, for example, I am now willing to bet (i) at even odds that later (after the nth trial) I'll be willing to bet at odds of 2 : 1 that the (n + 1)st draw will be red, and (ii) at even odds that after the nth trial I'll be willing to bet at odds of 1 : 2 that the (n + 1)st draw will be red. It would first be necessary to specify n in some good way, and there remains then the difficulty that if the experiment is inconclusive (if, for example, about half the draws are red and half black) I should be willing to bet neither at odds of 1 : 2 on red nor at odds of 2 : 1 on red; and I know this quite well before the experiment starts.

This is not to say that no behaviouristic sense can ever be made of embedded partial beliefs; clearly we often have beliefs about our future and past beliefs, and perhaps even about our present beliefs, and it is often possible to understand these in a behaviouristic way. It may be that the present example shows that some, quite special,

[35] See, in particular, de Finetti's discussion in *Theory of Probability*, chapter 11, vol. II.

sorts of embedded belief cannot be given a behaviouristic interpretation. It may also be that the probabilities in the classical
account are not to be understood as partial beliefs. What is perhaps
more to the point is that the account in terms of beliefs about future
beliefs is false to the principle of the classical account that the
probabilities are constant, that it is not they but our beliefs about
them that change through time.

It should be clear that this is, from the point of view of a serious
subjectivism, not just an annoying puzzle, but a profound problem
in epistemology and the foundations of probability. Subjectivism is
deeply committed to the identification of probability and partial
belief. What is important in probability must thus be comprehensible in terms of partial belief. The classical concept of Bernoulli
trials is a very fundamental, if not the fundamental, concept in the
classical theory of probability. It is essential not only to the laws of
large numbers—which, since they establish the relationship between
probability and relative frequency, are the basis of probabilistic
reasoning—but also to the classical limit theorems that govern the
normal distribution and its relation to sampling and to statistical
tests of relevance. A probabilist who cannot make legitimate use of
these methods and techniques is not much of a probabilist at all.
Further, a committed subjectivist will see the problem of Bernoulli
trials, and the problem of embedded probabilities in general, as a
serious difficulty in the theory of probability. He will be convinced
that unless good sense can be made of these, the entire theory of
probability is based upon confusion, and that all the theorems and
methods of probability and statistical reasoning are so much idle
nonsense. Of course the mathematical theory of measure is a perfectly respectable and (let us assume) well-founded part of mathematics, but the question of its application to reasoning about
stochastic phenomena is not decided by this: number theory, too, is
well founded, but this does not assure that it is well applied in
numerology.

The technique of the de Finetti representation theorem offers a
precise and philosophically satisfying resolution to this problem. To
gain some appreciation of the spirit of that theorem, let us return to
the example of the experiment involving draws from one of the two
urns. One of the urns has been selected, and balls will be drawn from
it. The classical description says first that either $P(S_i) = 2/3$ for all
trials i, or $P(S_i) = 1/3$ for all trials i, and also that

$$P[P(S_i) = 2/3] = 1/2; \quad P[P(S_i) = 1/3] = 1/2$$

as well as that the draws constitute independent trials; that is to say, that

$$P(S_i/S_j) = P(S_i)$$

when i and j are distinct trials, and that

$$P(t_k) = [p^n][(1 - p)^{(k - n)}]$$

where $n = F(t_k)$.

From a subjectivistic viewpoint there must be something wrong here, and we should hence start again, from a naïve position, to try to give a better description. We should try for a description in terms of our present beliefs, before the experiment; one which refers to neither probability nor partial beliefs in the content of these beliefs. Our partial beliefs before the experiment should not be about probability or partial belief, since an understanding of this is precisely what is at stake.

The first thing to say is this. The second part of the classical description is wrong. The trials are not independent. Notice first that, from the naïve point of view, the most plausible degree of belief in S_i (for any i) before the experiment starts is 1/2. That follows from the equivalence to the single-urn experiment in the case of any one draw, and it is also the value of the expectation of P in the classical description. Rather than introducing the expectation of an unknown probability which determines the strength of (reasonable) belief, let us simply say that the strength of partial belief in (= probability of) success is 1/2. To see that the trials are not independent just notice that, keeping strictly to the identification of probability and partial belief, if the first ball is red, it is then a bit more likely that the urn includes two red balls, and hence the conditional belief in S_2 given S_1 should reflect this; that is to say, $P(S_2/S_1)$ should be a bit greater than $P(S_2)$, which latter should be 1/2. A plausible calculation for this is as follows: let "H" be the hypothesis that the urn includes two red balls and one black. Then

$$P(S_1/H) = P(S_2/H) = 2/3$$
$$P(S_1/\neg H) = P(S_2/\neg H) = 1/3.$$

Since the urns are indistinguishable, $P(H) = 1/2$. Further, though the draws are not independent, they would be independent were

H—that the urn contains two red balls and one black—to obtain. To put this in subjectivistic terms, if $P(X/H)$ gives reasonable odds for betting on X, the bet to be called off if H is false, then

$$P(S_1 \& S_2/H) = P(S_1/H)P(S_2/H) = 4/9;$$

similarly

$$P(S_1 \& S_2/\neg H) = P(S_1/\neg H)P(S_2/\neg H) = 1/9.$$

Again, since $P(S_1) = P(H) = 1/2$, a straightforward application of Bayes's theorem gives

$$P(H/S_1) = \frac{P(S_1/H)P(H)}{P(S_1)} = 2/3$$

$$P(\neg H/S_1) = 1 - P(H/S_1) = 1/3$$

So

$$\begin{aligned}
P(S_1 \& S_2) &= P(H)P(S_1 \& S_2/H) + P(\neg H)P(S_1 \& S_2/\neg H) \\
&= (1/2)(4/9) + (1/2)(1/9) \\
&= 5/18
\end{aligned}$$

$$P(S_2/S_1) = \frac{P(S_1 \& S_2)}{P(S_1)} = 5/9$$

Reasoning similarly about drawing black balls, we have:

$$\begin{aligned}
P(\neg S_1 \& \neg S_2) &= P(H)P(\neg S_1 \& \neg S_2/H) \\
&\quad + P(\neg H)P(\neg S_1 \& \neg S_2/\neg H) \\
&= (1/2)(1/9) + (1/2)(4/9) \\
&= 5/18
\end{aligned}$$

$$P(\neg S_2/\neg S_1) = \frac{P(\neg S_1 \& \neg S_2)}{P(\neg S_1)} = 5/9$$

This shows that it is implausible to regard the trials as independent. Given that the first ball is red (recall that the draws are with replacement) the chance is 5/9 that the second ball will be red, and 4/9 that the second ball will be black. Indeed, this calculation holds for all S_i and S_j, when $i \neq j$ and it reveals what is from a subjectivistic point of view a deep flaw in the classical description: if I took the draws to be independent, then I could not take S_1 to be evidence that makes S_2 slightly more probable, for if the draws are independent, then $P(S_2/S_1) = P(S_2) = 1/2$. Taking the draws to be independent would thus prohibit learning from experience. The subjectivistic response to this is to try to describe our present, pre-experimental or *prior* beliefs in such a way as to allow consequent belief changes to be determined by means of conditional beliefs (which do not change) applied to the actual experimental result. Thus if the actual experimental result is t_k, then our consequent degree of belief in the hypothesis H, that the chosen urn contains two red balls and one black, should be $P(H/t_k)$. And we should know this before the experiment. The question then is what properties these prior probabilities or pre-experimental conditional beliefs should have.

One response to this question has just been given: the belief in t_k is the weighted average or *mixture*

(i) $P(t_k) = \Sigma_i P(t_k/H_i)P(H_i)$

where the hypotheses H_i give the different possible constitutions of the urn. Each measure $P(X/H_i)$ is a classical Bernoullian measure, determined by the probability $P(S_j/H_i)$ of success. The mixture (i) is just what the classical description of the experiment calls the *expectation* of P. As we have seen, this mixture of Bernoullian probabilities is not itself Bernoullian.

A second way to describe the beliefs is in terms of one important feature of Bernoullian probabilities: namely that they are affected only by the frequency of success, and make no distinction in terms of the order in which successes occur. That is just to say, as pointed out above, that if P is a Bernoullian probability with $P(S_j) = p$, and $F(t_k) = F(u_k) = n$, then

(ii) $P(t_k) = [p^n] = (1 - p)^{(k - n)} = P(u_k)$

It is easy to see that this insensitivity to order is also characteristic of mixtures of Bernoullian probabilities:

Lemma. If P is a mixture of Bernoullian probabilities and $F(t_k) = F(u_k)$ then $P(t_k) = P(u_k)$.

This property is called *exchangeability*:[36] an exchangeable probability is just one that gives the same value to sequences of the same length which have the same frequency of success. The lemma says that every mixture of Bernoullian probabilities is exchangeable. From a subjectivistic point of view, exchangeability is a most

---

[36] De Finetti originally called it (in French) "équivalence". In more recent writings he uses "exchangeability". See, for example, *Theory of Probability* vol. I p. 8. The latter expression is now standard.

important feature of reasonable partial beliefs about certain kinds of situation or experiment, and this for several reasons: first, to say that beliefs are exchangeable involves no reference to unknown probabilities or embedded beliefs. It is thus a constraint that can be understood in subjectivistic terms. Secondly, non-Bernoullian exchangeable beliefs about the future have a sensitivity to experience that Bernoullian beliefs cannot have. Thirdly, the concept of exchangeability permits access to many of the classical results which look to depend on embedded probabilities. This access is by way of the de Finetti representation theorem. The theorem asserts that in a large class of cases the converse of the above lemma also holds: that every exchangeable probability of a certain sort is a mixture of Bernoullian probabilities. Let us first state the theorem a bit more precisely, and then go on to discuss its application briefly.

Not every exchangeable probability is a mixture of Bernoullian probabilities. Consider an experiment, like that described above, but which is to terminate after a certain number, $k = 2r$, of draws. Suppose that for some reason we consider it impossible to draw exactly r red balls and r black balls, but that every other relative frequency has positive probability. That is to say (where the constant Bernoullian probability of success is p) that

C_1 If $f(t_k) = 1/2$, then $P(t_k) = 0$.
C_2 If $f(t_k) \neq 1/2$, then $P(t_k) > 0$.

P cannot be Bernoullian, for if it were we should have that

$$p^r(1 - p)^r = 0$$

and hence that $p = 0$ or $p = 1$. But in this case any sequence containing some red and some black balls would have probability zero, and thus—contrary to C_2—some sequences with relative frequencies of success different from 1/2 would have probability zero. Though no Bernoullian probability can satisfy C_1 and C_2, these constraints are not incompatible with exchangeability: define P on sequences of length $k = 2r$ to divide its weight evenly on sequences which include more or less than r reds. It is also easy to see that

(iii) No mixture of Bernoullian probabilities can satisfy C_1 and C_2.

For suppose that P is a mixture of Bernoullian probabilities $P_1 \ldots P_n$. Then there are quantities $p_1 \ldots p_n$ ($P_i(S_j) = p_i$) and positive weights $q_1 \ldots q_n$ summing to one, such that for each t_k, where $F(t_k) = m$

$$P(t_k) = \Sigma_{i=1}^n q_i(p_i)^m(1 - p_i)^{(k-m)}$$

Now if P also satisfies C_1, then if $F(t_k) = r$,

$$P(t_k) = \Sigma_{i=1}^n q_i(p_i)^r(1 - p)^r = 0$$

Since the above quantity is zero, it must be a mixture of the two Bernoullian probabilities determined by $p = 0$ and $p = 1$. This entails that P must violate C_2, for these both assign zero to every sequence containing some reds and some blacks.

Although some exchangeable probabilities satisfy C_1 and C_2, none of them can be extended to exchangeable probabilities on the experiment in which the number of draws is not limited:

(iv) If P satisfies C_1 and C_2 on the k-draw experiment, and Q is an extension of P to the experiment in which the number of draws is not limited, then Q is not exchangeable.

To see why (iv) holds notice first that if P satisfies C_1 and C_2 on the k-draw experiment ($k = 2r$), then any extension of P must assign zero to every sequence which includes just r reds among the first k draws. But for any (rational) relative frequency f, there is some sequence of some length which includes just r reds among the first k draws and which has the relative frequency f of reds. Thus if Q is any extension of P and f is any relative frequency different from zero and one, there is some k and some sequence t_k with the frequency f of reds such that $Q(t_k) = 0$. Hence if Q is in addition exchangeable, for every such f there is some k such that every sequence of length k and relative frequency f must be assigned zero by Q. Q would thus have to assign zero to all extensions of every such sequence. That is to say that *every sequence which includes some reds and some blacks has some finite extension which is assigned zero by Q*. From this it follows (with the help of the axiom of choice) that *for some finite quantity m, every sequence of length $\geq$ m which contains some reds and some blacks is assigned zero by Q*. Q would thus have to be zero on all sequences of length $\geq$ m save the sequence of all reds and the sequence of all blacks. But this is incompatible with C_2.

We can now formulate the de Finetti representation theorem. Let us say that an exchangeable probability P on the k-draw experiment is *extendable*, just in case some extension of P to the experiment in which the number of draws is not limited is exchangeable. We have just seen that the extendable exchangeable probabilities are of two sorts: first, mixtures of the Bernoullian probabilities determined by $p = 0$ and $p = 1$ (i.e., those that assign zero to every sequence containing some reds and some blacks); secondly, those that assign zero to no finite sequence.

De Finetti representation theorem. Every extendable exchangeable probability is a mixture of Bernoullian probabilities. Indeed, the class of extendable exchangeable probabilities is precisely the result of taking all mixtures of Bernoullian probabilities.

The preceding discussion puts things in terms of draws from urns for the sake of simplicity and completeness. It should be clear however that the concepts and results apply to stochastic phenomena quite generally: repeatable trials of any sort, if they are exchangeable, can be treated by the de Finetti theorem. If P is any exchangeable and extendable probability on sequences t_k of given length k, then for some m there are Bernoullian probabilities $P_0 \ldots P_m$ and weights $p_0 \ldots p_m$ such that

$$P(t_k) = \Sigma_{i=0}^{m} p_i P_i(t_k)$$

for each sequence t_k.

The case of tosses with a bent coin is a classic example. We may have no clear opinion at all, before the coin is tossed, about the direction or degree of its bias. In particular there will be no concrete hypotheses corresponding to those giving the constitutions of urns in the above discussion. There are in fact two important steps in moving from the urn model to the general case. One of these is that the degrees of bias may form a continuum and not, as in the different proportions in the urns, a finite set. This gap is filled by the continuous form of the theorem: if P is any exchangeable and extendable probability then where π_i is the Bernoullian probability with probability i of success ($0 < i < 1$) there is a unique measure μ such that

$$P(t) = \int_0^1 \pi_i(t) d\mu(i)$$

for each finite sequence t. Here, quite as in the finite case, the continuous weighting function μ can be thought of as giving the probabilities of the various biases p_i.

The second difference from the finite and discrete case is that, in the case of the bent coin, we have no apparent meaning for the various values $\mu(i)$. It is easy to think of the weights assigned to the Bernoullian probabilities in the urn example as the probabilities of various constitutions of the urn. Here there is a certain possible state of the world, more or less likely, and about which we may have more or less precise and informed opinions. Indeed, in the above exposition, these could even be formulated as hypotheses, and the Bernoullian probabilities as conditionalizations of the given exchangeable probability. There is, however, no such ready interpretation in the case of the bent coin. From a classical point of view, nothing prevents us from reading $\mu(i)$ as the probability that the Bernoullian probability of heads (or success) is π_i, but this interpretation is not legitimate from a subjectivistic point of view, for, from this point of view, Bernoullian probabilities are not states of the world about which one can have opinions. It is thus a confusion to think of the de Finetti theorem as giving a subjectivistic *reduction* of classical Bernoullian probability. Such a reduction would show how to eliminate reference to embedded or unknown probabilities, and the theorem does not do that. It does, however, give what might be called the subjectivistic content of expectations of Bernoullian probabilities, and in this way it gives a subjectivistic interpretation of a large and important class of embedded probabilities. In particular, the classical laws of large numbers and limit theorems—the fundamental truths on which probabilistic reasoning is based—can be formulated in subjectivistic terms.

As interesting as this is, the importance of the theorem is not restricted to making probability safe for subjectivism. It is deeply significant that the work of certain kinds of embeddings can be done by conditionalization. That was the spirit of the above discussion of the urn case. Whether one is a subjectivist or not, one can agree that it is a great advance to see that what seems to be reasoning about probabilities (taking expectations of Bernoullian probabilities) can as well be thought of as reasoning in terms of conditional probabilities; the work that is done by embedded probabilities can as well be done by probability conditionals.

The theorem shows that embedded probabilities of a critical sort, namely those that figure in expectations, are not needed in probabilistic inference. Whatever holds for inference involving the expectations of Bernoullian probabilities will hold as well for exchangeable probabilities, since every exchangeable probability has a representation as a mixture or expectation of Bernoullian probabilities. The general effect of the theorem can be roughly characterized by returning to the comparison of subjectivism with positivistic moral theories. On certain of those theories values are not in the world but in the way we intend it. Value judgements in which the values are embedded present a great obstacle to these theories, for it is not clear how to get the value out of its specific place in the content and into the act of evaluation. Subjectivism has an obvious and obviously analogous problem; if probability is just strength of partial belief, then how to account for probabilities (such as Bernoullian probabilities on the classical account) that have quite precise functions in the content of probability judgements? The representation theorem shows that and how it can be done in the general and crucial case of Bernoullian probabilities; so long as your partial belief function is exchangeable, it works just like the expectation of Bernoullian probabilities, but without the troublesome (from a subjectivistic point of view) confusions involved in the classical description.

The wider class of situations to which exchangeability applies includes all those sequences of events which, though regular, since they consist of trials and outcomes of a clearly specifiable kind, are nevertheless not constituted or individuated by order in time. Sequences generated by gambling devices, by shuffling and tossing under the right conditions, are of this sort, as are many sequences observed in nature; thus, for example, from the point of view of genetics the genotypes of offspring from given parents form an exchangeable sequence. These sequences are thus neither chaotic nor causally determined. They are, further, those in which we seek no deeper comprehension or more detailed laws which would reduce or eliminate the stochastic features: increased accuracy in predicting dice throws, coin tosses, or draws from an urn is not a serious scientific goal. It may be an article of faith of various determinisms that a sufficiently complete description of a coin and its tossing would permit certain prediction of its outcome, but this is of little interest to the probabilistic study of exchangeable phenomena.

Exchangeability, it is worth pointing out in this connection, is a condition of probabilistic knowledge, not part of the content of what is known. Since it is a condition of knowledge, not known itself in the same way, exchangeability is what Kant, and philosophers in the critical tradition that he founded, call a *transcendental* condition. Kant, of course, would deny that knowledge could have any such condition. Indeed, he thought that the a priori universality of order in time was a transcendental precondition of any knowledge about the world, and thus that exchangeability could be no more than an admission that one was ignorant of the causal order upon which knowledge always depended. It is however possible and plausible, if not easy, to apply the general Kantian method of the transcendental deduction to knowledge of stochastic situations, where exchangeable beliefs rather than causally nomological beliefs are a priori justified. Stochastic knowledge of genetic structures is a good example of knowledge of this sort. The generalized Kantian method would try to uncover the fundamental exchangeable processes that underlie our knowledge of such phenomena. If this runs counter to the spirit of the Kantian project, it is no less incompatible with de Finetti's empirical idealism, but that should not deter us from making use of the methods and results of these thinkers in ways and areas where they would resist that application.[37]

[37] From a philosophical point of view the question can be put as follows: how are the transcendental deduction and the categories transformed if the table of judgements includes chance or partial judgement? See Vickers, "On the Reality of Chance" for a discussion of this.

3
Carnapian Logical Probability

3.1 *The space of possible theories of probability*

POSITIVISM divided human experience and discourse into three classes: analytic, synthetic, and non-cognitive. Corresponding to these there are three sorts of theory of probability. Roughly described, these are distinguished by the categories into which they put probability statements. For logicists, probability statements are analytic, for empiricists they are a posteriori, and for subjectivists they are non-cognitive. These positions permit many nuances and combinations. Subjectivism has been discussed in the preceding chapter. It may ease later discussion to sketch some features of logicism and frequentism in a brief and preliminary way.

The logical interpretation of probability takes probability statements to assert logical connections of a partial or metricized sort between hypotheses and evidence. It is in this way like Hume's probability of chances, and may be seen as a consequence when that view is subjected to the transformations discussed in section 5 of chapter 1. The logical connections in question are now taken to be among sentences or propositions, and the algebra of sentences or propositions provided by truth-functional connection now replaces the discarded algebra of ideas and comprehensions. The changes in the concept of analyticity now permit its application to statements of the form "The probability of A is p". Such a statement is analytic if it follows by logic alone from the definition of probability. This represents a considerable liberation along just the lines remarked by Frege, for it would be at best awkward to apply the classical notion of analyticity—inclusion of the predicate idea in that of the subject—to such judgements. Further, the task of logicism here is clearly marked out: its programme will consist in large part of providing an adequate definition of probability to function as a premiss in the appropriate demonstrations. Logical consequences of the definition, augmented by definitions of other key concepts, will be analytic probability statements.

As logic now applies to sentences or propositions, these become the objects of probability and probabilistic relations, and probabilistic or partial judgement follows the path of Fregean assertive force. In Hume's account, the probability of chances entered into the composition of the judgement and helped to hold its parts together. Just as assertion is divorced from this copulative function, so is probability, which, from the point of view of logicism, is a metrical generalization of Fregean assertion.

Logical probability most plausibly generalizes the relation of logical implication or conditionality. That was true of Hume's theory, and it remains so in the later theory. In modern logics these notions are sharply distinguished. Conditionality is understood as the material conditional or its universal quantification. Then implication is either a metalinguistic relation between sentences or a strengthened and non-truth-functional conditional satisfying additional constraints. There are accordingly two ways to think of logical probability: as a generalization of implication, or as a generalization of conditionality. Reichenbach generalized the material conditional to define probability in the object language, and Carnap generalized the metalinguistic relation of implication.[1]

The main thrust of empirical or a posteriori theories of probability is to provide an understanding of probability statements as statements which depend upon experience for their confirmation. There are two varieties of empiricism in probability: one treats probabilities in terms of *propensities* of substances or situations, and the other depends upon *relative frequencies*. Since the theory of the next chapter has certain affinities with frequentism—it might be characterized as logical frequentism, to distinguish it from the empirical frequentism of Reichenbach and von Mises—a brief sketch of some features of frequentism will be useful for later exposition.

(Empirical) frequentism differs from logicism both with respect to the form it gives to probability judgements, and with respect to the account it provides of their evidence. The present chapter is concerned mainly with Carnapian logicism, according to which a probability judgement takes the form of a relation between sentences—structurally like logical implication. For frequentism, a probability judgement usually expresses a relation between properties or classes—the relative frequency with which one of these

---

[1] Reichenbach in *The Theory of Probability* and Carnap in *Logical Foundations of Probability*.

occurs in the other. Other forms of probability judgement may be considered but they will usually reduce to this fundamental relation.

As far as evidence is concerned, for logicism the support of probability judgements is logical and definitional. Frequentism, true to its name, is explicit that probability statements are confirmed by statements of finite relative frequencies. The content of a probability statement may be infinite, when the properties concerned have infinite extensions, and then evidence statements about increasingly large finite subclasses of this extension (properly structured) provide increasingly strong evidence for the statement. Frequentism has difficulties of several sorts with infinities. There is first the ambiguity of relative frequency when the infinite extensions in question have no canonical order. If A is a finite non-null class, then the relative frequency of B in A is just the quotient:

$$\frac{\text{number of things in A} \cap \text{B}}{\text{number of things in A}}$$

If, however, A is (denumerably) infinite, then some use must be made of limits—the relative frequency of B in A should be the limit of the relative frequencies among finite subclasses. But in the case in which the intersection of A and B is infinite, different orderings of the extensions will give different values for the limit, and if infinitely many As are also non-Bs then for some orderings no limit will exist, and for any rational quantity between zero and one inclusive there will be some orderings of A and B such that the relative frequencies of finite subclasses, so ordered, will approach that quantity as a limit.[2] This means first that some canonical ordering of extensions must be assumed in order to assure that probability is univocal, and secondly, that in some cases probability is just not defined. Frequentism takes in fact a fairly strong position on meaningfulness. Not only are statements where the appropriate limits do not exist ruled out, but many single-case probabilities—in which probability is attributed to a proposition or to the relation of conditionality between propositions—are also not accounted for.[3] So the probability that inflation will slow down if Smith is elected will be defined

[2] To make the relative frequency of A in B m/n (where m and n are positive integers) just let the first m of each n objects be in A $\cap$ B, and the remaining n – m be in B – A. For an example in which no limit exists, see note 21 to chapter 4 below.

[3] This question is discussed in more detail in my paper "Phenomenology of Partial Belief".

only if the two statements "inflation will slow down" and "Smith is elected" can be analysed as propositional functions of a shared parameter: "Inflation will slow down in year t" and "Smith is elected in year t", for example, where instances of these forms are temporally ordered. And such relative frequencies would clearly give little basis for sound prediction. Further, a proposition may be analysable into function and argument in several different ways, and such different analyses may give different relative frequencies for the same proposition. Thus, "The chance that a will defeat b is P" may be analysed as expressing the frequency of a property of a, of b, or of the couple (a,b).

With respect to the form of judgement, frequentism has no need to admit any probabilistic generalization of simple assertion. Probabilistic judgements are straightforward assertions, true or false, about relative frequencies. Thus, where logicism generalizes the act of judging, to make of it a partial or probabilistic act, frequentism puts what probability there is—in the form of relative frequency—not into the act, but into the content of judgement. Relative frequencies are empirical facts in the world, judgements about them are true or false. There is no need to allow partial judgements.

3.2 *The general algebraic setting of Carnapian logical probability: probabilities on Boolean algebras*

The business of the present chapter is an exposition of Carnapian logical probability. The theory in question differs in many respects from probability as Carnap analysed it in *The Logical Foundations of Probability* and other writings, but the main lines of that development are preserved. Details and vocabulary may vary to ease the integration of the discussion into a more general framework. In the present section measure-theoretic probability, not necessarily Carnapian, is briefly considered. The concern is mostly terminological, but a few results are cited, and some first steps are taken towards formulating and answering in a Carnapian framework the question of the relation between logical probability and probability as it is defined and studied in measure theory.

From the abstract point of view of measure theory, a probability (measure or function) is a numerical function of a certain simple sort, defined on a Boolean algebra. In the present context Boolean algebras may be thought of as set-theoretic structures. If Z is a non-empty set, then a *Boolean algebra* of subsets of Z is any collection of subsets of Z which includes Z itself as a member, includes the complement with respect to Z of each of its members, and is closed under the formation of finite unions; if A and B are members of the algebra, then their union $A \cup B$ is also a member. Given Z we write Ω_Z, or sometimes just Ω where the context permits, to denote a Boolean algebra of subsets of Z. In what follows, barring explicit mention to the contrary, Z is presumed to be finite or denumerably infinite. If Z is finite then Ω_Z is necessarily finite, but if Z is denumerably infinite, then Ω_Z may be finite, denumerably infinite, or non-denumerably infinite. Some acquaintance with these matters is presumed.[4] We recall that every Boolean algebra includes the null set as a member, and that Boolean algebras are closed under the formation of finite intersections of their members.

A Boolean algebra is said to be a *sigma* or *limit* algebra if it is closed under the formation of countable unions, that is to say, if whenever Δ is a denumerable subfamily of Ω, $\cup \Delta \in \Omega$. Sigma algebras are also closed under the formation of countable intersections.

An *ascending chain* in a Boolean algebra Ω is a sequence

$$\{A_1, A_2, \ldots\}$$

of members of Ω each of which is a subset of its successor. The element $A \in \Omega$ is a *limit* of this chain if,

(i) each A_i is contained in (i.e., is a subset of) A;

(ii) A is contained in any member of Ω that contains all the A_i.

Similarly, a *descending chain* is a sequence each element of which contains its successor, and a limit of a descending chain is an element contained in every element of the chain and which contains any element of Ω that is contained in all members of the chain.

Sigma algebras may alternatively be characterized in terms of limits: a Boolean algebra Ω is a sigma algebra if Ω includes a limit of each of its ascending chains. This is equivalent to saying that Ω contains a limit of each of its descending chains. The upper limit of

---

[4] Expositions are to be found in most elementary books on modern algebra. Halmos's *Lectures on Boolean Algebras* are clear and simple. Sikorski's *Boolean Algebras* is a thorough theoretical treatment. From a logical point of view that in Rosenbloom, *The Elements of Mathematical Logic* is quite useful.

an ascending chain is the union of its members; the lower limit of a descending chain is the intersection of its members.

An *atom* of a Boolean algebra (of sets) is a non-null element which contains no distinct non-null element as a subset, and the Boolean algebra Ω is said to be *atomic* if every non-null element contains some atom. We cite without proof three standard principles governing Boolean algebras. Some of the later development depends upon these.

2.1 Ω is atomic if and only if for each non-null element A of Ω, there is a unique collection of atoms, $\Delta(A) \subseteq \Omega$ such that $A = \cup \Delta(A)$.

A Boolean algebra is said to satisfy the *finite descending chain condition* if each descending chain includes its own limit as an element. This is equivalent to the analogous condition in terms of ascending chains.

2.2 Every Boolean algebra that satisfies the finite descending chain condition is atomic.

Example (i). Not every atomic Boolean algebra satisfies the finite descending chain condition, however. Let Z be the natural numbers and Ω the collection of all its subsets. Then the unit sets—for $n \in Z$—are the atoms of Ω, and the sequence,

$$Z, (Z - \{1\}), (Z - \{1,2\}), \ldots$$

is an infinite descending chain in Ω. The limit of this chain is null, but every member of the chain is non-null.

Every finite Boolean algebra satisfies the finite descending chain condition, for no finite algebra can include infinitely many distinct elements. Further we have:

2.3 If Ω satisfies the finite descending chain condition, then Ω is finite.

Satisfaction of the finite descending chain condition is thus equivalent to finiteness, and these entail, but are not entailed by, atomicity.

Every Boolean algebra can be extended to a sigma algebra, its closure under denumerable unions and complements. The intersection of denumerably many sigma algebras is a sigma algebra, and the intersection of all sigma algebras that are extensions of a given Boolean algebra is the smallest sigma algebra that contains it. For the development of probability theory a few special kinds and characters of Boolean and sigma algebras are of particular interest.

Given a Boolean algebra Ω_z, a countable family $\Delta \subseteq \Omega_z$ is a *partition* of Z if (i) the members of Δ are non-null and pairwise exclusive, and (ii) the union of the members of Δ is just Z. More generally, Δ is a partition of the element B of Ω if the members of Δ are non-null and pairwise exclusive and their union is B. Each union of non-null members of a partition is a distinct member of the algebra. If Δ is a denumerably infinite partition in an algebra Ω, there are then uncountably many distinct unions of non-null members of Δ. Hence any sigma algebra which includes an infinite partition has non-denumerably many members. From this it follows that:

2.4 There are no denumerably infinite sigma algebras.

For, if $X_1 \ldots$ is a denumerably infinite sequence of distinct and non-null members of a sigma algebra Ω, then the elements Y_i

$$Y_i = X_i - \cup\{X_j | j \neq i\}$$

form a denumerably infinite collection of pairwise disjoint members of Ω. Thus the collection

$$\{Y_1 \ldots [Z - \cup \{X_j\}]\}$$

is a denumerably infinite partition of Ω, and hence Ω is non-denumerably infinite.

A similar conclusion can be reached by making use of the notion of *constitution*: if $\Delta \subseteq \Omega$ is a subcollection of an algebra Ω, then a constitution of Δ is a set which includes for each member X of Δ either X or Z – X, but not both. If Δ is denumerably infinite then Δ has non-denumerably many distinct constitutions. If each of these has a non-null intersection, then these intersections are all distinct members of the algebra. Thus:

2.5 If Ω is a sigma algebra including a denumerably infinite sub-family Δ each constitution of which has a non-null intersection, then Ω is non-denumerably infinite.

A Boolean algebra Ω_z is *compact* if and only if every partition of Z in Ω_z is finite. Alternatively:

2.6.1 Ω_z is compact if and only if every collection of pairwise disjoint members of Ω_z is finite.

Compactness can also be defined in terms of intersections or chains and limits:

2.6.2 A Boolean algebra Ω is compact if and only if every denumerable subcollection of Ω with null intersection has a finite subset with null intersection.

2.6.3 A Boolean algebra Ω is compact if and only if no infinite descending chain in Ω has a null limit.

Finite Boolean algebras are trivially compact. Hence the finite descending chain condition entails compactness. Example (i) above, the set of all subsets of the natural numbers, is a sigma algebra which is (non-denumerably) infinite, not compact, and does not satisfy the finite descending chain condition. As 2.6.3 makes clear, as concerns sigma algebras, compactness is just the finite descending chain condition restricted to descending chains with null limits: in a finite Boolean algebra every chain includes its own limit, in a compact Boolean algebra every chain which has a null limit includes its own limit. Again, in a compact Boolean algebra every partition is finite, but in a finite—and hence atomic—Boolean algebra there is a unique finest and finite partition; every non-null element of the algebra is the union of members of this partition.

Example (ii). The set of all subsets of the natural numbers which are either finite or have a finite complement is a Boolean algebra but not a sigma algebra. The union of all sets of the form $\{2n\}$ is the set of even numbers. This set and its complement are both infinite, so it is not a member of the algebra. So this algebra is not closed under denumerable unions. Nor is it compact, for the collection of all single membered subsets is an infinite partition.

Example (iii). A simple modification of example (ii) gives a denumerable and compact Boolean algebra that is *not* a sigma algebra: let Ω include every finite set of odd numbers and the complement in the natural numbers of every finite set of odd numbers. Ω is obviously closed under complement, and brief reflection will assure that it is closed under finite union and intersection as well. It includes the set N of all natural numbers and the null set. Ω is thus a Boolean algebra. Since the collection of finite sets of odd numbers is denumerable, so is the collection which includes these and their complements. Every partition in Ω is of the form

$$\{X_1 \ldots X_k, [N - (X_1 \cup \ldots \cup X_k)]\}$$

where $X_1 \ldots X_k$ are finite sets of odd numbers. Every partition is thus finite, and, by 2.6.1, Ω is hence compact. Ω is not closed under denumerable unions, for the set of odd numbers is not a member of it, yet this set is the union of the infinite partition $\{\{1\}, \{3\}, \ldots\}$

of unit sets of odd numbers. Ω is hence denumerable, compact, and not a sigma algebra.

Example (ii) also makes clear how compactness is the restriction of the finite descending chain condition to chains with null limits: there are infinite descending chains in Ω:

$$\{N \supset (N - \{1\}) \supset (N - \{1, 3\}) \supset \ldots\}$$

is an example. The limit of this chain is the set of even numbers, which is not a member of the algebra and not a member of the chain. But every descending chain in Ω with a null limit has a null member and is finite (cf. 2.6.3).

From the abstract point of view of measure theory, a probability (measure) is just a numerical function with certain simple mathematical characteristics. These characteristics display certain clear analogies to the laws of probability intuitively considered. In this and the following section these analogies are made precise and a few characteristics of them are established.

Probabilities (that is to say, probability functions or measures) are functions defined on Boolean algebras. If Ω_Z is a Boolean algebra, then a *probability* on Ω_Z is a function, P, that assigns a non-negative real number to each member of Ω_Z in accordance with the following two principles:

Principle of normalcy. $P(Z) = 1$.

Principle of finite additivity. If A and B are disjoint members of Ω_Z then $P(A \cup B) = P(A) + P(B)$.

In consequence of these, every probability assigns zero to the null set, and probability values never exceed one. The following generalized form of finite additivity is also a consequence:

If Δ is a finite subfamily of Ω_Z, the members of which are pairwise disjoint, then

$$P(\cup\Delta) = \Sigma_{A\epsilon\Delta}P(A).$$

The condition of finite additivity may be generalized to define *denumerably additive* probabilities on sigma algebras. In this case the above condition holds with "denumerable" in place of "finite". The principle of finite additivity is then an immediate consequence.

Notice that if Ω is a finite Boolean algebra then every finitely additive probability on Ω is also (trivially) denumerably additive; for every subfamily of a finite Boolean algebra is finite. If Ω is a Boolean algebra which is not a sigma algebra (as in example (ii) above) then the union of a denumerably infinite subfamily of Ω may fail to be a member of Ω. The definition of denumerable additivity thus presupposes a sigma algebra as the domain of definition. On the other hand, no additional presuppositions are required to assure the existence of the denumerable sum:

$$\Sigma_{A\epsilon\Delta}P(A)$$

for if P is a probability then its value never exceeds one. Thus if $A_1 \ldots A_n$ are members of Ω,

$$P(A_1 \cup \ldots \cup A_n)$$

is no greater than one. Hence the values of P for unions of finite subfamilies of Ω are all no greater than one, and hence the set of these values has a least upper bound which is no greater than one. If a probability P on a Boolean algebra Ω is not denumerably additive, then either

(i) Ω is not a sigma algebra, or

(ii) Ω is not compact. (Corollary to 2.8, below.)

An example of the first sort is provided by example (ii) above—the sets of natural numbers which are finite or have a finite complement. With Ω as given there, define P on Ω to assign zero to all finite sets and one to all infinite sets, i.e., to those with finite complements. Then for each n, $P(\{n\}) = 0$. These unit sets form a denumerable partition of $N = Z$ and

$$\Sigma_{n\epsilon Z}P(\{n\}) = 0 \neq P(Z)$$

It may also be remarked that if Ω' is a sigma algebra that includes the Ω of example (ii), then the P here defined has no denumerably additive extension on Ω'. The Ω of example (ii) is not a sigma algebra.

An example of a probability on a (non-compact) sigma algebra that is not denumerably additive can be constructed in the algebra that consists of all subsets of the natural numbers. The standard and simple interpretation of probability as (not necessarily empirical) relative frequency assigns probabilities to sets $X \subseteq N$ in accordance with the rule:

P(X) = relative frequency of X in N.

To define this frequency, N and each of its subsets must be taken in a given order. In the present example this is just the standard order of magnitude—1, 2, . . . Then for each $n \geq 0$, let

$N(n) = \{0, 1 \ldots (n-1)\}$

and for a finite subset $X \subset N$, let $C(X)$ be the cardinality of X. (So $C(N(n)) = n$.) Then define

$P(X) = \lim_{n \to \infty} 1/n \, C(X \cap N(n))$

when this limit exists. This last provision is essential, for there are many sets $X \subseteq N$ for which the given quotients do not converge as n increases without bound.

Now let $\chi \subseteq \Omega$ be the collection of subsets of N for which P is defined, then

(i) Both the null set and N are in χ.

(ii) If $X \in \chi$ then $0 \leq P(X) \leq 1$.

(iii) If X and Y are members of χ that have no members in common, then their union is in χ and $P(X \cup Y) = P(X) + P(Y)$.

So P is, where defined, a finitely additive probability. Certain values of P are easily calculated:

If X is finite, then $X \in \chi$ and $P(X) = 0$.

Hence P is not denumerably additive, since the unit sets $\{n\}$, for $n \in N$, are a denumerable partition of N, and P assigns zero to each of them but one to their union. We have further that

$P(\text{even numbers}) = P(\text{odd numbers}) = 1/2$

and in general that

$P(\text{integers mod } n) = 1/n$, for each $n > 0$

$P(\text{prime numbers}) = P(\text{powers of ten}) = 0$.

Probabilities on non-compact Boolean algebras may fail to be denumerably additive. Denumerable additivity does not however require that the base algebra be compact: with Ω as above let P assign 1 to all sets of natural numbers which include zero as a member and zero to all other sets. Then P is a denumerably additive probability.

If Ω is a Boolean algebra but not closed under denumerable unions, then the presuppositions for the definition of denumerable additivity—the existence of the union of a denumerable family of pairwise disjoint sets—may not be satisfied, and hence this definition may not be applicable. There is still, however, the possibility of partial application of the definition in an algebra which is not a sigma algebra but where in some cases the unions do exist. The property in question is simply defined:

The probability P is said to be (denumerably) *disintegrable*[5] on the Boolean algebra Ω_Z if for every (denumerable) partition, Δ, of Ω_Z and every element B of Ω_Z,

$$P(B) = \Sigma_{A\epsilon\Delta} P(A \cap B).$$

If Ω is a sigma algebra then disintegrability on Ω is equivalent to denumerable additivity: to see this notice first that a denumerably additive probability on a sigma algebra will always be disintegrable, for if Δ is a denumerable partition and B an element of a sigma algebra Ω, then the sets $A_i \cap B$, for $A_i \epsilon \Delta$, form a denumerable and pairwise disjoint subfamily of Ω. So if P is denumerably additive,

$$P(B) = P(B \cap \cup \Delta) = \Sigma_{A\epsilon\Delta} P(A \cap B).$$

Conversely, if P is disintegrable on a sigma algebra Ω, and if Δ is a denumerable and pairwise disjoint subfamily of Ω, then $\cup\Delta$ is an element of Ω, as is $C = Z - \cup\Delta$. Hence $\Delta' = \Delta \cup \{C\}$ is a denumerable partition of Z, so by disintegrability:

$$P(\cup\Delta) = \Sigma_{A'\epsilon\Delta'}P(A' \cap \cup\Delta) = \Sigma_{A\epsilon\Delta}P(A).$$

Disintegrability is the locus of an important relation between logic and probability. The basis of this relation is stated as a theorem:

2.8 If Ω_Z is a compact Boolean algebra and P a finitely additive probability on Ω_Z, then P is disintegrable.

Proof. Let Δ be a denumerable partition of Z and B an element of Δ. Then the collection of sets formed by intersecting members of Δ with B, written:

$$\Gamma = \{A_i \cap B \mid A_i \epsilon \Delta\}$$

is a partition of B. And the collection

$$\Gamma' = \Gamma \cup \{Z - B\}$$

is a partition of Z. Hence—since Ω_Z is compact—Γ' is finite.

$$\Gamma' = \{(Z - B), (A_1 \cap B), (A_2 \cap B) \ldots (A_n \cap B)\}$$

and

$$B = (A_1 \cap B) \cup (A_2 \cap B) \cup \ldots \cup (A_n \cap B).$$

---

[5] See Dubins, "Finitely Additive Conditional Probabilities, Conglomerability and Disintegration".

Hence

$$P(B) = \Sigma_{i=1}^{n} P(A_i \cap B)$$

Further, for every k,

$$[(A_1 \cap B) \cup \ldots \cup (A_k \cap B)] \subseteq B$$

so for every k,

$$P[(A_1 \cap B) \cup \ldots \cup (A_k \cap B)] \leq P(B)$$

which proves the theorem.

In the light of the remark that precedes it, this theorem leads to an important corollary:

Corollary. Every probability on a compact sigma algebra is denumerably additive. (For finite additivity and compactness entail denumerable additivity.)

A probability on a Boolean algebra Ω_Z is said to be *regular* if the values zero and one are reserved exclusively for the null set and Z, respectively. The probability defined above, in terms of relative frequency, is not regular. A part of the interest of regularity, as well as that of its absence, depends upon conditional probabilities.

Logical probability traditionally and plausibly generalizes the relation of implication. Hume's probability of chances did this, and so did Carnap's confirmation functions. In accordance with this intuition, if A implies B, then the probability of B conditional upon A should be one, and if A implies the negation of B this should be zero. There is some unclarity here in the case of a condition A which is inconsistent, and which hence logically implies both B and not-B. The above principle would entail that in this case the probability of B conditional upon A should be both zero and one. Some modification or attenuation of the principle is thus required. In the case of abstract probabilities on Boolean algebras, this modification may take the form of leaving conditional probability undefined in certain cases. One standard definition is in terms of non-conditional probability: if Ω is a Boolean algebra and P a probability on Ω, then if $A \in \Omega$ and $P(A) > 0$, we define

$$P(B/A) = P(A \cap B) / P(A)$$

writing "$P(B/A)$" for the probability of B conditional upon A. In the case of regular P, the condition that $P(A)$ be positive is equivalent to restricting conditionals to non-null antecedents. The first consequence of this definition is that when it is defined, the one-place function of X, P(X/A), is a probability on Ω. If P is denumerably additive, so is P(X/A). If P is regular then P(B/A) is zero only when A ∩ B is null, and P(B/A) = 1 only when A ⊆ B.

P is said to be (denumerably) *conglomerative* if for every denumerable partition $\Delta = \{A_i\}$ and quantities p and p′, if

$$p \leq P(B/A_i) \leq p', \text{ for all } A_i \in \Delta$$

then $p \leq P(B) \leq p'$. Conglomerativity is equivalent to dis-integrability[6] and we have that if Ω is a sigma algebra, then P is con-glomerative on Ω if and only if P is denumerably additive on Ω. Hence every probability on a compact sigma algebra is disintegrable, con-glomerative, and denumerably additive.

The general and philosophical significance of these results is that a structural and non-probabilistic feature of an algebra (com-pactness) entails quite strict constraints on what probability func-tions can consistently be defined on the algebra: if Ω is compact, then there are no (finitely) additive probabilities on Ω which are not also denumerably additive. Hence, in the presence of compactness there is no room to discuss the advisability or plausibility of denumerable additivity as if it were an additional constraint; some-thing to be required or not in addition to the laws of finitely additive probability. This relation between compactness and additivity takes on yet more weight in the following section. There we discuss probabilities on first-order theories, which are typically (though not invariably) compact in the logical sense. There also the objects to which probability attaches—sentences of a formal language—have each a finite logical structure.

The issues of regularity, conditionality, and denumerable addi-tivity are treated in a bit more detail later in this and the following chapter.

---

[6] The proof is not easy. It is given by Dubins in the paper cited in the previous note. De Finetti, in *Theory of Probability* vol. I, pp. 177 f. and *Probability, Induction and Statistics*, section 5.19, founded and began the discussion of conglomerability. Dubins continues the investigation and Schervish, Seidenfeld, and Kadane, in "The Extent of Non-Conglomerability of Finitely Additive Probabilities", give a com-prehensive account of the relations between countably and finitely additive prob-abilities. I am grateful to Isaac Levi for calling this last paper to my attention.

3.3 First-order theories and their representing algebras

Carnap thought of probability as a logical and metalinguistic concept. The objects to which probability values attach are sentences. More fundamentally, the basis of probability is a relation between sentences: a two-place metalinguistic function which gives the degree or extent to which one of the sentences *confirms* the other. The sentences in question are typically given or found in a formal language with explicit logical structure. To set the stage and vocabulary for the treatment of this we begin by recalling a few features of formal languages and theories.[7]

The *vocabulary* of a first-order language consists of predicates (including relational predicates of finite numbers of arguments), also function-symbols, individual constants, individual variables, various marks of punctuation, and the logical connectives and operators (truth-functional connectives, quantifiers, description operators, and so on). The *expressions* of the language are just all finite strings of these symbols. The (*well-formed*) *formulas* of the language are those expressions constructed according to the formation rules of the language; the formulas of a formal language correspond to the grammatical expressions of a natural language. Those formulas which include no free variables are the *sentences* of the language; these are the linguistic objects to which truth-values attach. Fixing the interpretations of predicates, function symbols, and individual constants in a structure determines the truth-value of every sentence of the language.

Given a language, the predicate logic of first-order determines a relation of logical implication between sets of sentences and sentences of the language. In view of the completeness of standard axiomatizations of this logic, this implicative relation can be thought of in axiomatic, deductive, and syntactical terms (then the set Γ of sentences logically implies the sentence A if there is a *derivation* of A from Γ) or equivalently in terms of models or interpretations (then Γ logically implies A if A is true in every model of Γ).

The relation of logical implication on a given language can also be extended in various ways. Again, these extensions can be thought of in either syntactical or semantical terms. In the first case, new rules or axioms are added to some axiomatization of (pure) first-order

---

[7] See Shoenfield, *Mathematical Logic*, chapter 2 for a thorough exposition.

logic. Then certain new derivations are licensed, and the class of derivations is expanded. A set Γ implies a sentence A in the expanded sense if there is a derivation in the expanded sense of A from Γ. If the extension is semantically defined, then it amounts to restricting the class of models or interpretations. In this case Γ implies A in the expanded sense if A is true in every model of Γ of the restricted sort.

Every syntactical extension of first-order logic determines a semantical extension: in the simplest case, that of an axiomatic extension, the restricted class of models includes just those models in which the new axioms are true. If the extension is by way of rules of inference, then the class of models is such that application of the rules to sentences which hold in all the models never leads to a sentence which fails to hold in some model in the class.

The determination does not run in the other direction, however: not every class of model can be described axiomatically or in terms of rules. When generalized or extended notions of implication are in question, there is thus no assurance that one can move back and forth between proof-theoretic and model-theoretic vocabularies, as is the case in pure first-order logic. The model-theoretic vocabulary is looser and more figurative; there are sets of models which are not precisely specifiable. This looseness supports a certain economy of expression, and for that reason we shall, in the next few pages, treat extended notions of implication in semantical terms.

Given a language, by a *first-order theory* we mean any extension of the pure logic of first-order in the language. Theories are to be thought of in terms of classes of model: every class of models determines a theory and vice versa. Obviously not every theory of this sort can be grasped or described, but this will cause no confusion so long as it is kept in mind. If T is a theory, we distinguish L(T), the language of T, from S(T), the set of sentences of the language L(T), and both of these from the set V(T) of *theses* of T; the set of those sentences in S(T) which are true in every model for T. We write $\vdash$ and $\vDash$ respectively for the syntactical and semantical relations of logical implication in pure first-order logic. So if Γ and A are sentences, $\Gamma \vdash A$ asserts that there is a derivation of A from Γ in (some standard axiomatization of) pure first-order logic, and $\Gamma \vDash A$ asserts that A is true in every model of Γ. The *valid* sentences of a given language are those that hold in all models or, equivalently, that are derivable without the use of premisses. We recall that these relations are *compact*; that is to say, that if Γ logically implies A, then some finite subset of Γ logically implies A. Consequently, every logically inconsistent set of sentences has a finite logically inconsistent subset. The relations between this logical compactness and the algebraic notion of the preceding section are discussed below.

Given a language, and hence its formulas and sentences, the relation of logical consequence supports a definition of logical closure. We say that a set Γ of sentences is *logically closed* if every logical consequence of Γ is a member of Γ: that is to say if

$\Gamma \vDash$ A entails A ϵ Γ, for every sentence A

$\Gamma \vdash$ A entails A ϵ Γ, for every sentence A.

The set of all sentences is logically closed and every logically closed set of sentences is a subset of it. It is the union of all logically closed sets. The set of valid sentences is logically closed and is a subset of every logically closed set. It is the intersection of all logically closed sets. If Γ is any set of sentences, the *logical closure of* Γ is just the set of all (sentences which are) logical consequences of Γ. Alternatively, the logical closure of Γ is the intersection of all logically closed supersets of Γ. If Γ is inconsistent then the logical closure of Γ is the set of all sentences. The logical closure of the null set is the set of valid sentences. If Γ is logically closed then the logical closure of Γ is Γ itself. Since theories are in every case extensions of first-order logic, the set V(T) of theses of a theory is always logically closed and always includes the set of all logically valid sentences in S(T). Pure first-order logic can thus be regarded as the "null" theory; that theory which places no restrictions on the class of models.

The theories in question here are presumed consistent when the contrary is not remarked. If T is a (consistent) theory then the standard logical notions can be relativized to T: Γ is *T-inconsistent* if there is no T-model in which every sentence in Γ is true. A sentence is *T-necessary* if it is true in every T-model, and a set Γ of sentences *T-implies* a sentence A if A is true in every T-model in which all members of Γ are true. We may sometimes not distinguish sentences from their unit sets; thus a sentence A T-implies a sentence B if B is true in every T-model of A, and *T-equivalent* sentences are those that T-imply each other. It is natural to extend this condition to define T-equivalence among sets of sentences: sets of sentences are T-equivalent when they have all and only the same T-models. A slight abuse of language lets us say that a subset Γ and a member A of S(T) are T-equivalent when A is true in all and only T-models of

Γ. The relations between logical and algebraic structures are revealed in what has become a standard development, following the original construction of Tarski and Lindenbaum.[8] The correspondence thus established provides a foundation for logical probability—defined for sentences—which follows the lines of the measure-theoretic concept—defined for elements of Boolean algebras. The logical construction is briefly sketched here; the main concern is to illuminate the translation of measure-theoretic probability into logical probability.

Given a (consistent) theory T, a *T-maximal* set of sentences (of S(T)) is one which is included in no distinct T-consistent set of sentences. Clearly every T-inconsistent set is T-maximal, and every T-maximal and T-consistent set includes V(T) as a subset. (For if A is a T-necessary sentence that is not a member of the T-consistent set X, then X $\cup$ {A} is distinct from X, includes X, and is T-consistent.) If M is a T-model then the set $\Delta(M)$ of all those sentences in S(T) that are true in M (sometimes called the *diagram* of M) is always T-maximal and T-consistent. It is T-consistent since M is a model for it. It is also T-maximal, for, if A is not a member of $\Delta(M)$, then A is not true in M. Thus $\neg$ A is true in M and $\neg$ A ϵ $\Delta(M)$. So $\Delta(M)$ $\cup$ A is inconsistent and T-inconsistent. That is to say that adding a new sentence to $\Delta(M)$ results in a T-inconsistent set. Thus $\Delta(M)$ is included in no distinct T-consistent set. This leads to a form of *Lindenbaum's theorem*:

3.1 If T is a consistent theory, then every T-consistent set of sentences has a T-consistent and T-maximal extension.

Proof. If Γ is T-consistent then Γ has T-models. Let M be one of these models. Then Γ $\subseteq$ $\Delta(M)$, so $\Delta(M)$ is a T-maximal and T-consistent extension of Γ.

It should be emphasized that the brevity and ease of this proof depend on the figurative and imprecise notion of *theory* in use here. In particular, the phrase "Let M be one of these models" presumes a very strong application of the axiom of choice to a set (the set of T-models of Γ) which may not be well-defined. In contrast to this, the use of the axiom of choice in the standard proofs of Lindenbaum's theorem is much more modest and controlled.

[8] See articles V, XII, and XVII in Tarski, *Logic, Semantics, Metamathematics*. What is sometimes referred to as Lindenbaum's Theorem is Theorem 55 on p. 98 of this work. For a more recent exposition see chapter 5 of Shoenfield, *Mathematical Logic*.

Given a theory T, the collection of T-maximal and T-consistent subsets of S(T) is, if not well defined, at least described and characterized. This collection forms a space, Z. Each "point" of this space is a T-maximal and T-consistent set of sentences. The set V(T) of theses of T is thus a subset of each of these sets, and, indeed, V(T) is just their intersection. For a given sentence A (presumed always to be a member of S(T)) we can thus define the set of those members of Z of which A is a member:

$$A^\$ = \{x| \ A \ \epsilon \ x \ \epsilon \ Z\}$$

$A^\$$ is just the set of T-maximal and T-consistent extensions of A. (Or, more properly, of $\{A\}$.) It is null when A is T-inconsistent, and is the space Z when A is T-necessary. The mapping $\$$ thus maps S(T) into the collection of subsets of Z. This mapping is canonical in the sense that the correspondence of logical and algebraic structures is just what it should be. It is a many–one mapping of sentences to sets of sentences that always takes T-equivalent sentences to the same image set. In fact, the mapping $\$$ partitions S(T) into mutually exclusive and collectively exhaustive equivalence classes. Given T, S(T), and Z, we denote the collection of images of members of S(T) under $\$$ by $\Omega(T)$. So each member of $\Omega(T)$ is the image of sentences of S(T), and if A is any sentence of S(T), then $A^\$ \ \epsilon \ \Omega(T)$. Since each member of $A^\$$ is the diagram of some T-model, $A^\$$ can be thought of as the set of T-models in which A is true.

Thus defined, $\Omega(T)$ is always a Boolean algebra of subsets of Z. The logical and algebraic structures correspond in the obvious way:

$$[\neg A]^\$ = Z - A^\$$$
$$[A \ \& \ B]^\$ = A^\$ \cap B^\$$$
$$[A \lor B]^\$ = A^\$ \cup B^\$$$

A set Γ T-implies a sentence B if and only if

$$\cap \{A^\$| \ A \ \epsilon \ \Gamma\} \subseteq B^\$$$

If Γ is a set of sentences, then we write $\Gamma^\$$ for the set of the images of members of Γ under $\$$:

$$\Gamma^\$ = \{A^\$| \ A \ \epsilon \ \Gamma\}$$

Then Γ is T-inconsistent if and only if $\cap [\Gamma^\$]$ is null, and Γ and Δ are T-equivalent if and only if $\cap \Gamma^\$ = \cap \Delta^\$$. A *T-partition* is a set Γ of sentences such that:

(i)   each member of Γ is T-consistent
(ii) distinct members of Γ are pairwise T-inconsistent
(iii) the set $\{\neg A | A \in \Gamma\}$ of negations of members of Γ is T-inconsistent.

This last condition amounts to saying that Γ is disjunctively T-necessary; so, if $\Gamma = \{A_1 \ldots A_k\}$ is finite, (iii) becomes

(iiia) $A_1 \vee \ldots \vee A_k$ is T-necessary.

Notice that Γ is a T-partition if and only if $\Gamma^\$$ is a partition in $\Omega(T)$.

Since the set of sentences on a fixed vocabulary is always denumerable, and since $\$$ is a many-one mapping of $S(T)$ onto $\Omega(T)$, it follows that $\Omega(T)$ is always denumerable.

A theory T is said to be *finite* if the set Z of maximal T-consistent subsets of $S(T)$ is finite. If T is finite, then the representing algebra $\Omega(T)$ is a finite Boolean algebra, and every T-partition is finite. Again, if T is finite, there is a finite set Γ of members of $S(T)$ such that every T-consistent sentence is T-equivalent to some disjunction of members of Γ.

Given a theory T, the algebra $\Omega(T)$ provides a structural representation of the logical relations imposed by T. The logical bases and preconditions for logical probability defined in terms of a theory are represented by structural algebraic conditions which are themselves bases and preconditions for measure-theoretic probability on the representing algebra.

From the point of view of probability, the algebraic distinction between sigma algebras and Boolean algebras which are not closed under denumerable unions is of some importance. It is thus of some interest in discussing logical probability to see what is characteristic of those theories that are represented by sigma algebras. The answer to this is simple and plausible: sigma algebras are sometimes called *limit* algebras, since they are just those Boolean algebras in which chains have limits. Recall that the limit of an ascending chain

$$A_1 \subseteq A_2 \subseteq \ldots$$

is the union of the members of the chain, and that the limit of a descending chain is the intersection of the members of the chain. An ascending chain in an algebra $\Omega(T)$ represents a sequence of sentences each member of which T-implies its successors (for the algebraic image of T-implication is $\subseteq$) and, conversely, a descending chain represents a sequence of sentences each of which is T-implied by its successors. If an ascending chain of representing sets in the algebra $\Omega(T)$ has an upper limit, this will be a set that represents some sentence in S(T) which is a "T-implicative upper limit" of the sequence of propositions represented by members of the chain; a sentence which is T-implied by its predecessors and which T-implies any other sentence that has this property. If T is a theory in which the Ω-rule (see the example following proposition 3.8 below) holds, then $(\forall x)F(x)$ will be the lower limit of the chain

$\{F(0), [F(0) \& F(1)], [F(0) \& F(1) \& F(2)] \ldots\}$

and $(\exists x)F(x)$ will be the upper limit of the chain

$\{F(0), [F(0) \vee F(1)], [F(0) \vee F(1) \vee F(2)] \ldots\}$.

Let us put the above argument a bit more explicitly with the aid of some definitions and a theorem:

Given a theory T, an *ascending T-implicative chain* in S(T) is a sequence of sentences each of which T-implies its successor. An *upper limit* of such a chain is a sentence (of S(T)) that is T-implied by every member of the chain and T-implies any other sentence with this property. Notice that if any member of an ascending chain is T-inconsistent, then all of its predecessors are T-inconsistent, and if any member is T-necessary, then so are all of its successors. Distinct upper limits of an ascending chain are always T-equivalent, since each T-implies the other. The theory T is said to be *convergent* if every ascending T-implicative chain has an upper limit.

Descending T-implicative chains are defined symmetrically— each sentence T-implies its predecessor—and a lower limit is a sentence that T-implies every member of the chain and is T-implied by any sentence that shares this property. The set of negations of members of an ascending (descending) chain is always a descending (ascending) chain, the negation of a limit of the first is a limit of the second. Hence T is convergent if every descending chain has a lower limit. The above informal argument supports the following theorem:

3.2 T is convergent if and only if $\Omega(T)$ is a sigma algebra.

Since $\Omega(T)$ is always at most denumerable, that there are no denumerably infinite sigma algebras (2.4), entails:

3.3 T is convergent if and only if $\Omega(T)$ is a finite Boolean algebra and T is a finite theory.

Finite Boolean algebras are those that satisfy the finite descending chain condition (cf. theorem 2.3 above). These are algebras which include only finitely many distinct elements. The logical analogue of this is a finite theory: a theory in which only finitely many distinct things can be expressed. Of course such a theory will have infinitely many distinct sentences, but they will fall into just finitely many T-equivalence classes. If $\Omega(T)$ is finite, then T will have finite expressive power in this quite precise sense. In such a case an ascending T-implicative chain can have only finitely many members which are not T-equivalent to each other (for if there were infinitely many, $\Omega(T)$ would have to include infinitely many distinct members to represent them). This is just to say that an ascending T-implicative chain $\{A_1 \vDash_T A_2 \vDash_T \ldots\}$ must include some member A_i which is T-equivalent to all of its successors. Such an element will be T-implied by every member of the chain, and will be T-equivalent to any other sentence with this property. It will thus be an upper limit of the chain. Hence if T is convergent and $\Omega(T)$ is a finite Boolean algebra, then every ascending chain in T will include an upper limit as a member.

We recall that sigma algebras can be alternatively characterized in several ways:

(i) Sigma algebras are those Boolean algebras in which every descending (ascending) chain has a lower (upper) limit.

(ii) Sigma algebras are Boolean algebras that are closed under the formation of denumerable unions.

(iii) Sigma algebras are Boolean algebras that are closed under the formation of denumerable intersections.

In view of 3.3 these yield alternative characterizations of finite theories:

(i) Finite theories are those in which descending (ascending) implicative chains have lower (upper) limits.

(ii) T is a finite theory if and only if for every $\Gamma \subseteq S(T)$ there is some sentence B in S(T) which holds in just those T-models in which some member of Γ is true.

(iii) T is a finite theory if and only if for every $\Gamma \subseteq S(T)$ there is some sentence B in S(T) which holds in just those T-models in which all members of Γ are true.

Every Boolean algebra can be extended to a sigma algebra: intuitively, this extension amounts to adding new elements to the algebra to close it under the formation of denumerable unions. If the Boolean algebra in question is denumerably infinite, then—since there are no denumerably infinite sigma algebras—non-denumerably many new elements will have to be added to close it in this way. Hence, though every Boolean algebra can be extended to a sigma algebra, not every first-order theory can be extended to a convergent theory, for this extension would require adding non-denumerably many sentences. In a convergent theory whatever could be expressed by an infinite conjunction or disjunction can be expressed by some sentence of the theory. We have seen that the only theories with this character are finite; whatever could be expressed by an infinite conjunction or disjunction in such a theory is already expressed by some finite part of that conjunction or disjunction.

If T is a convergent theory and $\Gamma \subseteq S(T)$, then there is some $B \in S(T)$ such that

$$B^{\$} = \cap [\Gamma^{\$}]$$

If Γ is also logically closed, then, since $\Gamma \vDash_T B$, $B \in \Gamma$. Further, for every $A \in \Gamma$, $B \vDash_T A$, and—since Γ is logically closed—no sentence not in Γ is entailed by B. Convergence thus entails the following principle:

Finite axiomatization principle. If Γ is a T-closed subset of $S(T)$, then Γ is the T-closure of some sentence in Γ.

The finite axiomatization principle also entails convergence. To see that notice first that if Γ is any subset of $S(T)$ and Γ^0 is the T-closure of Γ then

$$\cap [\Gamma^{\$}] = \cap [\Gamma^{0\$}]$$

Hence if Γ is any subset of $S(T)$ and Γ^0 is its T-closure, then the finite axiomatization principle entails that there is some B in $S(T)$ such that

$$B^{\$} = \cap [\Gamma^{\$}] = \cap [\Gamma^{0\$}]$$

which is the third formulation of convergence.

3.4 If $S(T)$ includes an infinite T-partition then $\Omega(T)$ is not a sigma algebra, and T is not convergent.

Proof. If Γ is an infinite T-partition, then $\Gamma^{\$}$, the image of Γ in $\Omega(T)$, is an infinite partition in $\Omega(T)$. Since $\Omega(T)$ is denumerable, by 2.4 it cannot be a sigma algebra.

If $\Gamma \subseteq S(T)$ then a *constitution* of Γ is a set that includes for each member of Γ either it or its negation but not both. The image of a constitution of a set of sentences will always be a constitution of the representing algebra $\Omega(T)$, and the latter has a non-null intersection just in case the former is T-consistent. Theorem 2.5 thus supports:

3.5 If $\Gamma \subseteq S(T)$ is denumerably infinite and if each constitution of Γ is T-consistent, then $\Omega(T)$ is not a sigma algebra, and T is not convergent.

Proof. $\Omega(T)$ includes an image $A^\$$ of each sentence $A \in S(T)$. Each constitution of Γ yields a corresponding constitution $\Gamma^\$$ in $\Omega(T)$. Since the constitutions of Γ are T-consistent, the intersections of the constitutions of $\Gamma^\$$ are non-null. Hence by 2.5, since $\Omega(T)$ is denumerable, it cannot be a sigma algebra.

3.6 If T is a convergent theory then there is a finest and finite T-partition Γ: every T-consistent subset of $S(T)$ is T-equivalent to some disjunction of members of Γ.

Proof. If T is convergent, and hence finite, then $\Omega(T)$ is a finite and, by 2.2, atomic Boolean algebra. Let Γ consist of sentences which correspond to the atoms of $\Omega(T)$. If Δ is a non-null subset of $S(T)$, then $\Delta\$ = \{A\$|A \in \Delta\}$ is non-null and finite. If Δ is T-consistent then $\cap \Delta\$$ is a non-null member of $\Omega(T)$ and is hence the union of atoms of $\Omega(T)$. Δ is thus T-equivalent to the disjunction of the corresponding sentences in Γ.

Compact Boolean algebras are those in which no infinite descending chain has a null limit. This is just the restriction of the finite descending chain condition to chains with null limits. Alternatively, a Boolean algebra is compact if every partition in it is finite, or, again, if every denumerable subcollection with null intersection has a finite subset with null intersection. This final condition corresponds to the standard definition of compactness for logical theories: a first-order theory T is *compact* just in case every T-inconsistent subset of $S(T)$ has a finite T-inconsistent subset. The correspondence between theories and their representing algebras then gives the following theorem:

3.7.1 T is a compact theory if and only if $\Omega(T)$ is a compact Boolean algebra.

In view of the finite axiomatization principle every convergent theory, since it is finite, is trivially compact. The alternative formulations of compactness for Boolean algebras give rise to alternative formulations for theories:

3.7.2 T is a compact theory if and only if every T-partition is finite. (Recall that Γ is a T-partition if and only if $\Gamma^{\$}$ is a partition in $\Omega(T)$.)

3.7.3 T is compact if and only if no descending T-implicative chain, every member of which is T-consistent, has a T-inconsistent limit.

Although every finite theory is compact, not all compact theories are finite. The distinction parallels that between compact and finite Boolean algebras pointed out in the previous section: in a compact theory every T-partition is finite, but there may be no finest T-partition as there always is in a finite theory. In contrast to 3.7.3, which asserts that descending T-implicative chains with inconsistent limits include their own limits, in a finite theory every T-implicative chain includes its own limit.

If a theory T is compact, then when Γ T-implies A, Γ has a finite subset that T-implies A. T is said to be (*finitely* or *decidably*) *axiomatizable* if there is a (finite or decidable) set $Ax(T) \subseteq V(T)$ such that

$$\Gamma \vDash_T A \Leftrightarrow Ax(T) \cup \Gamma \vDash A$$

for every Γ and A. If T is axiomatizable and $\Gamma \vDash_T A$, then—by the compactness of logical implication—there is some finite subset of $Ax(T) \cup \Gamma$ which logically implies A. There is thus some finite subset of Γ, call it Γ^F, such that $Ax(T) \cup \Gamma^F$ logically implies A, and hence Γ^F T-implies A. Thus

3.8 If T is an axiomatizable theory, then T is compact.

The following is a simple example of a theory that is not compact (and hence not axiomatizable). Take the vocabulary of T to include the one-place predicate F, and denumerably many distinct constants 0, 1, 2, . . . In addition to the rules and axioms of first-order logic, T-inference makes use also of the following rule Ω:

$$\Omega \quad \{F(0), F(1) . . .\} \vDash_T (\forall x)F(x)$$

T is consistent, and the class of T-models is just the class of structures in each of which every object has one of the names "0", "1", . . . T is not compact, since the set

$$\{(\exists x) \neg F(x), F(0), F(1) . . .\}$$

is an infinite and T-inconsistent set, every finite subset of which is

T-consistent. This shows that the rule Ω is not reducible to rules that apply to only finitely many premisses, and that it cannot be expressed in axioms.

Example (i) of section 2 above described a non-compact sigma algebra, the set of all subsets of the natural numbers. In view of theorem 2.7, it is essential to this example that the algebra in question be non-denumerably infinite, and it is thus not possible to translate it into an example of a non-compact and convergent first-order theory.

3.4 *Characteristics of logical probability*

Logical probability is a metrical generalization of the relation of logical implication. That is a fundamental principle that has traditionally guided its development. This principle entails that logical probability should (weakly) increase monotonically with logical implication; that is to say, that the probability of a sentence should never exceed that of any of its logical consequences, and hence that logically equivalent sentences have always the same logical probability. In addition to this, logical probability is always additive over finite disjunctions of pairwise incompatible disjuncts and always assigns one to every logically necessary sentence or proposition. The generalization of logical relations in terms of first-order theories supports a generalization of these laws: if T is a consistent first-order theory then a *T-probability* is a function P defined for sentences in S(P) and such that

If A and B are T-equivalent then $P(A) = P(B)$

If A, B is T-inconsistent then $P(A \vee B) = P(A) + P(B)$

If A is T-necessary then $P(A) = 1$.

The following theorem is the basis for the relations between logical and measure-theoretic probability.

4.1 If P is a T-probability then there is a unique probability P' on $\Omega(T)$ such that $P'(A^{\$}) = P(A)$ for all sentences A in S(T). If Q is a probability on S(T) then there is a unique T-probability Q^0 such that for each $X \in \Omega(T)$ and all $A \in X$, $Q^0(A) = Q(X)$. Further, the correspondences ' and ^{0} are inverses: $P'^0 = P$, and $Q^{0'} = Q$.

The proof of 4.1 is almost immediate, given the groundwork of the preceding section. In view of the first clause in the above definition of T-probability, a T-probability can always be expressed as a probability on T-equivalence classes of sentences. Again, A and B are T-equivalent if and only if $A^\$ = B^\$$. The stated correspondence is then obvious.

In view of this theorem, clarity will be served by not distinguishing the functions P and P' or the functions Q and Q^0. We shall use the same notation for a T-probability and the corresponding probability on $\Omega(T)$.

As concerns conditional probability, there are three approaches: non-conditional probability can be taken as basic and conditional probability defined in terms of it. Then the probability of B conditional on A, written P(B/A), is just the quotient

$$\frac{P(A \,\&\, B)}{P(A)}$$

when the denominator is not zero. It is however also possible to develop conditional probability first and then to define non-conditional probability in terms of it,[9] taking the T-probability of a sentence to be just its probability conditional on some T-necessary sentence. Finally, the two may be defined independently and related by theorems based on their separate definitions. In the present section the first of these courses is followed. The alternatives are discussed below and explored in later sections and chapters.

The logical relations enforced by a first-order theory T correspond to structural relations on the algebra $\Omega(T)$: T is a finite theory (that is to say, there are only finitely many T-equivalence classes) if $\Omega(T)$ is a finite Boolean algebra. T is compact if $\Omega(T)$ is compact, and T is convergent if $\Omega(T)$ is a sigma algebra. Since there are no denumerably infinite sigma algebras, the restriction to theories with denumerable sets of sentences means that convergent theories are finite. Section 3.2 reveals some of the ways in which the structure of a Boolean algebra constrains and determines probabilities defined on the algebra. Theorem 4.1 can be exploited to draw similar conclusions about logical probability from the correspondence between algebraic and logical structures.

We recall that a probability P on a Boolean algebra Ω is *disintegrable* if for every (denumerable) partition Δ of Ω and every element B of Ω

---

[9] As does Carnap. See also Renyi's discussion in *Foundations of Probability*.

$$P(B) = \Sigma_{A \in \Delta}P(A \cap B).$$

The analogous property of T-probabilities is derived directly from this definition: a T-probability P is *disintegrable* if and only if for every T-partition Γ and every sentence $B \in S(T)$

$$P(B) = \Sigma_{A \in \Gamma}P(A \& B)$$

Clearly P is disintegrable on S(T) if and only if its homonym is so on $\Omega(T)$. It follows that

4.2 If P is disintegrable and Γ is a T-partition, then for every sentence B in S(T)

$$P(B) = \Sigma_{A \in \Gamma}P(B/A)P(A)$$

4.2 depends on the definition of conditional probability in terms of non-conditional probability. It can also be formulated in the context of an independent development of conditional probability. This is done below. We recall also that all and only disintegrable probabilities on Boolean algebras are conglomerative. This applies as well to probabilities on first order theories: P is *conglomerative* on S(T) if and only if for every T-partition Γ and every sentence $B \in S(T)$, if $p \leq P(B/A) \leq p'$ for all A in Γ, then $p \leq P(B) \leq p'$. Since all and only conglomerative T-probabilities are disintegrable these terms are sometimes used interchangeably in the sequel.

First-order theories fall into three classes: finite theories, infinite compact theories, and infinite non-compact theories.[10] If T is a finite theory, then the Tarski–Lindenbaum algebra of T is a finite, compact, and atomic Boolean algebra and is hence a sigma algebra. The finite axiomatization principle entails that there are finitely many maximal T-consistent sentences, corresponding to the atoms of the representing algebra, and a T-probability is completely determined on S(T) by the values it assigns to these: any assignment of non-negative numbers summing to one to the maximal T-consistent sentences fixes a T-probability.

---

[10] Scott and Krauss, in "Assigning Probabilities to Logical Formulas", provide a thorough theoretical treatment of the question. The relations between structural characteristics of logical theories and properties of probabilities defined on them are explored in two recent and elegant papers by Amer: "Classification of Boolean Algebras of Logic and Probabilities Defined on them by Classical Models" and "Extension of Relatively ς-additive Probabilities on Boolean Algebras of Logic". In particular, Proposition 5 of the first of these suggested theorem 4.3 below. Amer and I were both at work on these matters in 1981 and we discussed them briefly then.

If T is an infinite and compact theory, then the representing algebra $\Omega(T)$ is an infinite and compact Boolean algebra which is not a sigma algebra. There is hence not in general a finite subset of S(T) such that the definition of P on that class determines P everywhere in S(T). Every T-partition is however finite, so every T-probability is denumerably conglomerative.

Finally, infinite, non-compact theories, represented by infinite, non-compact Boolean algebras which are not sigma algebras, permit probabilities which are not denumerably additive or disintegrable. Denumerable disintegrability is however always a possibility in such a case:

4.3 If T is an infinite theory which is not compact then there are T-probabilities which are denumerably disintegrable and T-probabilities which are not denumerably disintegrable.

Proof. For the first part, let Γ be a maximal T-consistent subset of S(T) and define P:

$$P(A) = 1 \leftrightarrow A \in \Gamma$$

then P is a two-valued T-probability which is easily seen to be denumerably disintegrable.

For the second part we give first a lemma.

Lemma 1. If T is a theory and if $\Gamma \subset S(T)$ is such that

(i) For every $A \in S(T)$ either $A \in \Gamma$ or $\neg A \in \Gamma$ (i.e., Γ is a constitution of S(T)).
(ii) Every finite subset of Γ is T-consistent

then the function P defined for members of S(T)

$$P(A) = 1 \leftrightarrow A \in \Gamma$$

is a (finitely additive) T-probability.

Notice that if the theory T is compact then sets Γ satisfying (i) and (ii) will be maximal T-consistent sets. When compactness does not obtain, however, these sets—which are maximal—may fail of T-consistency. That they determine finitely additive T-probabilities shows clearly the way in which compactness determines denumerable additivity. The proof of the lemma is straightforward and omitted. Suppose now that T is a non-compact theory. Then there is a (denumerably) infinite T-partition Γ. Since no proper subset of a T-partition is a T-partition, if Δ is any finite subset of Γ Δ is not a T-partition and the set

$$\Delta^- = \{\neg A | A \in \Delta\}$$

is T-consistent. Now let $\Gamma^- = \{\neg A | A \in \Gamma\}$. By a familiar construction Γ^- can be extended to a set $\Gamma\#$ satisfying (i) and (ii) of the lemma. Where $S(T) = \{A_1, A_2 \ldots\}$ define

$$\Gamma^-_0 = \Gamma^-$$

$\Gamma^-_{i+1} = \Gamma^-_i \cup \{A_{i+1}\}$ if A_{i+1} is T-consistent with every finite subset of Γ^-_i

$\Gamma^-_{i+1} = \Gamma^-_i \cup \{\neg A_{i+1}\}$ otherwise

and let $\Gamma\#$ be the union $\Gamma^-_0 \cup \ldots \cup \Gamma^-_i \ldots$ Then $\Gamma\#$ satisfies (i) and (ii) of the lemma and hence determines a T-probability P as there described. Since P assigns one to every sentence in $\Gamma\#$, it assigns zero to every member of the T-partition Γ. It follows immediately that P is not denumerably disintegrable.

The relation between compactness and disintegrability can be stated as a theorem:

4.4 If T is compact then every T-probability is (denumerably) disintegrable.

We have so far taken conditional probability to be defined in terms of non-conditional probability. It is also possible and useful to take conditional probability to be the general case of which non-conditional probability is a special instance. Conditional probability may be thought of by analogy to logical implication: as a relation between sentences. Given a theory T and sentences A and B of S(T), P(B/A) will then give the probability of B conditional on A. Since it should in any event be required that whenever A T-implies B, P(B/A) = 1, and that the probabilities of B and its negation, conditional on the same sentence A, should sum to one, the antecedents for which P is defined must be restricted to T-consistent sentences. From the point of view of the representing algebras $\Omega(T)$, this means that the image sets under the mapping $ should be non-null.

If conditional probability is defined in terms of non-conditional probability, then conditioning is restricted not only to consistent or non-null antecedents, but further to those that have positive probability. That is to say that, in this simple case, when $\Omega(T)$ is a sigma algebra and $P(A^\$)$ is positive, one can define:

$$P(B/A) = P(B^\$/A^\$) = \frac{P[(A \& B)^\$]}{P(A^\$)}$$

If, however, conditional probability is developed independently, and not defined in terms of absolute or non-conditional probability, it will then be possible to define conditional probabilities $P(X/A)$, $P(X/A^s)$, in general for T-consistent A or non-null A^s. The possibility can thus be left open that $P(B/A)$ be defined even when $P(A)$ is zero.

Let us now look briefly at the question of independently defined conditional probabilities. A consistent theory T with sentences $S(T)$ and representing algebra $\Omega(T)$ is presumed. P is a conditional T-probability if and only if:

(i) For each T-consistent sentence A in $S(T)$ and each B in $S(T)$, $P(B/A)$ is a real number between zero and one inclusive.

(ii) P is invariant for the replacement of T-equivalent arguments at both places.

(iii) If A is T-consistent and T-implies B, then $P(B/A) = 1$.

P is *regular* if the converse of (iii) holds as well.

(iv) If A is T-consistent and $\{A, B, C\}$ is T-inconsistent, then $P[(B \lor C)/A] = P(B/A) + P(C/A)$

(v) If A, B is T-consistent then $P[(B \& C)/A] =$ $P(B/A)P[C/(A \& B)]$

The first four of the above laws yield the laws of non-conditional T-probability when any T-necessary sentence is put in the place of A. When A is T-necessary, $P(X/A)$ is just non-conditional T-probability. In this case the fifth principle yields the usual definition of conditional T-probability under the assumption of regularity. Even without that assumption, the fifth principle is still a law of T-probability when A is T-necessary.

The independent definition of conditional probability on Boolean algebras is precisely analogous to the above. Given a Boolean algebra Ω_Z of subsets of a set Z, P is a conditional probability on Ω_Z if for each non-null member X of Ω_Z, and each Y and W in Ω_Z:

(i) $0 \le P(Y/X) \le 1$

(ii) If $X \subseteq Y$ then $P(Y/X) = 1$

(P is *regular* if the converse of condition (ii) holds as well.)

(iii) If X is not null and $X \cap Y \cap Z$ is null, then $P[(Y \cap W)/X] = P(Y/X)P[W/(X \cap Y)]$

Just as conditional T-probability may be defined for T-consistent antecedents of zero probability, so conditional probabilities on Boolean algebras may be defined for non-null antecedents of zero probability. Relative frequencies provide a good example of this.

Let $N = \{0, 1, 2, \ldots\}$ be the natural numbers in their usual order. As above, in example (ii) of section 2.2, for each positive n let

$$N(n) = \{0, \ldots (n-1)\}$$

and take $N(0)$ to be ϕ. If X is a finite subset of N let $C(X)$ be the cardinality of X, so $C[N(n)] = n$ for each n. As in the earlier example let

$$P(X) = \lim_{n \to \infty} (1/n) C[X \cap N(n)]$$

when the limit exists. For X and Y subsets of N, with X non-null, let

$$P(Y/X) = \lim_{n \to \infty} \frac{C(X \cap Y \cap N(n)]}{C[X \cap N(n)]}$$

Then if $P(X) > 0$,

$$(a) \quad P(Y/X) = \frac{P(X \cap Y)}{P(X)}$$

Hence it is only in assigning values to $P(Y/X)$ in cases when $P(X) = 0$ and X is non-null that (a) differs from the definition of conditional probability in terms of non-conditional probability.

Consider now the Boolean algebra of example (ii) in section 3.2 above, the collection of all subsets of N which are either infinite or possessed of a finite complement. Call this algebra Ω_F. Ω_F is not a sigma algebra. It is however easy to see that the limit in (a) exists for X and Y members of Ω_F whenever X is not null: if X is infinite and Y finite, then the right side of (a) is zero. If X is finite then for some number m, $X \subseteq N(m)$ and the right side of (a) is equal to

$$\frac{C[X \cap Y \cap N(m)]}{C[X \cap N(m)]} = \frac{C[X \cap Y]}{C(X)}$$

If, finally, X and Y both have finite complements, then for some m, X and Y are both subsets of $N - N(m)$. Let

$$C[X \cap Y \cap N(m)] = r$$
$$C[X \cap N(m)] = x$$

Then $C[X \cap Y \cap N(m+m)] = r + n$, and $C[X \cap N(m+n)] = x + n$. So the right side of (a) is equal to

$$\lim_{n \to \infty} \frac{(r+n)}{(x+n)} = 1$$

Hence (a) gives a value to $P(Y/X)$ whenever X is non-null. The elementary arithmetic of limits assures that P is a conditional probability on Ω_F, defined even when $P(X) = 0$ for non-null X. P gives a clear meaning to picking a number at random from the member sets of Ω_F.

Conditional T-probability can also be defined, analogously to logical implication, with sets of sentences rather than sentences as antecedents. Then $P(B/\Gamma)$ is defined for T-consistent subsets Γ and members B of $S(T)$. The laws are obvious variations of those given above for sentences, the members of Γ being taken conjunctively. In the simplest case, when T is convergent and $\Omega(T)$ is a sigma algebra, when $P(\Gamma^\$)$ is positive we can define

$$P(A/\Gamma) = P(A^\$/\Gamma^\$) = \frac{P((A \,\&\, B)^\$ \mid B \in \Gamma)}{P(\Gamma^\$)}$$

Notice that if T is not convergent (see section 3 above) then there may be no *sentence* A of $S(T)$ such that $P(A^\$) = P(\Gamma^\$)$, but in the absence of such a sentence, $P(\Gamma^\$)$ is the lower limit of values of P for finite intersections of members of $\Gamma^\$$, and this is just the lower limit of the values of P for finite conjunctions of members of Γ. This would be the plausible value for $P(\Gamma)$ were it defined. This just supports the above definition in case the lower limit is positive.

The analogy of conditional probability with logical implication breaks down in one important way, namely as regards the effects of compactness. If T is compact, then any sentence T-implied by a set Γ of sentences is T-implied by some finite subset of Γ. Conditional probability is not, however, analogously compact. That is to say, it is not the case, even when T is compact, that for every Γ and B there is some finite $\Gamma^F \subseteq \Gamma$ such that

$$P(B/\Gamma) = P(B/\Gamma^F)$$

for the probability of a sentence B on sets

$$\Gamma^0 \subseteq \Gamma^1 \subseteq \ldots$$

need not change or stabilize in any regular way as the indices increase, as is the case for logical implication: whatever is T-implied by a set Γ is T-implied by every superset of Γ. It is, however, no violation of the laws of probability, nor is it even implausible, to assign

$$P[(\forall x)A(x)/\Gamma] = 1 - \epsilon$$

where $\Gamma = \{A(1),\ A(2)\ .\ .\ .\}$, and to assign also

$$P[(\forall x)A(x)/\Gamma^F] = 0$$

for each finite $\Gamma^F \subset \Gamma$. So long as ϵ is positive, the theory T may be compact. The reduction of conditional T-probability to conditionals with finite antecedents requires not only compactness but also convergence, and hence finiteness, of the base theory T. If T is convergent, and hence, *a fortiori*, finite, then T satisfies the finite axiomatization principle (3.3, above) and every T-closed subset Γ of S(T) is T-equivalent to some finite subset of Γ. In this case we have the reduction:

4.6 If T is convergent, P is a conditional T-probability, and Γ is a T-closed subset of S(T), then for each sentence B of S(T) there is some finite $\Gamma^F \subseteq \Gamma$ such that

$$P(B/\Gamma) = P(B/\Gamma^F)$$

Given a theory T with sentences S(T), an *extension* of T is any theory T′ such that

$$\Gamma \vDash_{T'} A \Leftrightarrow \Gamma \vDash_T A$$

for every sentence A in S(T). Hence if T′ is an extension of T, then every T′-probability is also a T-probability. In particular, since all the theories in question here are extensions of pure first-order logic, if T is any (consistent) theory then every T-probability is a pure-logical probability. There are in general alternative pure-logical probabilities on a given class S of sentences; all agree in assigning one to the theses of first-order logic and zero to logically inconsistent sentences, and all are invariant for (pure) logical equivalence, but these constraints leave the probabilities of contingent sentences undetermined. Of course what is contingent in one theory may not be so in another: the truths of arithmetic are contingent as far as pure logic is concerned, and the special sciences are contingent from the point of view of pure mathematics. As theories are extended, what was contingent becomes necessary or impossible, and probabilities based on these extended notions are more strictly constrained. The relativization of logical probability to a theory T is intended to provide a framework for considering the relations among these constraints and to answer the question how different varieties of probability may still be considered as falling under the concept of logical probability. One simple answer to that question, provided elsewhere,[11] is this: if T is any first-order theory and if P is any function that assigns one to every tautology and is additive on disjuncts of tautologically inconsistent disjuncts, then P is a T-probability if and only if P is invariant for T-equivalence. This provides a simple way of thinking of the network or collection of concepts of logical probability; it is determined by the network or collection of concepts of necessity. To the extent, for example, that truth is a limit of concepts of necessity, that function that assigns one to all truths and zero to all falsehoods is a limit of concepts of logical probability.

In a large and significant class of cases there is, however, no need to relativize the logical notions. In the simplest of these, the theories in question are finitely axiomatizable. If T is such a theory then there is some sentence $A(T)$ of $S(T)$ such that, where Γ is any subset of $S(T)$,

$$\Gamma \vDash_T B \Leftrightarrow \Gamma \vDash [A(T) \to B]$$

for every sentence B in $S(T)$. In this case, if P is any T-probability, and Q is any purely logical probability (that is to say, Q satisfies the above definition of T-probability, with pure first-order logic in the place of T) with $Q[A(T)] > 0$, then for every sentence B of $S(T)$

$$P(B) = Q[B/A(T)]$$

The extension of the definition of conditional probability to apply to sets of sentences as antecedents enables the generalization of this development for axiomatizable theories in general, even where the axiom set is not finite. In this more general case $Ax(T)$ will be not a sentence of $S(T)$ but a subset of $S(T)$ such that

$$\Gamma \vDash_T B \Leftrightarrow Ax(T) \cup \Gamma \vDash B$$

for all Γ and B. Hence if P is any T-probability, Q is any purely logical probability with $Q[\Gamma^\$] > 0$, and B any sentence, then

$$P(B) = Q[B/Ax(T)]$$

Pure-logical probability is thus the general case when only axiomatizable theories are in question. Since all axiomatizable theories are compact, the probabilities in question are always denumerably additive and denumerably conglomerative. This

---

[11] In Vickers, *Belief and Probability*.

comprehensive theory of pure-logical probability—comprehensive in the sense that it includes all axiomatizable concepts of necessity—provides also a general view of Carnap's vision of logical probability. At the beginning he thought of determining probability completely by axiomatic constraints on the metalinguistic measures. Later, after 1960 in particular,[12] he thought rather of narrowing the class of permissible measures. From the point of view of the present development the class of measures is constrained always by extending the logical theory on which probability is based and by reducing, in this way, the class of models. To the extent that probability is a logical concept, it requires just invariance for logical equivalence, unit probability for logical necessity, and additivity on disjunctions of logically incompatible disjuncts. That schema is specified by specifying the logic that determines the founding concepts of equivalence, necessity, and incompatibility. In the simple and powerful case of axiomatizable theories, this is done not by placing requirements directly on the probability measures or functions—a procedure which inevitably raises embarrassing questions of motivation and justification—but by the addition of axioms in terms of which the founding logic is determined. The issue of justification is thus displaced; one asks not what form probability should take, but what should be counted as necessary.

3.5 *The logical bases of additivity*

It is tempting to think of denumerable additivity and denumerable disintegrability as stronger requirements, in addition to finite additivity, which may further constrain probabilities. This temptation is a confusion in the case of probabilities based on compact theories, for—as theorem 4.4 shows—if T is compact then no T-probability can fail to be denumerably disintegrable and denumerably additive. In the case of non-compact theories, however, denumerable disintegrability may hold for some (finitely additive) probabilities and not for others. The distinction between these two sorts of probability is not to be made on logical grounds alone, and stronger notions of reasonableness and plausibility must be introduced to discuss it. De Finetti in particular has argued that in

---

[12] See Carnap, "A Basic System of Inductive Logic".

many cases denumerable disintegrability is an implausible constraint to put upon probability, that there are quite plausible finitely additive probabilities that it would rule out.[13] This argument depends upon certain striking examples. We turn to one of these now.

This example depends upon a simple numerical theory T_0. The vocabulary of T_0 includes the single individual constant a, the denumerable list A_1, A_2 . . . of one place predicates, and the one place predicate E. The theory is interpreted in ordinary arithmetic. E is interpreted as the even positive integers. The predicates A_i are interpreted as a cover or partition of the positive integers, each member of which includes one even and two odd integers

$$A_1 = \{1, 2, 3\}$$
$$A_2 = \{5, 4, 7\}$$
$$A_3 = \{9, 6, 11\}$$

and so on. T_0 is just pure logic augmented by the axioms:

$$A_i(x) \rightarrow \neg A_j(x) \text{ for } i \neq j,$$

and augmented by the *omega* rule:

$$\neg A_1(x), \neg A_2(x) \ldots \vdash A_1(x).$$

These just assure that the A_i form a T_0 partition.

Now de Finetti argues first that $P[E(a) / A_i(a)]$ should in each case be defined, where a is the single individual constant of T_0, and further, that 1/3 is the most plausible value for each of these conditionals. This evaluation thus represents something like the judgement that the chance of a member of A_i being even is, for each i, 1/3. Let us call this principle (i):

(i) $P[E(a) / A_i(a)] = 1/3$ for $i = 1, 2 \ldots$

the second principle is that the chance of a number being even is 1/2:

(ii) $P(E(a)) = 1/2$.

Under the conditions of the example—that the set

$$\{A_1(a), A_2(a) \ldots\}$$

---

[13] In *Theory of Probability* vol. I, pp. 116–28. See also the appendix in vol. II, pp. 348–61. I am grateful to Isaac Levi for an illuminating critique of an earlier draft of this section.

is a logical partition in T_0—no P satisfying (i) and (ii) can be disintegrable, for (i) and disintegrability entail,

(iii) $P(E(a)) = 1/3$.

Thus, goes de Finetti's argument, disintegrability, and hence denumerable conglomerativity and additivity, are implausible constraints.

It should be remarked here that if conditional probability is defined in terms of non-conditional probability, then the relative frequency function will be undefined for the above conditionals, since $P(A_i(a))$ is zero for each i when P is relative frequency among the positive integers. The principle (i) would thus not hold. This seems to miss the point of the example, however, for the assignments (i) are intuitively plausible, and they are in fact those of the conditional relative frequency when this is given by the limit of the quotients

$$\frac{C(A_j \cap E \cap N(n))}{C(A_i \cap N(n))}$$

as n increases without bound.

We have seen, in section 2 above, that the relative frequency function is not denumerably additive, and thus that it is not denumerably conglomerative or disintegrable, and hence, from this point of view, the present example is not unexpected. Indeed the theory T_0, which includes an omega rule, is not compact, so even the source of the failure of denumerable additivity is pretty clearly isolable. The example deserves a bit more comment, however.

An important factor is the relativization to order implicit in (iii). As far as the relative frequency function is concerned, the distribution of the even numbers varies with the orders in which they and the integers are taken. This point may be emphasized by varying the example slightly.

Consider a theory T_1, with individual constant a and one place predicates E, A_1, and A_2. T_1 is pure logic augmented by the axioms

$$A_1(x) \rightarrow \neg A_2(x)$$
$$A_1(x) \vee A_2(x).$$

So T_1 is compact and A_1, A_2 is a T_1 partition. Now interpret E as the even numbers and let

$A_1 = \{1, 5, 2, 9, 13, 6 \ldots\}$

$A_2 = \{3, 7, 4, 11, 15, 8 \ldots\}$

So A_1 includes all integers of the forms $(8n - 7)$, $(8n - 3)$, and $(4n - 2)$; and A_2 includes all integers of the forms $(8n - 5)$, $(8n - 1)$, and $4n$.

Then with P conforming to conditional relative frequency we have,

(i) $P[E(a) / A_1(a)] = P[E(a) / A_2(a)] = 1/3$

and since $P(A_1(a))$, $P(A_2(a))$ are both positive, (i) holds whether or not conditionals are defined independently. Further, only finite additivity is needed to support

(iii) $P(E(a)) = 1/3$.

We thus arrive at the same contradiction of

(ii) $P(E(a)) = 1/2$

without use of denumerable disintegrability or of conditionals with antecedents of probability zero. It is thus clear that the root of the question is in neither of these disputed principles, but in the different ways in which (i) and (ii) depend upon order.

The lessons to be learned from these examples are clear and interesting. First, whatever other difficulties there may be in the requirements of denumerable additivity and in the definition of conditionals with antecedents of zero probability, the first example does not fairly call these into question. Secondly, it should be kept in mind that relative frequencies depend upon order. The principle (ii) is thus no more justified than is any other positive frequency. Indeed, the appropriate ordering of the positive integers for this example is clearly

$\{1, 3, 5, 7, 4, 9, 11, 13, 15, 16, 6, 8 \ldots\}$

3.6 Relative frequencies continued: thin sets, comparability, and the de Finetti hierarchy

When logical probability is conceived as a metrical generalization of logical implication, regularity—the requirement that the probability values one and zero are reserved for necessary and impossible propositions respectively—seems a plausible constraint to put on probability. When probabilistic reasoning is restricted to propositions involving finite samples this constraint causes no difficulty. But when infinite samples are in question, right reason seems often to make a clear distinction between what is impossible and what has probability zero. It is possible that a positive odd number picked at random should be prime, but the relative frequency of primes in the positive odd numbers, under the canonical ordering, is zero, and thus, to the extent that our probabilistic judgements conform to frequency in such cases, this chance should be the same as the chance that a positive odd number picked at random should be even, though this last is impossible. Again, in any case of an infinite partition, regularity requires that each member of the partition (being consistent or possible) should have positive probability. If probability is denumerably additive then this contradicts—what is often essential in probabilistic reasoning—that the several members of an infinite partition may be symmetrical and hence equiprobable.

As concerns conditional reasoning, it is often essential to take extremely unlikely propositions as hypotheses, and to compare the likelihoods of such propositions among themselves. If prior prejudices about regularity and additivity are put aside, questions such as the following arise at the outset:

(i) Among possible or consistent propositions of probability zero are some less likely than others? Or do all such fall into one homogeneous class of "practically impossible" propositions?

(ii) Can there be a general theory of conditioning on consistent antecedents of probability zero? (Not, obviously, if the standard definition

$$P(B/A) = \frac{P(A \& B)}{P(A)}$$

is adopted.)

(iii) Can the notion of probabilistic independence be extended to apply to propositions of probability zero?

This section provides a basis for the consideration of these questions. The development is in terms of relative frequencies in the natural numbers. Nothing further is said here about the application to probabilistic reasoning. The theory of zero probabilities in chapter 5 makes some use of these results and returns to the above questions in a general and modest logical framework.

The fundamental notions here are, first, that of *thin* sets of natural numbers. The thin sets are just those with relative frequency zero under the canonical ordering of the natural numbers. We make use also of a relation of *thinner than* among sets: a set A is (strictly) thinner than a set B if the relative frequency of A in A ∪ B is zero. This relation provides an answer to the first of the above questions, which answer then enables responses to questions (ii) and (iii). It is crucial to this account to establish the transitivity of the thinner-than relation.

It is often possible intuitively to compare the relative frequencies of thin sets among themselves. Thus, for example, both the (positive) integral powers of ten and the (positive) even powers of ten have relative frequency zero in the natural numbers in their canonical ordering, but the conditional relative frequency of even powers in integral powers is 1/2, and that of the integral powers in the even powers is one. Letting

$$N(n) = \{0, 1 \ldots (n-1)\}$$

$$D(k) = \{n| (\exists k)[n = 10^k\} = \text{integral powers of ten}$$

$$F^n(X) = \text{the relative frequency of X in } \dot{N}(n)$$

we have:

$$F^n[D(k)] = (1/n)\log_{10}(n)$$

Since the intermediate values of n—where n is not a power of ten—may be ignored in taking the limit (writing ≈ for equality in the limit as n increases without bound):

$$F^n[D(k)] \approx (1/n)\log_{10}(n).$$

So, writing F(X) for $\lim_{n \to \infty} F^n(X)$:

$$F[D(k)] = \lim_{n \to \infty} F^n[D(k)] = 0.$$

Similarly,

$$F^n[D(2k)] \approx (1/2n)\log_{10}(n).$$

Thus, in an obvious notation for conditional relative frequency:

$$F^n[D(2K) / D(K)] = \frac{F^n[D(2K)]}{F^n[D(K)]} = 1/2$$

and $F[D(2k) / D(k)] = 1/2$.

Since $D(2k) \subset D(k)$, $F[D(k) / D(2k)] = 1$.

The even and integral powers of ten are thus in a clear sense comparable. Indeed, their relation has the structure of that of the even and natural numbers. On the other hand, the square powers of ten have zero frequency in both sets. Letting:

$D(k^2)$ = square powers of ten

we have:

$$F^n[D(k^2)] \approx (1/n)\sqrt{\log_{10}(n)}$$

which yields,

$$F[D(k^2)] = 0$$
$$F[D(k^2) / D(k)] = F[D(k^2) / D(2k)] = 0$$
$$F[D(k) / D(k^2)] = 1$$
$$F[D(2k) / D(k^2)] = 1/2.$$

Again, the relationships replicate those among the natural numbers, the even numbers, and the squares.

This method of comparing zero frequencies is, however, not generally applicable. The even and odd powers of ten, for example, should be on a par, but, since they are disjoint, both the conditional relative frequencies are zero. De Finetti suggested a way to overcome this difficulty by generalizing the method.[14] His proposal is sketched and ramified here.

De Finetti's account of comparability defines the comparability of sets A and B not in terms of $F(B/A)$ and $F(A/B)$, but in terms of $F(A / A \cup B)$ and $F(B / A \cup B)$. In the case of odd and even powers of ten, for example, these are both 1/2. A few (idiosyncratic) definitions will help the exposition here. As stated above, the sets of natural numbers that have zero relative frequency in the natural numbers are called *thin* sets. More generally we say that A is *strictly thinner than* B, and write

A < B

when $F(A / A \cup B) = 0$. So the square powers of ten are strictly thinner than the powers of ten, and neither the odd nor the even powers of ten are strictly thinner than the others. If the above relative frequency is positive, i.e., if $F(A / A \cup B) > 0$, we say that B is *thinner than* A, and we write

---

[14] In de Finetti, "Les probabilités nulles".

$$B \lesssim A$$

Finally, if each of A, B is thinner than the other we say that they are *comparable* and we write

$$A \sim B$$

so, $A \sim B \Leftrightarrow A \lesssim B$ and $B \lesssim A$.

The even, odd, and integral powers of ten are all comparable.

Some consequences are immediate. If A is non-null, then A is thinner than A, A is comparable to A, and A is not strictly thinner than A:

$$A \neq \phi \Rightarrow A \lesssim A, A \sim A, \neg(A < A).$$

Comparability is symmetrical: if A and B are comparable, then B and A are comparable. If A is thinner than B, then B is not strictly thinner than A:

$$\text{If } A \sim B \Rightarrow B \sim A$$
$$\text{If } A \lesssim B \Rightarrow \neg(B < A)$$

If both the limits $F(A / A \cup B)$ and $F(B / A \cup B)$ exist, then their sum is no less than one, and if either is zero then the other exists and is one. Hence $A < B$ entails $A \lesssim B$. If the first of the above limits exists then not $A < B$ entails $B \lesssim A$. If both the above limits exist then $A < B$ or $B \lesssim A$ or $A < B$.

All non-null finite sets are comparable, and every non-null finite set is strictly thinner than any infinite set.

A few more principles, cited here as lemmas, are needed to establish the transitivity of these relations:

Lemma 1. If $F(C / A \cup C)$ exists then $A \subseteq B \lesssim C$ entails $A \lesssim C$, and $A \lesssim B \subseteq C$ entails $A \lesssim C$. If $F(A / A \cup C)$ exists then $A < B \subseteq C$ entails $A < C$ and $A \subseteq B < C$ entails $A < C$.

If A intersects neither B nor C and if both the quotients

$$\frac{F^n(B)}{F^n(A \cup B)} \qquad \frac{F^n(C)}{F^n(B \cup C)}$$

are positive, then their product cannot exceed

$$\frac{F^n(C)}{F^n(A \cup C)}$$

This leads to the second lemma:

Lemma 2. If A intersects neither B nor C and F(C / A ∪ C) exists, then A $\lesssim$ B $\lesssim$ C entails A $\lesssim$ C.

A similar argument gives,

Lemma 3. If F(C / A ∪ C) exists then A $\lesssim$ C and B $\lesssim$ C entail (A ∪ B) $\lesssim$ C.

We now have,

6.1 If F(C / A ∪ C) exists, then A $\lesssim$ B $\lesssim$ C entails A $\lesssim$ C.

Proof. Assuming the hypothesis, by lemma 1, (A ∩ B) $\lesssim$ C and (A ∩ C) $\lesssim$ C. Again, by lemma 1, (A ∩ – B ∩ – C) $\lesssim$ B. So, by lemma 3, the conclusion follows.

6.2 If F(A / A ∪ C) and F(C / A ∪ C) exist, then A ~ B ~ C entails A ~ C.

6.3 If F(A / A ∪ C) exists, the A $\lesssim$ B < C entails A < C, and A < B $\lesssim$ C entails A ~ C.

6.4 If F(A / A ∪ C) exists then A < B < C entails A < C.

The thin sets are ordered by < when the appropriate relative frequencies are defined and the limits exist. In particular, if π(A) is the collection of all predecessors of A under < , then no upper bound of π(A) is strictly thinner than A, and if B is an upper bound of π(A) such that F(B / A ∪ B) exists, then A and B are comparable. A is in this respect a least upper bound of π(A). Similarly, and in the same respect, A is a greatest lower bound of the set σ(A) of its successors under the relation < . If B is comparable to A then B is also and in this same respect a least upper bound of π(A) and a greatest lower bound of σ(A). It is, however, important to keep in mind that, in view of the failure of transitivity of comparability when the appropriate limiting relative frequencies do not exist, comparability does not partition the collection of thin sets into equivalence classes.

The set π(A) of predecessors of A under < is—by lemma 3—closed under finite unions. It is not closed under infinite unions. If A is a predecessor of B then B is not a predecessor of A. Further, if A is infinite, then π(A) is not null and includes always some infinite sets. To see this consider an infinite set {a_1, a_2 . . .} and let B be the subset of A consisting of those a_i with i prime. Then B is infinite and strictly thinner than A.

The thin sets form a partially ordered hierarchy. This hierarchy permits a usefully generalized concept of independence, and in this way provides an answer to the third of the questions put at the beginning of this section. The definition depends on taking some of the sets in question as a frame of reference: if $A \lesssim B \sim C$ and A and B are subsets of C, then we say that *B is independent of A conditional on C* if $F(B/A) = F(B/C)$. If A is not thin, i.e., if A is comparable to N, then the condition of this definition entails that B is also comparable to N, and—with $C = N$—independence in the standard and non-relative sense is a special case of conditional independence. Conditional independence is not in general symmetric: in particular if $A < B \sim C$, then $F(A/B) = F(A/C) = 0$ (if these are defined), whether or not B is independent of A conditional on C. The notion is nevertheless, even in this non-symmetric case, useful and plausible. If, for example, $C = N$ and B is the odd numbers, then B is independent of 1, 2 but not of $\{1, 2, 3\}$. Similarly $D(2k)$—the even powers of ten—is independent of $D(k^2)$ conditional on $D(k)$. In this last case all three of the sets in question are thin.

Although conditional independence is not in general symmetric, it is symmetric among comparable sets: if A and B are comparable, and B is independent of A conditional on C, then A is independent of B conditional on C. This follows from the fact that the equality in the definiens entails that the absolute difference:

$$\left| \frac{F^n(A \cap B)}{F^n(A)} - \frac{F^n(B \cap C)}{F^n(C)} \right|$$

approaches zero as a limit as n increases without bound. Since the hypothesis entails that $A \cap C = A$ and $B = B \cap C$, this entails that

$$\left| \frac{F^n(A \cap B)}{F^n(B)} - \frac{F^n(A \cap C)}{F^n(C)} \right|$$

also approaches zero with increasing n, and this yields the conclusion that A is independent of B conditional on C. In the particular case in which A and B are comparable and in which each is independent of the other conditional on $A \cup B$, we say that A and B are *locally independent*. This provides a quite general and plausible notion of independence among thin sets. To return to the example of the powers of ten, the square powers of ten and the even powers of ten are not locally independent, for $D(k^2) < D(2k)$, but

$$F^n[D(2k) / D(k^2)] \approx n / (\sqrt{n} + n)$$

so: $F[D(2k) / D(k^2)] = 1$.

3.7 *Analyticity and its effects*

Humean chance probability was analytic probability in the pre-Fregean sense of analyticity: a conditional chance judgement asserted the partial inclusion of the predicate idea in the idea of the subject. The notion of eidetic inclusion was then generalized so as to make non-probabilistic analytic judgement a limit case, in which the inclusion is total. It would be difficult to take the Humean account seriously as a foundation for chance probability today. Putting to one side its dependence upon the principle of indifference, it is nevertheless just inapplicable in too many cases and methodologically far too weak in most others; the foundations of an account of dispersion, for example, are quite beyond it. One source of this inadequacy is in the Humean and classical notion of analyticity itself. The barriers that Frege found to an adequate account of the analyticity of arithmetic judgements if the classical notion of analyticity is presumed also stand in the way of an analytic (in the classical sense) account of probability. Two of these barriers are important here. The first is structural. Arithmetic judgements are not typically of subject–predicate form, they are rather evaluations of functions at arguments. Once the presumption of subject–predicate structure is dropped, at least some of Kant's arguments that arithmetic is synthetic appear as arguments that the judgements of arithmetic are not subject–predicate judgements. In the same way, when probability is conceived measure-theoretically, probabilistic judgement is better conceived as the evaluation of a function—a probability measure—at an argument rather than as the assertion of a predicate of a subject. The second obstruction to an analytic account of arithmetic judgement is that on the pre-Fregean concept of analyticity the truth conditions of an analytic judgement do not lead out of the judgement itself: what is analytic should be obvious when one reflects properly upon the concepts that make up the judgement.[15] Frege's shift, to make analytic what follows by pure logic from definitions, completely breaks the ties of analyticity with obviousness, opens up great new areas for the application of analyticity, and points the way, as he tells us, to new methods in their investigation. Only when the canons of pure logic are clearly formulated and when adequate definitions are given can questions

---

[15] See the discussion of Frege's work in chapter 1, section 5 above.

of analyticity be raised. That the Fregean concept of analyticity was later undermined should not obscure the power of the sources that he tapped.

The Carnapian programme in logical probability works within these outlines. To show the analyticity of probability judgements, or of a certain type of them, one needs adequate definitions of the probabilistic concepts and an organon of their logic. At the beginning Carnap thought that for an appropriate language probability evaluations should be unique and decidable: given the language each metalinguistic assertion of the form $P(B/A) = p$, for fixed quantity p and sentences A and B of the language, should be analytically true or analytically false; either it or its negation should follow from the definitions.[16] Carnap's view was in this respect like Hume's, when Frege's transformation of the concept of analyticity is taken into account, and the resemblance extends to sympathy for the principle of indifference, which seemed to Hume to be involved in the very concept of equipossibility. Since the laws of probability (even augmented by regularity), which became the Carnapian definition from which analytic probability judgements would follow, are not categorical, more is needed to give the uniqueness and decidability of probability judgements. Carnap typically took up this slack by obvious applications of indifference or symmetry principles. Thus, for example, given a language with a finite number of logical equivalence classes, and hence for which there is a finest finite logical partition, one obvious symmetry condition requires that probability should be invariant for the thorough interchange of members of the partition. This uniquely determines probability, given the language of course. Carnap could defend this requirement (and various alternatives to it) against certain objections by employing the distinction of external from internal questions:[17] external questions regard the choice of a language, internal questions have to do with logic internal to the language. It would of course be possible to choose or to interpret a language in a lop-sided way. The example of partitioning the outcomes of coin tosses according to the number of heads, without regard for order, shows this. But this is an external question. Not

---

[16] "[T]he concept of probability on which inductive logic is to be based is a logical relation between two statements or propositions; it is the degree of confirmation of a hypothesis (or conclusion) on the basis of some given evidence (or premises) . . .": *Logical Foundations of Probability*, p. v (from the Preface to the first edition).

[17] See Carnap, "Empiricism, Semantics and Ontology".

every objection could be handled in this way, however, and Carnap was led to abandon symmetry conditions, at least as a priori constraints, and in consequence to give a more modest goal to the logicist programme in probability. The end of that programme would not be to show how probability evaluations are unique and decidable, but to reveal what classes of probability evaluations are permissible within the constraints of definition and logic.

The theory of the preceding sections, and its extension in the next section, are in this spirit. The general question is what the consequences are of various logical principles, and the source of most of these is the form of logical objects. The particular importance of convergence and compactness is in this respect evident, since the issue of denumerable additivity cannot easily be raised apart from them.

Another feature of the Carnapian theory should be remarked here. This is a consequence of the restriction of the arguments of probability to sentences or sets of sentences. In many cases probability seems to apply not to sentences or propositions, but to sentential or propositional functions. The relative frequency function on the integers is a good example of this. This function was treated above, in the previous section, by the device of an uninterpreted individual constant, a. P[E(a)] was understood as the chance that an integer is even, P[E(a) / A(a)] as the chance that a member of A is even. But this, as Frege pointed out,[18] is a way of thinking that is a source of deep obscurities in logic. We are invited to think of a as denoting a variable or randomly chosen integer. But no letter can do that. If a is a constant, then it must denote a certain integer, and hence P[E(a)] can take on only the values zero and one, according to whether the integer in question is odd or even. The right formula would recognize that the probabilities at issue apply properly to properties and their relations, to the properties A and E for example. One should then write something like P[E(x) / A(x)], with free variable x, to express the variability of the relation in question. Some proposals in this direction are advanced in chapters 4 and 5. As far as a strictly Carnapian framework is concerned, metalinguistic probability functions are defined on sentences, as are the syntactical concepts (theorem, derivation) and the semantical concepts (logical truth, implication) that they generalize. It is indispensable in both

---

[18] In Frege, "What is a Function?"

syntax and semantics to treat open sentences (putting aside substitution interpretations of quantification for the moment) but this is done either so as to make them essentially equivalent to sentences (thus an open sentence A(x) is true under the same conditions as its universal quantification) or in terms of intermediate concepts such as satisfaction, or finally by means of special constraints on the scopes of the quantifiers. None of these permits of good generalization for metalinguistic probability, and, indeed, when Carnap himself treats relative frequencies it is in terms of classes of sentences which differ among themselves in permuting individual constants. That is a bit like the aforementioned substitution interpretation of the quantifiers in which (∀x)A(x), (∃x)A(x) are said to be true when all, or respectively some, substitution instances of A(x) are true. The probabilistic version has it that the relative frequency of B in A is given by the relative frequency of truth among their substitution instances in a given class of individual constants. It takes nothing away from the substitution interpretation to insist that the quantifiers sometimes express logical relations which are not to be understood in this way. Scientific laws provide a clear example, and probabilistic relations among properties provide another. In at least some instances (the question is discussed in chapters 4 and 5) it is propositional functions that are related, not classes of their instances.

Again, the same point may be made about repeated sequences of trials. We may indeed line up trials of any heterogeneous sort and define success and failure in any clear fashion that suits us and the situation. This is not, however, the typical case and it has quite limited logical and epistemological interest. In the most interesting and general case the events in question are repeated instances of a phenomenon of given type. That is what is interesting about them, and that is why they merit statistical attention. The obvious structure in this situation is that of a common sentential or propositional function which is parametrized by an index or indices.[19]

[19] Cf. de Finetti's remarks to the contrary in "Foresight", 113 n. 1. Recent work by Łos ('Remarks on Foundations of Probability") and Fenstad ('The Structure of Logical Probabilities") extends Carnapian logical probabilities to open sentences in plausible ways. This is briefly discussed in section 2 of chapter 4 below.

3.8 *Embedded probabilities in a Carnapian framework*

Carnapian probabilities are metalinguistic operators. Hence probability assertions themselves can be assigned probabilities only when a meta-metalinguistic probability is defined on a first-level metalanguage in which probability occurs. Thus embedded probabilities are comprehensible only in terms of a structured hierarchy. Such assertions as that the probability is 1/2 that the probability of a head with this coin is 1/3 are then to be understood as being of the form:

(i) $P_1[``P_0(\text{'Heads with c'}) = 1/3''] = 1/2.$

There are structural problems of two sorts here, which may be pointed out by an example: (i) and

(ii) $P_1[``P_0(\text{'Heads with c'}) = 2/3''] = 1/2$

should imply, by the elementary arithmetic of expectations, that

(iii) $P_1(``\text{Heads with c''}) = 1/2,$

but the computations involved depend first upon resolving the question of computing with numerical designators—"1/3", "2/3", "1/2"—of different linguistic levels, and secondly upon relating the two probabilities P_0 and P_1. If the concept of probability is univocal, then one would expect P_1 to be at least partially constrained by P_0, or for there to be some generalized probability that combines them.

In both these respects metalinguistic probability is more than just analogous to the metalinguistic notion of truth. The unrestricted use of the concept of truth in languages of sufficient richness leads to paradox. A hierarchy of metalanguages with a corresponding hierarchy of truth predicates may however be defined without paradox.[20]

A sequence of languages, K_0, K_1 . . . is constructed, each of which, after K_0, is an adequate metalanguage of its predecessor. So in each case $K_{(i+1)}$ is an extension of K_i (each sentence of K_i is also a sentence of $K_{(i+1)}$) and $K_{(i+1)}$ includes also a name for each sentence of K_i, in addition to the truth predicate W_i for K_i. Any consistent distribution V of truth values to the sentences of K_i can then be expressed in a theory $T_{(i+1)}$ in the language $K_{(i+1)}$: if A is a sentence of K_i with the name (or Gödel number) A\$ in $K_{(i+1)}$ then:

$W_i(A\$)$ is a thesis of $T_{(i+1)}$ if and only if $V(A) = T$.

$\neg W_i(A\$)$ is a thesis of $T_{(i+1)}$ if and only if $V(A) = F$.

---

[20] See Kripke, "Outline of a Theory of Truth".

In view of the existence of paradoxical sentences, the distributions will not be everywhere defined—a sentence that says of itself that it is false will be neither true nor false. It is, however, consistent to require that what is true at any level remains so at higher levels: that if A is a sentence of K_i then $W_i(A\$)$ is a thesis of $T_{(i+1)}$ if and only if $W_{(i+1)}(A\$)$ is a thesis of $T_{(i+2)}$.

The situation in hierarchies of metalinguistic probabilities is structurally quite similar. At the base is a theory T_0 in a language K_0 in which no probability concepts occur. Then T_0 probability is defined for K_0. This definition can then be formulated in a meta-language K_1 for K_0 which includes the theory of syntax of K_0. Each expression A of K_0 has a name A\$ in K_1, and a predicate S_0 of K_1 represents the sentences of K_0, so $S_0(A\$)$ is a thesis of K_1 if and only if Λ is a sentence of K_0. A predicate T_0 of K_1 represents the theses of K_0, so $T_0(A\$)$ is a thesis of K_1 if and only if A is a thesis of K_0. The process is reiterated, giving rise to a hierarchy K_0, K_1 . . . of languages. In the standard case in question here, the successive languages are extensions of their predecessors, so every expression of any language is an expression of all succeeding languages. Further, the successive logics are always extensions of their predecessors, so whatever is a thesis of any language K_i is also a thesis of $K_{(i+1)}$. Simplicity is further served if each expression has the same name in all languages of higher levels. Thus if A is a sentence of K_0, and hence of all K_i, then A\$ names A in each of K_1, K_2 . . . In view of the presumption of extension, for each sentence A of any language K_i,

$$T_i(A\$) \rightarrow A$$

is a thesis of $K_{(i+1)}$.

In each case $T_{(i+1)}$ defines T_i probability. Thus, for each i, and every sentence A of K_i, the following are theses of $K_{(i+1)}$:

$$S_i(A\$) \rightarrow [0 \leq P_i(A\$) \leq 1]$$

$$T_i(A\$) \rightarrow [P_i(A\$) = 1]$$

and for sentences A, B, of K_i,

$$T_i[(A \rightarrow \neg B)\$] \rightarrow [P_i[(A \vee B)\$] = P_i(A\$) + P_i(B\$)]$$

is a thesis of $K_{(i+1)}$, as is

$$T_i[(A \longleftrightarrow B)\$] \rightarrow [P_i(A\$) = P_i(B\$)].$$

Conditional probability can also be defined at each level, quite as described in the preceding sections. It will be simplest to presume

$P_i(B/A)$ defined whenever A is a consistent sentence of K_i. Let us write

$C_i(A\$)$

to abbreviate $\neg T_i((\neg A)\$)$. So "$C_i$" represents consistency in T_i. Then the defining principles, appropriately expressed in the languages in question, will have as consequences that for sentences A, B of K_i,

(i) $C_i(A\$) \rightarrow [T_i((A \rightarrow B)\$) \rightarrow P_i(B\$/A\$) = 1]$

is a thesis of $K_{(i+1)}$, and that

(ii) $C_{(i+1)}[(T_i(A\$))\$] \rightarrow P_{(i+1)}[A\$ / (T_i(A\$))\$] = 1$

is a thesis of $K_{(i+2)}$.

The *regularity axiom* schema for P_i is

$$S_i(A\$) \rightarrow [T_i(A\$) \longleftrightarrow P_i(A\$) = 1].$$

$K_{(i+1)}$ expresses the requirement that P_i be regular if every instance of this schema, for an appropriate name A\$, is a thesis of $T_{(i+1)}$. If the regularity axiom (schema) holds in $K_{(i+1)}$ then—in view of the invariance of $P_{(i+1)}$ for $T_{(i+1)}$ equivalence—

(iii) $P_{(i+1)}[A\$ / (P_i(A\$) = 1)\$] = 1$

is a thesis of $K_{(i+2)}$ for every sentence A of K_i, when $P_i(A\$) = 1$ is consistent in $T_{(i+1)}$. If regularity holds in K_i, then the consequent of the principle (i) above can be asserted as a biconditional.

It should be emphasized that (i), (ii), and (iii) are schemata. They hold when the places marked by "A\$", "(A → B)\$", "B\$" are filled with appropriate expression names (which may be taken to be the Gödel numbers of expressions). The numeral "1" in these schemata is however a genuine and canonical name of the number one: it refers to the number one on its every occurrence in any of the languages above K_0 in the hierarchy. In schema (iii), for example, "1" occurs both as a constant of $K_{(i+1)}$—in the antecedent—and as a constant of $K_{(i+2)}$. Just as "A", "A\$" are informal metalinguistic variables, ranging over expressions and expression names, so an informal metalinguistic variable "p" may be introduced to range over numerals or numerical designators. This introduction is not as straightforward as quantification over expressions and expression names, for in the latter case the ranges of the variables are precisely and antecedently determined. Probability is, however, a real valued function and its range—the continuum in the closed unit interval—is non-denumerably infinite. But the class of numerical designators in any of the languages K_i is at most denumerable. Thus a requirement of the form "For every numerical designator, p, [. . . p . . .]" cannot be coherently formulated without prior determination of the class of designators in question. And it would not be easy to express the real-valued character of probability in first-order languages such as those in question here. In the development of the preceding sections the theory of real-valued functions is an informal presupposition; the metalinguistic probabilities defined there are real valued. The formalization of this informal theory, or of fragments of it, brings up the complications just mentioned.

There are two opposing forces here: probability must be strong enough to handle the object language and be weak enough to be handled in the metalanguage. The first of these forces controls an informal development like that of the earlier parts of this chapter; methods may be employed without being theoretically described. When probability theory is itself treated metalinguistically, however, fairly strict limits are placed on its power and complexity. Most noticeable among these are the limits introduced by representation in denumerable first-order languages, including the awkwardness of the first-order treatment of non-denumerable totalities and continuous functions. From this point of view, the models are most plausibly, if not necessarily, denumerable. The class of rational-valued probability functions takes on a certain importance in this light. From the standpoint of the general and informal theory of probability, rational-valued probability is at best a curiosity, virtually without interest once the fundamental and foundational place of the classical limit theorems is acknowledged. From the standpoint of metalinguistic understanding, however, the question is not so much what can be done, but rather how much of what can be done can be brought under a certain sort of theoretical control. In this situation rational-valued probabilities can play a significant role. These probabilities are closed under finite weighted mixtures, for example, and thus a general if restricted theory of means and moments about the mean is available for them, though it will lack the elegance and power of the classical and modern theory of probability integrals.

In the light of these considerations, the restriction to probabilities with denumerable ranges, which may, in the remainder of this section, be taken to be rational-valued, is a good compromise. Metalinguistic variables ranging over numerical designators will thus be presumed to have denumerable ranges, most plausibly the rationals in the closed unit interval. So if A is a sentence of a language K_i which is the domain of a probability P_i, then for each numerical designator p,

$$P_i(A\$) = p$$

is a sentence of the metalanguage $K_{(i+1)}$.

The laws of logical probability do not completely determine probability values for all sentences of the object language in question. This is a feature of the informal theory, and it is preserved in the formalization of that informal account. So, in each case, $T_{(i+1)}$ includes the theory of T_i probability in the form of constraints placed formally on the function symbol P_i in the theory $T_{(i+1)}$. These constraints determine the values of P_i only for T_i-necessary and inconsistent sentences of K_i. Values of the conditional probability P_i are determined only in cases of implication and inconsistency. It is however plausible to determine a probability P_i completely on sentences of K_i. Some of the examples of the preceding sections do this. This sort of determination may be represented formally. Let us say that the theory $T_{(i+1)}$ *decides* the probability P_i on K_i if for every sentence A of K_i there is some numerical designator p of $K_{(i+1)}$ such that

$$P_i(A\$) = p$$

is a thesis of $T_{(i+1)}$. Since every consistent T_i gives a collection of maximal T-consistent sentences of K_i, we have that if $T_{(i+1)}$ is absolutely consistent, then $T_{(i+1)}$ has a consistent extension that decides P_i.

One special case of decision is that of *two-valued* probabilities: probabilities P_i on languages K_i such that for each A of S_i just one of

$$P_i(A\$) = 0, \qquad P_i(A\$) = 1$$

is a thesis of $T_{(i+1)}$. If T is compact (but only then: recall the proof of theorem 4.3 above) then each such probability determines a maximal T_i-consistent subset of S_i:

$$\{A| \text{ ``}P_i(A\$) = 1\text{'' is a thesis of } T_{(i+1)}\}$$

is always consistent in T_i and, in the case of a two-valued P_i, is always maximal. And each maximal T_i-consistent subset of S_i determines a two-valued P_i. Each such P_i thus gives a complete and consistent theory $T_i{}'$, which is an extension of the theory T_i. If T_i includes ordinary first-order arithmetic, then $T_i{}'$ cannot be consistently represented in itself. That is to say, there can be no predicate B_i of K_i such that,

$B_i(A\$)$ is a thesis of $T_i{}'$ if and only if A is a thesis of $T_i{}'$.

This is just a consequence of Gödel's theorem on undecidability. Thus, in case T_i is compact and includes ordinary arithmetic, no two-valued P_i can be represented in T_i; there can be no predicate B_i of K_i such that

$B_i(A\$)$ is a thesis of T_i if and only if $P_i(A\$) = 1$.

The hierarchy of probabilities is thus quite analogous to the hierarchies generated by truth and provability. In none of these cases can the layered structure be reduced to a single theory. It is, however, possible to introduce constraints among the probabilities of various levels. The simplest of these is just to require that $P_{(i+1)}$ always agree with P_i where both are defined. This requirement can be formulated in $K_{(i+2)}$. We say that $T_{(i+2)}$ includes the *axiom (schema) of extension* (of P_i to $P_{(i+1)}$) if for each expression A of K_i,

$$S_i(A\$) \rightarrow [P_{(i+1)}(A\$) = P_i(A\$)]$$

is a thesis of $T_{(i+2)}$. We recall that successive languages and logics are here always extensions of predecessors. Thus P_i, S_i, and $A\$$ will be expressions of $K_{(i+2)}$ if the first two are expressions of $K_{(i+1)}$ and if A is an expression of K_i.

Another constraint between levels is *Miller's principle*.[21] This principle relates probabilities at adjacent levels by means of conditional probability. Put informally it says that the conditional probability at level $i + 1$ of A, given that the probability of A at level i is p, must be p:

Prob at $(i + 1)[A$ / Prob at $i(A) = p] = p$.

Here the condition "Probability at i of $A = p$" is a sentence of $K_{(i+1)}$, and A is a sentence of K_i. Since $K_{(i+1)}$ is an extension of K_i, A is also a sentence of $K_{(i+1)}$. Formulated as a schematic requirement on $K_{(i+2)}$, in which the theory of $T_{(i+1)}$ probability is formalized, Miller's principle says:

---

21 See Miller, "A Paradox of Information", and Jeffrey's review of it and related articles.

MP For each sentence A of K_i and each numerical designator p, if "$P_i(A\$) = p$" is a consistent sentence in $T_{(i+1)}$ then

$$P_{(i+1)}[A\$ / (P_i(A\$) = p)\$] = p$$

is a thesis of $T_{(i+2)}$.

It is noteworthy that Miller's principle does not entail that:

(i) $P_{(i+1)}[A\$ / (P_i(A\$) = P_i(B\$)] = P_i(B\$)$

is always a thesis of $T_{(i+2)}$. In particular $P_i(B\$)$ may not have a determinate value in T_i or $T_{(i+1)}$, though the left side of (i) be determined. This will typically be the case when $T_{(i+1)}$ does not decide P_i, and when $P_i(A\$)$ and $P_i(B\$)$ take on different values in different $P_{(i+1)}$ probabilities. This is just the ordinary case of unknown first-order probabilities that take on different values in a second-order distribution. Indeed, if (i) were always a thesis of $T_{(i+2)}$ we should have that

$$P_{(i+1)}[A\$ / (P_i(A\$) = P_i((\neg A)\$))\$] = P_i((\neg A)\$)$$

is always a thesis of $T_{(i+2)}$. And since Miller's principle entails that

$$P_{(i+1)}[A\$ / (P_i(A\$) = P_i((\neg A)\$))\$] = 1/2$$

is always a thesis of $T_{(i+2)}$, we should have that

$$P_i((\neg A)\$) = 1/2$$

is a thesis of $T_{(i+2)}$ whenever Miller's principle holds.

What are the relations between Miller's principle and the axiom of extension? That question has the simplest answer when $T_{(i+1)}$ decides P_i. Then the two principles are equivalent. To see this, notice first that if $T_{(i+1)}$ decides P_i then a sentence

$$P_i(A\$) = p$$

of K_i is consistent in $T_{(i+1)}$ if and only if it is a thesis of $T_{(i+1)}$. Hence, if $T_{(i+1)}$ decides P_i, then Miller's principle holds in $T_{(i+2)}$ if and only if

(ii) $(P_i(A\$) = p) \rightarrow P_{(i+1)}[A\$ / (P_i(A\$) = p)\$] = p$

is a thesis of $T_{(i+2)}$ for every sentence A of K_i and every numerical designator p.

If the axiom of extension of P_i to $P_{(i+1)}$ holds in $T_{(i+2)}$ then $P_{(i+1)}$ is determined on sentences of K_i by the values of P_i on those sentences. This does not determine $P_{(i+1)}$ on sentences of $K_{(i+1)}$ that are not sentences of K_i, and in particular it does not determine $P_{(i+1)}$ on sentences of the form

$P_i(A\$) = p.$

If, however, $T_{(i+1)}$ decides P_i, then every sentence of the above form is either a thesis of $T_{(i+1)}$ (and hence of $T_{(i+2)}$) or is inconsistent in $T_{(i+1)}$ and in $T_{(i+2)}$. Thus, since

$$P_{(i+1)}(Y/X) = P_{(i+1)}(Y)$$

is a thesis of $T_{(i+2)}$ when X is a thesis of $T_{(i+2)}$, we have the following lemma.

Lemma. If $T_{(i+1)}$ decides P_i then for every sentence A of K_i and every numerical designator p,

(iii) $(P_i(A\$) = p) \rightarrow (P_{(i+1)}[A\$ / (P_i(A\$) = p)\$] = P_{(i+1)}(A\$))$

is a thesis of $T_{(i+2)}$.

This leads to an expression of the relations among decision, Miller's principle and the axiom of extension:

8.1 If $T_{(i+1)}$ decides P_i then Miller's principle holds in $T_{(i+2)}$ if and only if the axiom of extension of P_i to $P_{(i+1)}$ holds in $T_{(i+2)}$.

Proof. Under the conditions of the theorem, if the axiom of extension holds in $T_{(i+2)}$ then for every A and p,

(iv) $(P_i(A\$) = p) \rightarrow (P_{(i+1)}(A\$) = p)$

is a thesis of $T_{(i+2)}$. This, in company with the lemma, implies that Miller's principle holds.

Conversely, Miller's principle and the lemma imply that (iv) is a thesis of $T_{(i+2)}$ for every A and p. Since $T_{(i+1)}$ decides P_i, for every sentence A of K_i there is some p such that

$P_i(A\$) = p$

is a thesis of $T_{(i+1)}$, and hence of $T_{(i+2)}$. Hence, if the axiom of extension does not hold in $T_{(i+2)}$, for some A and p,

$p = P_i(A\$) \neq P_{(i+1)}(A\$)$

is consistent in $T_{(i+2)}$, contradicting that (iv) is always a thesis of $T_{(i+2)}$. This completes the proof of the theorem.

When $T_{(i+1)}$ decides P_i, $P_{(i+1)}$ must assign either zero or one to any expression of $K_{(i+1)}$ of the form

$P_i(A\$) = p$

for each such sentence is either a thesis or inconsistent in $T_{(i+1)}$. In this case, Miller's principle seems to have no genuine employment, as it should when $P_{(i+1)}$ may assign other positive values to these sentences. We turn now to the consideration of this more general case.

We consider the representation with the aid of Miller's principle of a finite discrete distribution.

Suppose that (i) $T_{(i+2)}$ decides $P_{(i+1)}$, and further that (ii) for a given sentence A of K_i there are distinct $p_1 \ldots p_k$, all positive and less than one, such that

$$[P_i(A\$) = p_1] \vee \ldots \vee [P_i(A\$) = p_k]$$

is a thesis of $T_{(i+1)}$ (and hence of $T_{(i+2)}$). Since the p_j are distinct, the disjuncts are pairwise inconsistent in $T_{(i+1)}$, and hence in $T_{(i+2)}$. Suppose further that (iii) for some $q_1 \ldots q_k$, all positive, for each $j = 1 \ldots k$:

$$P_{(i+1)}[(P_i(A\$) = p_j)\$] = q_j$$

is a thesis of $T_{(i+2)}$. Under these assumptions

$$q_1 + \ldots + q_k = 1.$$

Hence each sentence

$$P_i(A\$) = p_j$$

is a consistent non-thesis of $T_{(i+2)}$, and hence each is a consistent non-thesis of $T_{(i+1)}$. If, now, Miller's principle holds in $T_{(i+2)}$, then we have that for each j,

$$P_{(i+1)}[A\$ / (P_i(A\$) = p_j)\$] = p_j$$

is a thesis of $T_{(i+2)}$, and hence that

$$P_{(i+1)}(A\$) = \Sigma_{j=1}^{k}(p_j)(q_j)$$

is a thesis of $T_{(i+2)}$. This is a standard use of higher-order probabilities, as in the case of a coin known to be biased in one of the ways $p_1 \ldots p_k$, but where the knowledge of which bias holds is probabilistic. We have in this case that the axiom of extension of P_i to $P_{(i+1)}$ cannot hold in $T_{(i+2)}$, for if it did, we should have that

$$P_i(A\$) = \Sigma_{j=1}^{k}(p_j)(q_j)$$

is a thesis of $T_{(i+2)}$, and not all of the sentences

$$P_i(A\$) = p_j$$

could be consistent in $T_{(i+2)}$.

4

Probability Quantifiers: Fundamentals

4.1 *Probability as a branch of logic*

Is probability a part of logic? Carnap held that in one important sense of "probability" it is. His view of probability can, it was argued in chapter 1, profitably be seen as the result of passing Hume's probability of chances through certain intellectual transformations, transformations concerning analyticity and logical form. Carnap insisted that many probabilistic questions, most notably those concerned with evidential relations, should be formulated and answered in logical terms and by logical means. The preceding chapter gave a formulation of some principles of Carnapian probability and applied those principles to a few issues—denumerable additivity, conditionals with zero antecedents, and embedded probabilities—that had not been explicitly considered by Carnap.

It is worth pausing briefly here to rehearse a few of the major points of Carnap's development.

1. Carnapian probability is, obviously, a metalogical concept. It is thus unlike generality, predication, and the truth functions, which are treated in the object language. Conditional logical probability generalizes the concept of logical implication; the probability of B conditional on A is (roughly) the proportion of models of A which are also models of B.

2. Carnap first looked for a definition of logical probability which would be sufficiently strong and specific to determine unique answers to all questions of conditional probability formulated within precisely characterized formal languages: given the definition and a particular language, the metalogic of the language would determine conditional probability for every pair of sentences (exception is made for inconsistent antecedents) in the language. His method was to look for additional principles with which to augment the non-probabilistic laws of deductive logic and which would place

increasingly strict constraints on the conditional probability or c-function. The laws of probability were the first of these, closely followed by regularity. Other principles were considered, some were rejected, some relativized to special applications.

3. In his later work, Carnap abandoned the search for a definition of probability which would determine it uniquely in all languages to which it is applicable. The end of the modified programme was rather to give good descriptions of the classes of functions that are permissible within logical constraints and symmetry considerations, perhaps applicable only within fairly narrow ranges. Other features of the approach remained, however, unchanged.

4. The arguments or objects of Carnapian probability are sentences of formal languages. It can be extended in certain ways to apply to sets of sentences and to open sentences, but it is most at home, like the relation of implication that it generalizes, in its application to the sentences of a formal language.

5. Embedded probabilities are accommodated by the Carnapian approach in a hierarchical way, as spelled out in section 3.8. That is a natural consequence of its association with logical implication. The logic of embedded probability will thus, as pointed out in section 2.3, be quite like the logic of embedded modalities on a Frege–Quine view of the nature of necessity. Better, as the complexity of the development of section 3.8 makes evident, the logic of embedded probability will be a greatly complicated form of the logic of embedded truth. The differences between truth and necessity are less important here than is the character they share of being predicates of sentences.

If probability is a logical concept, then the goal of probability logic should be an extension or a specialization of the goal of deductive logic in general. One critical part of this is the precise description of criteria of consistency for sets of sentences. Given consistency, and the usual understanding of negation, implication and validity are accounted for. Indeed, Carnap's mature view, when purged of its normative psychologism, points very much in this direction. Giving the right consistency criteria for classes of probabilistic judgements means extending the reach of logic to treat new classes of judgements; not to decide the truth of such judgements, but to lay bare the structure of implicative and consistency relations among them.

It will help in considering the relations between logic and probability to distinguish, as philosophers have, *pure* or *general* logic from *applied* logic, where the latter includes concern with such questions as the sources of error and confusion, and the methodology of argument. Carnap's principle of total evidence[1] comes under applied logic, and Peirce had applied logic in mind when he claimed that "interest in an indefinite community, recognition of the possibility of this interest being made supreme, and hope in the unlimited continuance of intellectual activity [were] indispensable requirements of logic".[2] Along the same lines, such requirements as coherence of partial belief are, if logical requirements at all (they might be said to be prudential, applying to action rather than to judgement), requirements of applied logic. Under pure or general logic we should include only necessary rules of thought; what Aristotle tried to codify in the *Prior Analytics* and Frege in the *Begriffschrift* and *Grundgesetze*.

Since applied logic makes extensive and perhaps even essential use of probabilistic reasoning, it would not be easy to exclude probability from applied logic, nor is it easy to see why anyone would want to do so. As far as pure or general logic is concerned, however, the issue is more delicate. The question is whether and to what extent a satisfactory account of probabilistic consistency can be provided in (pure) logical terms.

Putting things in this way underscores the importance of embedded probabilities and of accounting for them in a smooth way. Recursive embeddings are, in our day, a mark of the logical. If probability is logical, then embedded probabilities should be understandable in a recursive way. Think for a moment about the great contrast between pre- and post-Fregean accounts of logical generality: the classical account of generality was based on monadic quantification of the subject term of a judgement, and it understood this quantification in a pragmatic rather than in a semantical way; one who judged that all men are mortal intended that the term "man" be taken to have its full extension; one who judged that some men are mortal intended that this term be taken to have some undetermined and non-empty part of its extension. It is not clear on this account how "Some S is P and some S is not P" is consistent, nor can the theory account for the inference from $(\exists x)(\forall y)A$ to

[1] See Carnap and Jeffrey (eds.), *Studies in Inductive Logic and Probability* vol. I, pp. 69 ff. and Carnap, *Logical Foundations of Probability*, 211 ff.
[2] Peirce, "The Doctrine of Chances", p. 75.

(∀y)(∃x)A. Indeed, the classical account of logical structure has no recursive capacity whatever; judgements involving embedded logical operators are parsed hierarchically, as judgements about judgements. As Frege's succinct criticism of the Kantian table of judgements makes evident,[3] this doctrine, which flows from the dogma of subject and predicate, is an absolute barrier to a good understanding of inference.

This structure and its snags are familiar to us. The emotivistic account of ethical terms mentioned in section 2.1 breaks down when faced with embeddings. As concerns probability, the psychologistic accounts rehearsed in section 2.3 and the Carnapian metalinguistic account of section 3.8 are both led to construct complex hierarchies to interpret embedded probabilities. Not only is the application of probability to probability hard to understand for these views, but (quite like emotivism) embeddings within the scopes of logical operators resist uniform interpretation as well. In both cases—the Carnapian and the psychologistic—interpreting probabilities within the hierarchies requires principles relating probabilities at different levels. Psychologism requires postulates governing beliefs about beliefs; the metalinguistic treatment depends on something like Miller's principle or the axiom of extension. The status of these principles is or should be a source of embarrassment; the psychology of beliefs about beliefs is insufficiently developed to support the weight of recursive and partial belief attribution. Augmenting it with normative and prudential homilies leads back to the paralysis of ethical emotivism in the face of embedded expressions of attitudes. Miller's principle may be very plausible when appropriately restricted, but it is hardly a truth of logic, it leads to paradox if not employed with care, and it is quite unclear what sort of general logical support could be provided for it. It looks like what used to be called a synthetic a priori principle, but, even leaving aside the famous and crippling difficulties of this notion, such principles need transcendental support and can have only regulative force. Miller's principle is clearly constitutive and quite beyond transcendental justification.

It is not inaccurate to say that in the matter of embeddings probability has remained pre-Fregean. Frege's great insights about logical structure, his sophisticated Kantian view about the nature of pure logic, and the power of his methods, have left probability

---

[3] In *Begriffschrift*, section 4.

unaffected. Carnap certainly began the movement towards a Fregean theory of logical probability, but he never succeeded in seeing probability as a logical operator.

The interpretation of embedded probabilities will require some attention to matters of *scope*. In standard non-probabilistic logic, the scope of an operator is the shortest complete formula that immediately follows the operator; it is the material to which the operator applies. A large part of the power of Frege's quantifiers comes from the way in which they keep precise track of the scope of generality. Questions of scope arise in probabilistic contexts too.

An example will help to make this clear:

If h is a two-place function (a random variable) that assigns pairs of positive integers the values zero and one, we write

(i) $P(h = 0)$

for the probability with which h assigns zero to a randomly chosen pair from its range of application. It is sometimes useful to write free variables as placeholders. Then

(ii) $P[h(x,y) = 0]$

is just another way of writing (i). Logically considered, both (i) and (ii) are *terms*; they designate, name, or indicate a probability, and make no assertion about it.

A two-place function forms two one-place functions by instantiation. Thus if h is as above and m and n are positive integers, then

$h(m,y),$ $h(x,n)$

are one-place functions, each of which assigns to positive integers the values zero and one: $h(m,y)$ assigns one to an integer k just in case $h(m,k) = 1$. Given these one-place functions

$P[h(m,y) = 0]$ $P[h(x,n) = 0]$

are terms designating the probabilities with which these one-place functions take on the value zero. Here the use of variables as placeholders indicates the place of variation. Now for a given and determinate quantity p, between zero and one inclusive, the expressions

(iii) $P[h(m,y) = 0] = p$
(iv) $P[h(x,n) = 0] = p$

are not terms, nor are they propositional functions or open sentences. They are statements or propositions, each true or false. Though they include the variables x and y, (iii) and (iv) are not functional expressions that change truth value as these variables take on different values in their ranges. x and y are free variables in

$$h(m,y) \qquad h(x,n)$$

but these variables are bound and not free in (iii) and (iv). The context

$$P[\quad] = p$$

may thus be viewed as expressing a variable-binding operator in (iii) and (iv). It is thus appropriate to write the operator "P" with a subscript or suffix to indicate the variable bound. So (iii) and (iv) become

(v) $P_y[h(m,y) = 0] = p$

(vi) $P_x[h(x,n) = 0] = p$

For each integer m, the probability

(vii) $P_y[h(m,y) = 0]$

has a certain value. For purposes of illustration let us think of this as the relative frequency of integers y such that $h(m,y) = 0$. Similarly

(viii) $P_x[h(x,n) = 0]$

may be thought of as the relative frequency of integers x such that $h(x,n) = 0$. So, for example, if h assigns 0 to a pair of integers just in case their sum is even, we have that

$$P_x[h(x,2) = 0]$$

is 1/2.

If, now, variation is permitted at the place of "m" in (vii) and at that of "n" in (viii), the results are one-place functions or random variables. x is free and y is bound in

(ix) $P_y[h(x,y) = 0]$

y is free and x is bound in

(x) $P_x[h(x,y) = 0]$.

(ix) expresses a random variable. It takes on different values for different values of its free variable x. We may thus ask with what probability or relative frequency it takes on a certain value. So, for a given fixed quantity p, we can ask with what probability or relative frequency

(xi) $P_y[h(x,y) = 0] = p$

That is to say, we ask with what probability or relative frequency the random variable (ix) assigns the value p as the variable x takes on different values in its range. Similarly, for given p, the probability with which

(xii) $P_x[h(x,y) = 0] = p$

is just the probability with which the random variable (x) assigns the value p as the variable y takes on different values in its range.

These last probabilities may be written, again using suffixes to identify variables bound:

(xiii) $P_x(P_y[h(x,y) = 0] = p)$
(xiv) $P_y(P_x[h(x,y) = 0] = p)$.

(xiii) and (xiv) are terms designating probabilities. So if q is a given fixed quantity, then

(xv) $P_x(P_y[h(x,y) = 0] = p) = q$
(xvi) $P_y(P_x[h(x,y) = 0] = p) = q$

are sentences or propositions. Each is either true or false. The important difference between them is that of the patterns of the scopes of their variable-binding operators. If, for example, p and q are 1/2 and 1/3 respectively, then (xv) and (xvi) are the assertions

(xvii) $P_x(P_y[h(x,y) = 0] = 1/2) = 1/3$
(xviii) $P_y(P_x[h(x,y) = 0] = 1/2) = 1/3$

Neither of these implies the other; they are as logically independent as are

$(\forall x)(\exists y)[h(x,y) = 0]$
$(\forall y)(\exists x)[h(x,y) = 0]$

At least some confusions about embedded probabilities are avoided by the clear demarcation of scopes. The fallacious use of Miller's principle in section 3.8 above is precisely a matter of confused scopes. The proper form of the principle restricts replacements to rigid or canonical designators; that is to say to terms with the widest scope, or for which scope is irrelevant. Notice that in (xvii) and (xviii) there is no one function that gives probability, there are parametrized probabilities that give probability relative to a place of variation or variability. This makes probability function more like a logical quantifier; there is not one universal or existential quantifier; one cannot simply apply "all" or "some" to a propositional function. It is essential that the scope and variable of the quantifier be made explicit. This similarity invites writing (xvii) and (xviii) as

(xix) $[(1/3)x][(1/2)y](h(x,y) = 0)$
(xx) $[(1/3)y][(1/2)x](h(x,y) = 0)$.

A simple example will help in reading these: consider a universe of discourse consisting of the integers from 1 to 6

$$\{1, 2, 3, 4, 5, 6\}$$

and suppose that

$$h(1,1) = h(1,2) = h(1,3) = h(2,1) = h(2,2) = h(2,3) = 0$$

while h assigns one to every other pair. Then just one-third of the elements in the universe (namely 1 and 2) satisfy

(xxi) $[(1/2)y](h(x,y) = 0)$

for we have that $[(1/2)y](h(1,y) = 0)$ and $[(1/2)y](h(2,y) = 0)$: i.e., 1 and 2 are the only elements that satisfy (xxi). Thus (xix) holds in this interpretation, while inspection shows that (xx) does not.

$[(1/2)x]$, $[(1/3)y]$ and similar operators, always consisting of a non-negative quantity no greater than one and a variable, are *probability quantifiers*. In the remainder of this chapter a semantical theory is developed in which these quantifiers are interpreted and their logical behaviour charted. The next section includes a brief survey of precedent and related work. In section 4.3 and the sequel we turn to a more complete development of probability quantifiers in a general first-order setting.

4.2 *Precedents and parallels*

Probability quantifiers are not without precedents, both notational and conceptual. Perhaps best known is Reichenbach's notation for conditional probability. He wrote

$$A \ni B \atop p$$

where p is some given quantity between zero and one inclusive, to express conditional probability.[4] The notation presumes that A and B are sentential functions of the same free variable. Reichenbach was generalizing the *Principia Mathematica* notation for formal implication: Russell and Whitehead had written

(i) $\phi x . \supset_x \psi x$

----

[4] In *The Theory of Probability*.

to abbreviate

(ii) (x).ϕx $\supset$ ψx

Here they were following Peano who, though he lacked fully developed quantifiers, had nevertheless the notions of formal implication and bound and free variables on which (i) depends.[5] When Fregean notation is available, (i) becomes just a special case. The notation has thus fallen into disuse. In the modern theory the free variables of (i) are all read as universally quantified with greatest scope, so the subscripted variable is redundant.

The account of probability quantifiers given below differs from Reichenbach's in several respects. On the level of notation, there are both quantifiers of the form [Px] (for fixed quantity P) and of the conditional form—not unlike Reichenbach's. In both cases a variable is included in the quantifier so as to make scope and bondage explicit. Some of that is already clear in the examples of the preceding section, and richer examples will be given shortly. There are conceptual differences from Reichenbach's account as well. He understood probabilistic conditionals as assertions of empirical relative frequency. The concern of the present account is rather with the consistency conditions for sets of probabilistic assertions. We are thus interested less in particular contingent assertions than in the expressions of a formal language; typically a language in which the predicate and individual constants are uninterpreted. The question is thus one of providing a clear interpretation for probability quantifiers which permits them to mix with other probability quantifiers, with the standard quantifiers, and with other logical operators. Reichenbach's account was not as powerful as this, and, indeed, his only treatment of embedded probabilities is as probabilities of "higher level".[6] That is to say, embedded probabilities are interpreted in hierarchical terms.

The present investigation of probability logic is motivated by the logic of judgement, in particular by a concern to treat probability judgements in terms of the logic of generality. One might, on the other hand, start from probability theory, as it stands, and investigate logic from that point of view. These complementary directions

---

[5] See, for example, article 17 in the *Selected Works*. Although Peano did write "∃a" to mean that the class a is not null he seems not to have appreciated the notion of propositional function on which Fregean and Peircean quantification depends.

[6] See *The Theory of Probability*, chapter 8.

are not in competition, for they are directed at different questions. There is nevertheless some overlap of concern and results which may be briefly commented upon, if not studied in any detail.

When the theory of probability is applied to logical questions, the starting-point is measure theory. Some of the most fruitful work in recent probability logic has been on the basis of non-standard measure theory. This is not the place for an exposition of that theory;[7] let me just mention a few of its results and features.

Non-standard measure theory is based on the account of non-standard analysis developed by Abraham Robinson.[8] Perhaps the best-known character of non-standard analysis is the account it provides of infinitesimal numbers. Infinitesimals are numbers n that satisfy the condition

$$-r < n < r$$

for every positive real number r. Zero is an infinitesimal, and the only real infinitesimal. In non-standard models it can be shown that there are infinitely many non-zero infinitesimals, called *hyperreals*. The result of adding an infinitesimal to a real number is also a hyperreal, and the reciprocal of an infinitesimal is an infinite hyperreal. The standard real numbers are included in the hyperreals, which thus constitute a proper extension of the standard reals. The finite hyperreals are clustered about the reals; infinitesimal proximity is an equivalence relation which partitions the hyperreals into cells each of which includes just one standard real number, called the *standard part* of each proximate hyperreal. Hyperreals can be added, subtracted, divided, and multiplied, with the consequence that analysis can be given a thoroughly Leibnizean development without reference to limits.[9] One great advantage of non-standard measure theory is the plausible treatment it provides of the measure of finite non-null sets. In the usual standard measures on the unit square, probabilities being a conspicuous case, each finite set of points has measure zero. Thus, if one is thinking of infinite sequences of tosses of a coin with constant probability of heads, the probability of each point, or infinite sequence, is zero when calculated in terms of limits.

---

[7] See Bernstein and Wattenberg, "Nonstandard Measure Theory" and Loeb, "Conversion from Nonstandard to Standard Measure Space and Applications to Probability Theory".

[8] In Robinson, *Non-standard Analysis*.

[9] For a lucid introduction, see the first chapter of Keisler's *Elementary Calculus*.

A finite sequence of tosses is thought of as the set of all its infinite extensions (or the union of their unit sets). A finite sequence of tosses has positive probability, and is thus a set of positive measure which is at the same time the union of disjoint sets all of measure zero. This is not absurd only because measures are not perfectly additive. As de Finetti's arguments[10] make clear, one need not be a novice in measure theory to see denumerable additivity as an *ad hoc* constraint. Again, the standard theory of measure gives the same measure to points or finite or denumerable collections of them as it gives to the null set, and this may violate the quite strong intuitions that support the requirement of regularity.

Non-standard measure theory may in such cases assign positive infinitesimal measure to each point, zero to the null set, and the sum

$$\Sigma_{x \epsilon A} \, m\{x\}$$

to each measurable set A. Then finite and denumerable sets of points have infinitesimal measure, and for the standard sets the measure behaves just as it is supposed to: under plausible conditions m is infinitely close to the standard Lebesgue measure where both are defined.[11]

As far as probability is concerned this permits a finer distinction between the impossible and the highly unlikely. This distinction is accomplished below, following de Finetti's lead, in terms of the hierarchy of thin sets. There what is highly unlikely has probability zero, but it is compatible with this that its probability be positive conditional upon some unlikely condition. This violates regularity, as the approach in terms of infinitesimals does not, though the net results are roughly equivalent; whatever is highly unlikely has zero or infinitesimal probability on any likely condition.

Measure theory provides also a semantics for probability quantifiers. The basic idea for this is the concept of *probability model* for a language L. Given a first-order language L and a model M with domain D = D(M), for each n the extensions in M of formulas with n free variables form a Boolean algebra of subsets of D. One can thus define probabilities p_n on these algebras. Certain plausible assumptions assure that these probabilities obey Fubini-type

---

[10] Considered above in section 3.5. See also *Theory of Probability* vol. I, p. 10, and sections 3.11 and 6.3.

[11] Bernstein and Wattenberg, "Nonstandard Measure Theory", theorem 2.8.

constraints[12] among themselves. $\langle M, p_1 \ldots \rangle$ is then said to be a probability model for L. In particular, languages L that lack the standard universal and existential quantifiers lend themselves well to study in this way. Distribution (rather than, as in the present work, frequency) quantifiers can be defined.

$$(P_x > r) A(x)$$

where r is between zero and one inclusive, is satisfied by an assignment s in a probability model $\langle M, p_1 \ldots \rangle$ just in case the probability p_1 assigns a value greater than r to the set

$$\{d \mid t(x) = d \text{ for some } x \text{ variant } t \text{ of } s \text{ that satisfies } A(x)\}$$

H. J. Keisler laid the foundations for this work and Douglas Hoover has continued it.[13] They apply the method to various infinitary languages—languages which, though lacking the classical quantifiers, permit infinite disjunction and conjunction of formulas. The combination with non-standard measure theory (absent from the above sketch) has proven to be very fruitful with some sharp and deep results.

The most noticeable difference between the probability logics of Keisler and Hoover and those developed later in this chapter is the great power of the former. In contrast to the smooth strength of the hyperfinite development, the system of probability logic given here employs only the weak methods of standard predicate logic, for reasons to be spelled out below. Thus the definition of satisfaction in the hyperfinite theory includes reference to probability measures in the model. This would frustrate the ends of the present investigation which are to give, as far as possible, a logical account of probability.

Another contrast is in the treatment of embedded probabilities. Keisler's approach aims to reduce them to prenex occurrence, thus reducing embedded probabilities to the straightforward application of probabilities on product spaces, by way of a hyperfinite form of the Fubini theorem.[14] This is what opens the way to a smooth and unified application of non-standard measure theory, something that

---

[12] See section 5.5 below for a brief explanation of the Fubini theorem and its import.

[13] Keisler, "Hyperfinite Model Theory", and Hoover, "Probability Logic" and "A Normal Form for $L(\omega 1 P)$, with Applications".

[14] "Hyperfinite Model Theory", theorem 1.12.

would be difficult if the probabilities remained, as they do in the present work, embedded. For this reason Keisler's quantifiers do not mix with the standard universal and existential quantifiers (some of the work of which is accomplished by infinite formulas), since their occurrence would greatly complicate the definition of satisfaction and apparently block the reduction to prenex normal form and the elimination of quantifiers in certain cases. Indeed in remarking on the absence of the standard quantifiers Hoover writes that they "are not probabilistic notions".[15] That might be disputed (particularly in view of the distinction made in the non-standard theory between zero and infinitesimal probability; between probability one and probability infinitesimally close to one), but the point is that it makes evident the difference of approach—from the present point of view the question is put the other way round: which of the probabilistic notions are logical?

If probability has not traditionally been treated as a quantifier, there are nevertheless certain precedents for doing so. Perhaps the most obvious of these is Reichenbach's generalization of formal implication, mentioned above. Reichenbach was not the first to think along these lines; Peirce remarked on the possibility of defining probability quantifiers in a footnote to one of his first records of the definition of quantifiers.[16] It is not apparent that he gave the subject any further thought, though he did work extensively in probability along what might be called logical frequentist lines.

In 1909, in a remarkable work published in German in 1913, Łukasiewicz [17] generalized the Fregean concept of truth value to apply to propositional functions, which he calls 'indefinite propositions". The truth value of an indefinite proposition is ". . . *the ratio between the number of values of the variables for which the proposition yields true judgements and the total number of values of the variables*" (p. 17). The relative (conditional) truth value of indefinite propositions is the quotient of the truth value of their conjunction and that of the antecedent. Łukasiewicz then argues that these truth values provide an adequate account of probability, free from

[15] "A Normal Form for L(ω1P)", 607.

[16] In Peirce, *The Collected Works of Charles Saunders Peirce*, 3.393.

[17] Łukasiewicz, "Die logische Grundlagen der Wahrscheinlichkeitsrechnung". References here are to the English translation, "The Logical Foundations of Probability". I am grateful to Ernest Adams for calling this paper to my attention.

many of the difficulties that plague subjectivistic and empirical views.

Łukasiewicz considers neither infinite interpretations nor embedded probabilities. He treats only monadic propositional functions and he writes the truth value or probability as the value of a function applied to an indefinite proposition or propositions, not as a quantifier or operator. He nevertheless announces and defends two themes central to the present approach: logicism, and the requirement that probability involve always a free parameter:

If probabilistic propositions are interpreted as indefinite propositions and probability fractions are interpreted as truth values, then all the principles of the probability calculus can be obtained from this assumption in a strictly deductive manner by the algebra of logic.[18]

Łukasiewicz proves a form of a theorem relating multivariate probabilities (e.g. P(Ax & Ay)) and single variable probabilities (P(Ax), P(Ay)) (see theorem 4.1 below) as well as a form of Bayes's theorem (chapter 5, 2.6 (2)) for finite domains. The paper is certainly one of the earliest important works in probability logic, clearly ahead of its time. It also includes excellent critical discussions of some of Bolzano's and Grelling's views.

More recent predecessors are the works of Łos and Fenstad mentioned in section 3.7, n. 19 above, in which probabilities are defined for open sentences on the basis of measures on sets of models, and an insufficiently noticed 1974 paper by Ernest Adams, "The Logic of Almost All". Although Adams does not in that paper define probabilities on open sentences, the semantical relations between open sentences and product spaces are given close and fruitful examination.

The work of Łos and Fenstad also shares some of the motivations of the present approach. It is directed at defining probabilities of open sentences in a first-order language. This is done, as far as possible, in logical terms and without extra-logical assumptions. The technique centres around a representation theorem which can be roughly described as follows.

Carnapian logical probabilities on sentences of first-order languages can be extended to apply as well to open sentences with no change in the axiomatic definition; the extensions are normal and

---

[18] 'Logical Foundations'', 42. See also especially sections 16 and 17.

finitely additive. In themselves such functions have little interest beyond that of those restricted to closed sentences. The leading idea of Łos, followed up by Fenstad, is to use measures on sets of assignments to give a richer structure to probabilities of open sentences. If, that is to say, A is an open sentence of a language L, then the set A^M of assignments that satisfy A in the model M is assigned a certain value $v_M[A^M]$ which can be thought of as the probability of A in the model M. If M is finite then this can easily be done in a suitable way. If, for example and illustration, A has just one free variable, x, then A^M is just the set of all assignments s such that $M \vDash_s A$. The values of v_M can then be set so that

$v_M[A^M]$ = the relative frequency of x-variants of s that satisfy A

which is independent of the choice of s (when only x is free in A) and is equal to

$1/m\ C(A^M)$.

That is, it is the relative frequency of the set M|A| in the domain of M.

At the centre of this work is a representation theorem which asserts that if P is any extended Carnapian probability, defined on the formulas of a first-order language L, then where L{M} is the set of all models of L, there are measures v_M and a probability q on L{M} such that

$$P(A) = \int_{L\{M\}} v_M[A^M]\, d\, q(M)$$

for all formulas A of L. That is to say that extended probabilities on sentences can always be represented as weighted averages of probabilities on sets of assignments in a model, the weights being given by a probability on the set of models.

An analogous structure, though not the representation in terms of decomposition, is found in the expectation theorem, 4.5.2, below.

Fenstad, in particular, is interested in applications of the representation theorem in which statistics for finite models are inferential conditions in the calculation of expectations for larger and infinite models. That is an important issue in inductive logic, but it is not the point of the present inquiry. The main differences between this and the Łos–Fenstad approach are, first, that their technique is based upon measure-theoretic foundations, and, secondly, that its application to embedded probabilities would apparently require a hierarchical development—some version of that sketched in section 8 of chapter 3 above.

4.3 *Probability quantifiers: principles and semantics*

Kant took the first task of transcendental philosophy to be the deduction of the forms of judgement and the categories of thought. One important difference between the two editions of the first *Critique* is a shift of emphasis concerning the parts or direction of this task: in the first edition, categories are fundamental—if judgements provide a "route" to them—while in the second edition the priority has passed to the forms of judgement.[19] In Frege's version of the deduction, the passage is complete: "Never . . . ask for the meaning of a word in isolation, but only in the context of a proposition"[20] takes the question out of the mind and puts it into the realm of thoughts. It is now the structure of thoughts, and not the form of thought, that is at issue. This structure is, further, very simple: it always involves or represents the application of a function to an object. Frege gave a precise account of what it means for an object to fall under a concept, an account which he then generalized so as to make it completely pervasive. Generality (Everything is ϕ, or Something is ϕ) became the application of a second-crder concept (That of applying to everything, or to something) to a first-order concept.

One way to think of probability is as a metrical second-order concept. Then a first-order concept ϕ falls under the second-order concept "probability p" just in case the proportion of objects that fall under ϕ is p, quite as ϕ falls under 'everything is—" just in case all objects fall under ϕ. Now just as Frege's account accommodates embedded generalities and keeps track of their scopes with no ramification of orders beyond the second, so embedded probabilities are also accommodated within the same simple structure, awaiting only an explication of "the proportion p of objects fall under the concept ϕ". The same point can be made, following the lines of the discussion of section 2.2 above, in a Tarskian rather than a Fregean vocabulary,

---

[19] See Henrich's "The Proof-Structure of Kant's Transcendental Deduction".
[20] Frege, *Grundlagen*, p. xxii.

avoiding the hypostatization of logical objects. Then one says that an expression "the probability of ϕ is p" is satisfied when the proportion of objects that satisfy ϕ is p. Or, to make explicit the relativity to a variable, that an assignment of objects to variables satisfies "the probability of ϕx is p" when the proportion of assignments each of which agrees with the given assignment for all variables save (perhaps) x and which satisfy ϕx, is p.

Conditional probability can also be treated in this way. Then an assignment satisfies "the probability of ψx given ϕx is p" when the proportion of its x-variants that satisfy ϕx which also satisfy ψx is p.

These ideas are the foundation for the logic of probability quantifiers, developed in the remainder of this chapter. We turn now to an informal exposition of that logic, including a description of some of its results to be established in later sections.

The major motivating principle of probability quantifiers is the development of probability within pure or general logic to the extent that this is possible. The great difficulty of precisely defining *general logic* can perhaps be avoided by agreeing that however it is defined, the semantics of first-order logic as developed by Frege and Tarski fall quite within its confines. Then, as the above remarks suggest, the question is just to what extent such notions as "the proportion of objects falling under a concept" or "the proportion of assignments satisfying a formula" can be given a meaning in general logic. It is essential here to separate the case of finite domains from the general case, and, again, to mark off denumerably infinite domains from domains of higher orders of infinity. As concerns the second of these questions, beginning with classical first-order logic means that the standard domains are all denumerably infinite. That is the smallest class of models that suffices for a full theory of (first-order) logical consistency. The extension of general logic to provide a logical account of probability should be conservative, both in the precise and technical sense that validity and consistency in non-probabilistic logic should be unaffected by it, and also in the ordinary sense that the modifications in the Frege–Tarski semantics required to accommodate probability should be as modest as possible: the domains should be denumerably infinite, individual variables should range over the entire domain, n-place predicates should be interpreted as sets of n-adic vectors in the domain.

As concerns finite domains, no expansion or modification of the models themselves is required. If M is a standard, finite model, then an assignment s to variables will satisfy "the probability of A(x) is p" just in case the proportion of x-variants of s that satisfy A(x) is p. This definition is schematic as concerns the letter "p"; that is to say, it signals a system of definitions for the satisfaction of expressions such as "the probability of A(x) is 1/2". The object language will include no variables ranging over probabilities. The schematic letter "p" thus occurs both to mark the place of an expression designating a proportion (in the definiens, on its second occurrence) and to mark the place of a name of such an expression (in the definiendum, on its first occurrence). That should not be the source of any great unclarity, since the correspondence between rational number designators—fractions—and rational numbers is pretty well understood, but it should be kept in mind. It should also be kept in mind that the language of probability quantifiers will be relatively poor in expressive power as concerns truths *about* probability; it will interpret expressions in which probability is used, but will not interpret expressions in which probability is mentioned. It will provide no interpretation for such assertions as "the probability of A is greater than that of B". It is in this respect like the language of standard first-order logic as concerns its quantifiers; that language interprets assertions in which generality is used, but not expressions in which it is mentioned.

In the general case of denumerably infinite models the determination of proportions and ratios is not as straightforward as in the finite case; for, as the discussions of sections 3.1 and 3.5 above make evident, in infinite domains relative frequencies depend on order. Hence in a standard, denumerable first-order model, the proportion of x-variants of a given assignment that satisfy a formula will not in general be well-defined. In view of this the concept of first-order model will be modified to include as domains only denumerable sets which are also well-ordered and of type omega: isomorphic to the natural numbers. Independently of the logic of probability quantifiers this is not an unnatural requirement. Indeed, on a certain rather Kantian view of infinity it is quite plausible to think of the well-ordered, type-omega structure as the fundamental case, from which the standard unordered and denumerable model is derived by abstraction. To the extent that order in time is a necessary and formal character of thought, order may properly be counted a logical concept. This is an important question for the present approach, for it is just the limits of logic that are at issue. One might, of course, think of ramifying the constraints on order to allow variations of order type, but in a preliminary development that seems not advisable. Distinguishing different orders of the same domain is conservative in the second of the senses mentioned above; it is a modest complication.

This complication is also conservative in the first of the above senses: validity and consistency of formulas in non-probabilistic first-order logic are completely unaffected by the introduction of ordered models. Whatever is valid or consistent in standard and unordered models remains so when models are taken to be ordered. The consideration of multi-variate probability quantifiers will require further assumptions about ordering, and these are briefly discussed below in anticipation of a fuller treatment in section 5.5.

In section 4.1 above, the notation for probability quantifiers was informally sketched. Consider now the rational quantities between zero and one inclusive. Each such quantity may be named or designated by a (not unique) *rational number designator*. Although the correspondence between these quantities and their names or designators is not unique, each quantity does have a unique reduced expression: a fraction in lowest terms. We may thus presume a biunique correspondence between rational quantities (understood between zero and one inclusive) and the expressions that designate them. That said, we can now say that for each rational number designator, P, and each variable x, [Px] is a probability quantifier. This is just a general way of saying that "[1/2x]", "[9/10y]", and so on are all probability quantifiers.

No interpretation is thus provided for irrational probabilities. The main reason for this is the principle that guides the development of probability quantifiers, namely to interpret probability, and embedded probability in particular, as far as possible in logical terms and with as little modification of standard first-order logic as is feasible. The languages in question should have denumerable alphabets and expressions of only finite length. There are thus insufficient notational resources to allow for real-valued probability quantifiers. The notation could be expanded to allow for this, thus allowing the closure of probability values under all limit operations, and not just when the limiting values are rational, but this would still not assure that probability was everywhere defined. The rational-valued theory, though lacking the power of a real-valued development, is nevertheless strong enough to allow the formation of finite weighted averages, which, since the probability in question may not be denumerably additive, is about as much as can be usefully employed. Again, there seems nothing particularly probabilistic in the complications of extending the logical treatment of denumerable and well-ordered totalities to account for continuous magnitudes. As far as the problems of logic and probability are concerned, the rational-valued case enables an examination of them in a simple foundational setting.

The interpretation of embedded probabilities in a general logical framework is a large part of the motivation for the development of probability quantifiers. From the point of view of syntax this requires a notation for keeping track of scopes and variables, and the notation of probability quantifiers can obviously do this. We presume a standard development of the syntax of first-order languages, with expressions, predicates of finite degree, individual constants and variables, quantifiers, connectives, and the usual punctuation. The terms include the individual variables and constants as well as the result of putting a function symbol together with an appropriate number of terms. This syntax is then modified by the addition of one schematic formation rule (probability conditionals are considered in the next section):

Rule of formation for formulas including probability quantifiers. If A is a formula, x a variable, and P a rational number designator (of a quantity between zero and one inclusive) then [Px]A is a formula.

As remarked above, it must be kept in mind that each probability quantifier includes a specific constant numerical designator: "[1/2x]" and "[9/10y]" are probability quantifiers, "[Px]" and "[Qy]" are not. These last occur only in the informal metalanguage. It should also be emphasized that the formula A may be any formula whatever; the variable x need not occur free in it, and A may include other probability quantifiers, as well as connectives and standard quantifiers, to any level of complexity and embedding. The semantics to be given below will interpret all such formulas as a matter of course.

Given the now-modified definition of formula, embedded probabilities are expressed as easily as, and quite on a par with, embedded generality. Probabilities may occur within the scopes of connectives, standard quantifiers, and other probability quantifiers, with no more linguistic hierarchization than that required for standard first-order languages. Of course, this is so far only on the level of notation, but it is worth remarking that a large part of Frege's solution of the problem of generality was solved at just this notational level: to get away from the strictures and enforced complexity of the hierarchical account of generality; move generality out of the act of judgement and into the content of what is judged. Or, to put this as a comment on the Carnapian account of embedded probabilities, to get away from the strictures and enforced complexity of the hierarchical account of (embedded) probability; move probability out of the metalanguage and into the object language.

As concerns semantics, the smooth and recursive interpretation of embedded probabilities will require integration of the rule for satisfaction of expressions of the form [Px]A in the standard definition of satisfaction. The models in question are just standard first-order models, with the additional complication that the denumerable domains are always well-ordered and of type omega. Given a probabilistic first-order language, K, as described above, an *interpretation* M for K consists of a well-ordered and denumerable set D(M) in which the individual constants, function symbols, and predicates of K are interpreted in the usual way: we write $|E|^M$ for the interpretation of the expression E in M. Then if P is a k-place predicate, $|P|^M$ is a set of k-tuples of members of D(M). If f is a k-place function symbol, $|f|^M$ is a function which assigns some member of D(M) to each k-tuple of members of D(M). If a is an individual constant then $|a|^M$ is a member of D(M). All languages are presumed to include an identity predicate, and this is always interpreted normally: as the set of pairs $\langle m,m \rangle$ for m a member of D(M).

The semantical rules for the non-probabilistic fragment are formulated in the classical Tarskian way. The individual variables are presumed to be given in order, as are the individual constants. Given an ordered domain D(M) an *assignment* to the terms is a function s which assigns to each term (i.e. individual variable or individual constant) some member of D(M) with the restrictions (i) that all assignments agree in assigning to the kth individual constant the kth member of the domain, and (ii) that all assignments conform to the structure of functions: the result of applying the function $|f|^M$ to $< s(t_1) \ldots s(t_k) >$ must always be just $s(f(t_1 \ldots t_k))$. As far as variables are concerned, the order within an assignment is independent of the order of the domain. Assignments are *x-variants* if and only if they agree for all terms except (perhaps) for the variable x.

Notice that for each variable x and assignment s the ordering of the domain induces an ordering of the x-variants of s. The jth x-variant of s in this ordering is just like s except that it assigns the jth member of the domain $D(M)$ to x. So if $D(M)$ is $\langle m_1, m_2 \ldots \rangle$, then the first x-variant of s assigns m_1 to x, the second x-variant of s assigns m_2 to x, and so on. Given the ordered domain $D(M)$ this is called the *canonical ordering* of the x-variants of s.

An atomic formula $A(t_1 \ldots t_k)$ is *satisfied* by the assignment s in the interpretation M if the elements $s(t_1) \ldots s(t_k)$ stand in the relation $|A|^M$. If A is a formula, we write

$$M \underset{s}{\vDash} A$$

to abbreviate "s satisfies A in M". So

$$M \underset{s}{\vDash} A(t_1 \ldots t_k) \text{ iff } <s(t_1) \ldots s(t_k)> \epsilon |A|^M$$

The negation of a formula is satisfied by just those assignments which fail to satisfy the formula. An assignment satisfies a conjunction just in case it satisfies both conjuncts. Disjunctions are satisfied where at least one of their disjuncts is satisfied, a conditional is satisfied except when its antecedent is satisfied and its consequent not satisfied, and a biconditional is satisfied by those assignments which agree for its two sides.

A universal quantification, $(\forall x)A$, is satisfied by an assignment in an interpretation if every x-variant of that assignment satisfies the formula A in that interpretation. Similarly for existential quantification, $(\exists x)A$, with "some x-variant" in place of "every x-variant".

This completes the definition of satisfaction for non-probabilistic formulas. As remarked above, the introduction of ordered domains leaves the classical semantics of the non-probabilistic fragment unaffected.

The additional clause in the definition of satisfaction for probabilistically quantified formulas is this: an assignment s satisfies a probabilistically quantified formula [Px]A in an interpretation M just in case the formula A is satisfied by the proportion P of x-variants of s. We turn now to the precision of this definiens.

Consider an interpretation M with a denumerably infinite domain $D(M)$. For each variable x and each assignment s let

$$I(s,x) = \langle s_1, s_2 \ldots \rangle$$

be the canonical ordering of the x-variants of s, where s_j is the jth assignment in this ordering (that is to say, the assignment that assigns the jth element of D(M) to x). And for each n = 1, 2 . . . let

$$I^n(s,x) = \langle s_1, s_2, \ldots s_n \rangle$$

be the first n assignments in I(s,x). Given a formula A, let

$$F^n(A,s,x)$$

be the proportion or relative frequency of the first n x-variants of s that satisfy A. That is to say

$$F^n(A,s,x) = 1/n[\text{number of sequences in } I^n(s,x) \text{ that satisfy A}]$$

A direct recursive definition of F^n, following the structure of formulas, is blocked, since, for example, the proportion for a conjunction is not determined by the proportions for the conjuncts: the relative frequencies of A and B in a reference class D(M) leave the relative frequency of (A & B) quite undetermined. This is one great difference between probability logic and the logic of two-valued measures. It is precisely at this point that mathematical induction on formulas in terms of their rank or structure becomes inapplicable in probability logic. This is a clear difficulty in the way of a smooth and thorough mixture of logic and probability. The above definitions open the way to overcoming it.

Given a denumerable structure M, a formula A, a sequence s, and a variable x, the sequence

$$F^1(A,s,x), F^2(A,s,x), \ldots$$

is an infinite sequence of rational numbers, between zero and one inclusive. In some cases this sequence *converges rationally*; that is to say, there is a rational number r, such that as n increases without bound $F^n(A,s,x)$ becomes and remains arbitrarily close to r. In case there is such a number r, *the proportion of x-variants of s that satisfy A in M* is defined to be that number, and in this case we write

$$F(A,s,x) = r$$

and we say that F(A,s,x) is *(rationally) defined*. If F(A,s,x) is not defined, that is to say if the sequence {$F^n(A,s,x)$} does not converge to a rational value, then no proportion of x-variants of s satisfies A in M. In this case the negation clause in the definition of satisfaction has as a consequence that s satisfies ¬ [Px]A, for every rational designator P. The clause defining satisfaction of probabilistically quantified formulas can now be put explicitly:

If P is a rational designator between zero and one inclusive, x a variable, and A a formula, then the assignment s satisfies the formula [Px]A in the interpretation M if and only if

$$\lim_{n \to \infty} F^n(A,s,x) = P$$

This clause functions as an integral part of the expanded definition of satisfaction. If $F(A,s,x)$ is defined (that is, if the above limit exists and is rational) then $F(\neg A,s,x)$ is defined in the same sense and turns out to be just $1 - F(A,s,x)$. If A and B are incompatible in the structure M (that is to say, if no assignment satisfies both A and B in the structure M) then, if both $F(A,s,x)$ and $F(B,s,x)$ are defined, $F(A \vee B, s,x)$ is defined and turns out to be the sum of $F(A,s,x)$ and $F(B,s,x)$. These truths mean that the standard probabilistic laws governing additivity will be consequences of the definition of satisfaction. It is worth remarking that it does not in general follow from the fact that both $F(A,s,x)$ and $F(B,s,x)$ are defined that $F(A \& B, s,x)$ is also defined, and that $F(A \vee B, s,x)$ may be defined though either or both of $F(A,s,x)$, $F(B,s,x)$ are undefined. Examples are easy to come by.[21]

The definitions of truth in a model, of validity, and of implication are standard: a formula is *true* in a model if satisfied by every assignment in that model, and a formula is *valid* if true in every

---

[21] For an example of the first sort consider a model with the natural numbers in their canonical order as domain. Let $|A|^M$ be just the even numbers, and let $|B|^M$ include the odd numbers up to a certain number n_1, the even numbers between n_1 and n_2, the odd numbers between n_2 and n_3, and so on ($n_1 < n_2 < n_3 < \ldots$). Then $F^n A(x) \& B(x), s,x) = 0$ for each s. If, however, the interval between n_1 and n_2 is sufficiently large, then $F^{n_2}(A(x) \& B(x), s,x)$ approaches arbitrarily close to $1/2$. Again, for n_3 sufficiently large, $F^{n_3}(A(x) \& B(x), s,x)$ becomes arbitrarily close to zero. Thus if the differences $n_{k+1} - n_k$ expand rapidly enough, then as n increases $F^n(A(x) \& B(x), s,x)$ will fluctuate perpetually between close to $1/2$ and close to zero. Hence $F(A(x) \& B(x), s,x)$ does not converge and is undefined. But $F(A(x), s,x)$ and $F(B(x), s,x)$ are both defined and equal to $1/2$. For an example of the second sort let the extension of A fluctuate: including the even numbers up to n_1, then no numbers between n_1 and n_2, and so on, while the sequence $n_1, n_2, \ldots$ expands as above. Let the extension of B be just the even numbers. Then $F(A,s,x)$ is undefined, and $F(B,s,x)$ and $F(A \vee B, s,x)$ are both $1/2$. For an example of the third sort, define the extension of A to fluctuate in this same way, while the extension of B fluctuates with the same period but in the opposite way: to include no numbers up to n_1, then the even numbers between n_1 and n_2, and so on. Then both $F(A,s,x)$ and $F(B,s,x)$ are undefined, but $F(A \vee B, s,x) = 1/2$.

model. A set Γ of formulas *implies* a formula A if any assignment that satisfies every member of Γ in any structure M also satisfies A in M. The following abbreviations are used:

$M \vDash A$ for A is true in M

$\vDash A$ for A is valid

$\Gamma \vDash A$ for Γ implies A

These definitions need to be expanded in two ways: to interpret conditional probabilities and to interpret multivariate probabilistic quantification. Before turning to these expansions, we mention a few metatheoretic consequences of the development so far.[22] The proofs are straightforward combinations of the usual inductions and the elementary arithmetic of limits.

3.1 Let M be an interpretation, A a formula, x a variable, and t a term. Then

(1) Assignments which agree for all variables in A also agree in satisfying or not satisfying A.
(2) If no variable is free in A then either A is true in M or $\neg A$ is true in M.
(3) If t is a term, x a variable, and s is an assignment such that $s(t) = s(x)$; then if B is the result of replacing each free occurrence of x in A by t, no replacement occurring within the scope of a quantifier of any variable of t, s satisfies A in M if and only if s satisfies B in M.
(4) For each assignment s there is at most one quantity P such that s satisfies [Px]A in M. (Recall that the correspondence between rational numbers and their canonical designators is biunique; each rational is represented by a fraction in lowest terms.)

Although the logic of probability quantifiers is not axiomatizable (this is established in section 4.5 below) there are a few basic rules governing inference which suffice for many of the arguments in the sequel. From the point of view of probability theory, the most fundamental of these are additivity (3.4, below) and the principle 5.3 which allows the elimination of unembedded probability quantifiers in favour of cardinality assertions in the finite case. From a logical and deductive point of view, however, the ways in which

---

[22] These are quite analogous to the basic lemmas and theorems in Tarski, "The Concept of Truth".

probability quantifiers bind variables and govern scope are equally significant. It should be recalled that the rules of formation allow for vacuous quantification: [Px]A is well formed whether or not x is free in A. And the definition of satisfaction applies also to such formulas.

The first theorems show how probability quantifiers relate to the standard universal and existential quantifiers. An assignment s satisfies a formula [1x]A in an interpretation M just in case the proportion of x-variants of s that satisfy A in M is one, or, as it is sometimes put, just in case almost every x-variant of s satisfies A. If the domain of M is infinite, then it is compatible with this that any finite number of x-variants of s may fail to satisfy A. On the other hand, if every x-variant of s satisfies A, then A is satisfied by almost every x-variant of s. Hence

3.2 (1) $(\forall x)A \vDash [1x]A$, but not the converse

(2) $\neg [0x]A \vDash (\exists x)A$, but not the converse.

In finite models this distinction between "every" and "almost every" does not exist: if the proportion of x-variants of s that satisfy A is one, then every x-variant of s satisfies A. So

3.3 If C_k is a sentence expressing that there are exactly k objects (k a positive integer) then

(1) $C_k, [1x]A \vDash (\forall x)A$

(2) $C_k, [0x]A \vDash \neg (\exists x)A$.

3.2 (1) formulates a law of probability—that whatever holds of everything has unit probability. Another law is additivity, which holds in the following form: if a conjunction has zero probability, then the probability of the corresponding disjunction is the sum of the probabilities of the disjuncts. It will help in formulating this to introduce an informal notational convention. "P", "Q" are informal metalinguistic variables, used to formulate laws in which they mark the place of arbitrary numerical designators. When these variables occur, we may write "P + Q", "PQ" to indicate the numerical designator which designates the sum or the product of those quantities indicated by whatever designators are put in the place of "P" and "Q". This convention is always dispensable, at some sacrifice of economy and clarity of expression. Thus, the additivity principle could be formulated without employing it as follows:

(i) If "P", "Q" are any rational designators, and "R" designates the sum of the quantities designated by "P" and "Q", then

[0x](A & B), [Px]A, [Qx]B ⊨ [Rx](A ∨ B)

It will, however, be simpler to state this principle using the convention:

3.4 (1) [0x](A & B), [Px]A, [Qx]B ⊨ [(P + Q)x](A ∨ B)

The law of negation also holds. The above notational convention is extended here in an obvious way.

3.4 (2) [Px]A ⊨ [(1 – P)x] ¬ A

The zero and one quantifiers have the sense of "almost none" and "almost all". These "almost" quantifiers function in certain ways like universal and existential quantifiers. Here are some of those ways:

3.5   (1) If x is not free in A then ⊨ [1x]A ∨ [0x]A
       (2) If A is true in M, then [1x]A is true in M
       (3) [1x]B entails [1x](A → B) and [0x]A entails [1x](A → B)
       (4) [0x]A entails [0x](A & B).

Theorem 3.5 is a consequence of 3.2 and the additivity principle. 3.5 (3) has the consequence that

(i) ⊨ [1x]([1x]A → A)

When we turn to the logic of probability quantifiers which are neither zero nor one the situation is a bit more complicated. Here is a distribution property for the conditional:

3.6 (1) [1x](A → B) ⊨ [Px]A → [Px](A & B)

The generalization of this for Q different from one obviously does not hold. That the biconditional with probability one gives an equivalence relation is shown by the following theorem

3.6 (2) [1x](A ⟷ B) ⊨ [Px]A ⟷ [Px]B

and this, together with 1.2 (1) supports the extensionality of probability quantifiers in the following clear sense.

3.6 (3) (∀x)(A ⟷ B) ⊨ [Px]A ⟷ [Px]B

Here is a simple law (it is a consequence of 3.6 and the additivity principle) governing the antecedents of conditionals in which the quantified variable is not free:

3.7 If x is not free in A then [Px](A → B) ⊨ A → [Px]B

but the generalization of (i) above, with "P" in the place of "1" does not hold. The following theorem gives conditions under which formulas can be moved into quantifier scopes.

3.8 (1) If x is not free in A then A & [Px]B $\vDash$ [Px](A & B)

(2) If in addition P is positive then the converse implication holds as well: [Px](A & B) $\vDash$ A & [Px]B

(3) [Px](A & B), [1x]A $\vDash$ [Px]B.

4.4 *On principles and consequences*

In section 4.1 above it was argued that one important task for logical probability is to expand logical techniques in such a way as to make possible the statement of consistency criteria for probability assertions. This requires a theory of the structure or logical form of such assertions, and the preceding section is the first stage in such a theory. The theory of probability quantifiers pays particular attention to the problem of embedded probabilities and to the conditions of consistency for assertions in which they are involved. It was argued earlier, in chapter 1, that subjectivism and various kinds of psychologism are not plausible extensions of logic in this regard, and that their incapacities become clear and evident when embedded probabilities are in question. Again, the Carnapian theory of section 3.8, though it offers something closer to a logical account of embedded probabilities, does this only with difficulty and under the weight of various non-logical principles.

The system of probability quantifiers treats embedded probabilities with just the same ease as the classical theory of quantification treats embedded generality. In the sequel this system is extended to account for probability conditionals and multivariate probabilistic quantification. In the present section a few foundational questions and related issues are briefly discussed.

It is first necessary to insist that the logic of probability quantifiers makes no pretence of providing a definition or reduction of probability. There is here no answer to the question "What is probability?" Indeed, that question may well have no good answer; except to say that probability is what our theories of probability say it is or must be. There is, then, no attempt to analyse or account for the content of probability judgements, to say what it is that one asserts in a statement of probability. There is no attempt to say in what consists the evidence for probability assertions, or what their empirical meaning is or should be. Although the present account involves relative frequencies, it in no way entails or should even suggest that probability assertions are assertions of relative frequencies; no more than the account of consistency provided by first-order logic entails or suggests that ordinary discourse makes assertions about denumerable structures. In both cases the abstract structures function as possible interpretations to demonstrate the consistency of statements with reference to a certain theory of their forms. The ultimate test of the adequacy of these accounts and of the structures they call into being is just the extent to which they provide an adequate and systematic account of consistency: an account that conforms to pre-systematic intuitions and also extends these intuitions in rewarding ways. Again, there are properly speaking no such objects as probabilities in the logic of probability quantifiers, just as there are no general ideas in the Frege–Tarski account of generality. There are sentences involving probability quantifiers, but these quantifiers are quite without reference in the interpreting structures. Those structures include ordered domains and subsets and functions in these domains, but there are no entities to be identified as probabilities. It is, for example, not right that probabilities are proportions or relative frequencies with which the extensions of predicates occur in the domain, for this description ignores the probabilistic quantification of complex, including probabilistic, formulas. This becomes even more evident when multivariate probability quantifiers are introduced in section 5.5. If one takes a strictly Fregean approach, then probability quantifiers are second-order concepts, as suggested in section 4.1 above, but the semantics of the previous section eschews that in favour of Tarskian satisfaction.

Theorem 3.5 (1) of the preceding section says that when the variable x is not free in the formula A, then [1x]A v [0x]A is valid. That implies that sentences (formulas in which no variable is free) can have probability only in a degenerate sense; if a sentence A is true in the structure M then so is [1x]A, if A is false in M, then [0x]A is true in M. The reason for this is that all probability (in the genuine sense) requires, on the present approach, a parameter. That is entailed by the way in which variables and scopes are tracked in embedded occurrences. In extensional contexts—and the semantics of probability quantifiers is completely extensional, as the law 3.6 (3) makes clear—the extensions of predicates, function-symbols, and individual constants in a sentence determine its truth value, either true or false. No sentence can be one-half true or almost false.

If A is a sentence and P less than one, then (A & [Px]A) is inconsistent. An argument for subjectivism has sometimes been made from this: namely that if we were to assign objective probabilities to sentences or propositions, then we should have to assign only the values zero and one,[23] and thus no objective account of probability can be realistic. In particular, if probability is to serve as a standard for degree of belief, then an objectivistic theory will always set a standard which is too high, as Ramsey put it, to expect of mortal men.

In its strongest form this argument purports to show that no objectivistic account of probability can be correct: the objects of probability are sentences or propositions; by excluded middle each sentence or proposition is either true or false; on objectivistic accounts these have probabilities one and zero respectively. It is, however, essential to probability that it can serve as a standard of belief, and no objectivistic account can allow for this, for all such accounts must set a standard that is too high for mortal men.

As it stands this argument presumes that sentences or propositions are the only legitimate bearers of probability, for it is to such objects that the law of excluded middle applies. It may be that sentences or propositions are the only legitimate bearers or objects of *partial belief* (though even this premiss seems unwarranted in view of the obvious difficulties it engenders for understanding *de re* belief), but it does not follow from this that they are the only legitimate bearers of *probability*, unless partial belief is the only legitimate sense of probability. That is itself a quite strong form of subjectivism, and this strong form of the argument should thus not persuade those who are not already convinced of subjectivism on other grounds.

In fact, if the issue of partial belief is put to one side for the moment, the most plausible common-sense view is that probability (in the non-degenerate sense) always requires some free parameters. That is true when it is defined for random variables, and single case probabilities always require an explication of the case as a propositional function. Generalization from a proposition to form a propositional function may be done in different ways, and these ways may give us different probabilities. The examples of section 4.2 above illustrate this.

---

[23] See, for example, Ramsey, "Truth and Probability".

In considering probability and belief, and particularly as regards the issue of consistency, it is salutary to keep in mind Hempel's question mentioned in the Introduction: a schoolchild does a sum on the blackboard. What is the function of the laws of arithmetic in our understanding of this event? The foundations of arithmetic must not render a good answer to this question impossible. Not the least advantage of Frege's account of generality over its predecessors is its excellence in this regard: it describes simple logical knowledge and deductive rules which are appropriate candidates for a *"canon of understanding* and of reason", in Kant's phrase.[24]

Hempel's question also tells us something about the foundations of probability: that it should always keep an eye on the sorts of account of ordinary probabilistic inference and belief that it renders possible or prohibits. Hume's theory of probability and partial belief, discussed in chapter 1 above, is always scrupulous in this regard, and—from this point of view at least, whatever may be its other shortcomings—is a worthy model. In general, one wants to avoid invoking complex assumptions, about measure theory, for instance, which may be unknown or even unknowable to the stochastically reasoning subject.

It is natural to distinguish, in judgement and belief, the believing act from the object or objects believed. These objects must presumably include propositions, or perhaps sentences of some ideal language, but also, in *de re* belief, propositional functions or open sentences. Accounts of consistency in belief or judgement will also respect the distinction between act and objects: beliefs may be said to be inconsistent when their (propositional) objects are inconsistent. The relativization of objective inconsistency to a logic then induces a corresponding relativization in the inconsistency of beliefs. Under plausible assumptions it can be shown that the logic governing consistency of belief determines the relation of logical equivalence for which belief is transparent or invariant.[25]

Consistency and inconsistency may also be applied to the acts of believing or judging, or, sometimes, to epistemic dispositions or tendencies to perform such acts. Two points, made in section 2.3 above, are relevant here: first, this does not eliminate the question of consistency of objects, since the acts as such can be consistent or inconsistent only with respect to their contents or objects. Secondly,

24 *Critique of Pure Reason*, A 53 = B 77.
25 See Vickers, *Belief and Probability*.

the account becomes pragmatic and consequential, either prudential or psychologistic, and is hence not logical. These accounts generally fare badly in the face of Hempel's question: psychologism in probability encounters just the same difficulties there as psychologism in arithmetic, namely it cannot account for the normative and a priori force of arithmetical and probabilistic laws. The tendency is to make the psychology required not scientific but transcendental: a collection of conditions for probabilistic thought which are not themselves thought or recognized as such, but which nevertheless govern the thought and judgement of all humans. One forgets that transcendental conditions can have only regulative, never constitutive, force. The introduction of prudential considerations to take over this task results, on the other hand, in an abstract and external notion of rationality, according to which those whose statistical knowledge is insufficient, among which must surely be counted all but an infinitesimally small fraction of humans—alive, dead, or yet to exist—can be rational only by fortuitous accident.

The system of probability quantifiers has several advantages in this respect. It mentions belief not at all, and it thus opens the way to accounting for consistency of belief as consistency of the objects believed. It is of course not ruled out that this account should be overlaid with a theory of consistency of acts of belief, including the probabilistic consistency of partial beliefs, but even without such a theory, a generous part of ordinary probabilistic inference is comprehensible purely in terms of the logical consistency of objects believed or judged. Some simple principles regarding embedded probabilities and the calculation of expectations are included in these rules of inference, as are principles relating frequencies and probabilities.

It should be emphasized that the logic of probability quantifiers neither includes nor constrains an account of belief. And it passes the test of Hempel's question very well: the function of the laws of probability in understanding ordinary probabilistic belief and inference can be restricted to pure or general logic of a very simple sort. This logic is quite free of empirical and transcendental psychological principles as it is of principles of prudence and rationality.

As concerns *de re* partial belief, the view of partial belief as represented by a probability on the sentences of a theory or language is severely hindered since it makes no provision for the application of propositional functions or open sentences to individuals. The language of probability quantifiers is not hindered in this way: one could define the analogue of Quine's *intensional abstraction* operator to give structured predicates which are both probabilistic and genuinely functional. Thus, to start with Quine's example, in

(i)   Tom believes xy[x denounced y] of Cicero and Catiline

belief is viewed as a relative term "predicable of objects some of which are propositions, attributes, or relations".[26] Proposition (i) is to be so understood as not to change its truth value when Tom, Cicero, or Catiline are differently named or described. Such variation internal to the intensional relational expression "[x denounced y]" would, however, change its referent. The point here is less semantical than formal. That is to say, it is less a question of interpreting (i), of how reference to intensions is to be understood, than of its logical form or structure. If propositions or sentences are the bearers of partial belief, then partial belief could not have the structure of (i), and (i) could not be varied to express, for example, that Tom believes the chance is 1/2 that Cicero has denounced someone. With probability quantifiers, however, one can write

(ii)   Tom believes x[[1/2y]x denounced y] of Cicero

in which the partiality is both objective (so partial belief is belief in a "partial" or probabilistic object) and applied to an open sentence.

Before turning to the elaboration of the semantics of probability quantifiers, one interesting point of difficulty in their application may be mentioned. This concerns the application of probability to assertions involving mass terms and continuous magnitudes. The representation of

(iii)   The chance of a randomly chosen object being a fair coin is 9/10

as

(iv)   [9/10x](x is a fair coin)

is plausible and natural. But

(v)   The chance that water is polluted is 3/4

cannot plausibly be written as

(vi)   [3/4x](x is polluted water).

---

[26] Quine, *Word and Object*, 168. The account is later (in chapter 6) modified to eliminate reference to intensional entities.

The reason for this is obvious; namely that the interpreting structures in use here are ordered collections of discrete objects or individual particulars. "Water" is a mass term, it does not "divide its reference", and (vi) could thus not be modelled in a structure in which 3/4 of the individual particulars are water. The difficulty is not peculiar to probability quantifiers, for standard first-order logic encounters the same problem in representing "Some water is polluted". Of course one can write

(vii) (∃x)(x is water & x is polluted)

but far from resolving the problem, this just ignores it. What is at issue is the logic of continuous magnitudes, and the discrete objects of first-order models provide a poor base for the study of this. This failure of probability quantifiers points up a way in which the system differs from the usual account of probability as a function defined on propositions or sentences. The latter applies probability only to an already formed object. Propositions involving mass terms may be assigned probabilities as easily as propositions of any other sort; that the logic of mass terms is not understood is no concern of probability. This is precisely what cannot be said with respect to the logic of probability quantifiers, for in that system the logic and the probability are inseparable.

4.5 *Cardinality and the Gaifman condition*

In standard first-order logic with identity, for each positive integer k, there are sentences that hold in all and only (normal) models of size exactly k. Given k and the distinct variables $x_1 \ldots x_k$, let $D(x_1 \ldots x_k)$ be the conjunction of the formulas $\neg(x_i = x_j)$ for distinct x_i and x_j. Then the sentence

$$C_k: (∃x_1) \ldots (∃x_k)[D(x_1 \ldots x_k) \,\&\, (∀y)(y = x_1 ∨ \ldots ∨ y = x_k)]$$

expresses that there are exactly k objects. It is only a slight complication of this to express that there are exactly j objects in the extension of a formula A of one free variable, y:

$$C_j(A,y): (∃x_1) \ldots (∃x_j)\{D(x_1 \ldots x_j) \,\& \\ (∀y)[A(y) ⟷ (y = x_1 ∨ \ldots ∨ y = x_j)]\}$$

There are also consistent sentences of first-order logic (with or without identity) which have no finite models: every non-null transitive, asymmetric, and connected relation has an infinite field, and these characteristics can be postulated of a relation R.

Inf: $(\forall x)(\forall y)(\forall z)\{[R(x,y) \rightarrow (R(y,z) \rightarrow R(x,z))]$ &
$[R(x,y) \longleftrightarrow \neg R(y,x)]\}$ & $(\exists v)(\exists w)R(v,w)$

The sentence Inf has no finite models, but it has denumerably infinite models. Inf cannot be said to *express* infinity as C_k expresses that there are just k individuals, for though it has only infinite models, it does not hold in *all* infinite models; it holds only when the relation-symbol "R" is appropriately interpreted. There can in fact be no sentence of standard predicate logic that holds in all and only finite models, nor can there be a sentence that holds in all infinite models.

When first-order logic with identity is augmented by the limit operations which interpret probability quantifiers, this situation is changed. We have first that if M is a model with domain of size (exactly) k, then every x-variant of every assignment satisfies

$$[(1/k)y](x = y)$$

for each assignment has just one x-variant that satisfies x = y. Thus

5.1 (1) $C_k \models (\forall x)[(1/k)y)](x = y)$, for every k > 0.

Applying 3.4 above yields

(i) $C_k, [0y](x = y) \models \neg (\exists y)(x = y)$
(ii) $C_k \models (\forall x)(\exists y)(x = y) \rightarrow (\forall x) \neg [0y](x = y)$

and since the antecedent of the conditional is a theorem of first-order logic with identity, we have that for every positive k,

5.2 (1) $C_k \models (\forall x) \neg [0y](x = y)$

The consequent of this is thus a sentence that holds in all and only finite models. From this it follows immediately that the logic of probability quantifiers is not compact; there are infinite sets of sentences that have no models and such that all finite subsets of them do have models:

$$\{(\forall x) \neg [0y](x = y), \neg C_1, \neg C_2 \ldots\}$$

is such a set.[27]

If M is a model with domain of size k, and if the extension of the monadic predicate A in M includes just j individuals, then

$$[(j/k)x]A(x)$$

---

[27] This argument was suggested by Brian Skyrms.

is true in M. Hence

5.3 (1) $C_k \vDash C_j(A) \longleftrightarrow [(j/k)x]A(x)$
(2) $C_j(A) \vDash C_k \longleftrightarrow [(j/k)x]A(x)$

Theorem 5.3 allows the reduction of probabilistically quantified formulas of just one free variable to cardinality expressions in the finite case.

If s is any assignment in a model M, then there is just one y-variant of s that satisfies x = y. Hence if M is infinite, for every assignment s, $F_n(x = y, s,x)$ is 1/n for every n greater than a certain quantity. Thus if M is infinite every s satisfies $[0y](x = y)$ and hence

5.4 (2) $\text{Inf} \vDash (\forall x)[0y](x = y)$
(3) $\text{Inf} \vDash (\forall x)[1y] \neg (x = y)$

(iii) $(\forall x)[0y](x = y)$

is a sentence that holds in all infinite models, and it is also a sentence that holds in *only* infinite models, for

$$\vDash (\forall x)[0y](x = y) \rightarrow \neg (\forall x) \neg [0y](x = y)$$

and (iii) thus contradicts a sentence that holds in all and only finite models.

How are the probabilities of quantified expressions related to probabilities of conjunctions of their instances? Since $(\forall y)(A(y) \rightarrow A(a))$ is a theorem of logic, it follows that P can never exceed Q when

$$[Px](\forall y)A(x,y) \text{ and } [Qx][A(x,a_1) \& \ldots \& A(x,a_k)]$$

are both true in the same model. If, then, for each positive k there is some quantity Q_k such that

$$[Q_k x][A(x,a_1) \& \ldots \& A(x,a_k)]$$

is true in a model M, and if $[Px](\forall y)A(x,y)$ is also true in M, then P is a lower bound on the quantities Q_k. It should be pointed out that the universally quantified expression $(\forall y)A(x,y)$ may have a probability with respect to the variable x even though not all (or even any) of the conjunctions $A(x,a_1) \& \ldots \& A(x,a_k)$ have probabilities with respect to x. A simple example will make this clear. Let M be a model with the natural numbers in their canonical order as domain. Let A be a two-place predicate, and interpret A in M as the union of the following sets:

E × N (i.e., $|A|^M$ includes all pairs $<e, n>$ where e is an even number and n any number)

The pairs $\langle m, 1 \rangle$ when m is odd and $0 < m < 10$

The pairs $\langle m, 1 \rangle$ when m is odd and $10^2 < m < 10^3$

And in general, the pairs $<m, 1>$ when m is odd and is between an even power of ten and the succeeding odd power of ten.

Then $M \models [(1/2)x](\forall y)A(x,y)$, for it is true of just half the numbers (namely the even numbers) that they stand in the relation A to every number. The relative frequency $F^n(A(x, 1), s, x)$ however, fluctuates as n increases. When n is an odd power of ten, this frequency is close to 1, when n is a positive even power of ten, it is close to 1/2. Thus it does not converge to a limiting value as n increases without bound, and thus $M \models \neg [Qx]A(x, 1)$ for every Q between zero and one inclusive. We have thus a one-membered conjunction of instances of $(\forall y)A(x,y)$ which has no probability with respect to x, though $(\forall y)A(x,y)$ itself does have a probability with respect to x. The example generalizes in an obvious way: Include in the extension of A in addition every pair $\langle m, k \rangle$ when k is any integer and m is odd and is between an even power of ten and the succeeding odd power of ten. Then no conjunction of instances of $(\forall y)A(x,y)$ has a probability with respect to x, though the truth of $[(1/2)x](\forall y)A(x,y)$ is unaffected.

If the probabilities of all conjunctions

$$A(x, a_1) \& \ldots \& A(x, a_k)$$

exist, then—since the sequence of these probabilities must be monotonically non-increasing as k increases—they converge about a limiting value as k increases without bound. We saw above that this limiting value provides an upper bound on the probability of $(\forall y)A(x,y)$, if the latter is defined. The question naturally arises of finding a useful lower bound for this probability. Notice first that if even one member of the domain of the model M lacks a name (that is to say, if there is some $m \in D_M$ such that for no constant a does $|a|^M = m$) then $[0x](\forall y)A(x,y)$ may hold in M even though

$$[1x][A(x, a_1) \& \ldots \& A(x, a_k)]$$

holds for every k; just suppose that $|A|^M$ includes a pair $\langle m, n \rangle$ if and only if n has a name. Indeed, in this case

$$(\forall x)[A(x, a_1) \& \ldots \& A(x, a_k)]$$

is true in M for every k, while $(\forall x)\neg(\forall y)A(x,y)$, and hence $[0x](\forall y)A(x,y)$, is also true in M.

At least a part of what is at issue here is the way in which one thinks of generalization: if every individual has a name, then the import of the universal quantifier is just the conjunctive import of its instances, and that of the existential quantifier is the disjunctive import of its instances. That is what is meant by speaking of the quantifiers in terms of infinite conjunction and disjunction. On the other hand, if models are not so restricted, then the meanings of "all" and "some" are not to be thought of in this way.[28]

The situation is similar in the Carnapian theories of the last chapter, allowance being made for the differences between the two approaches. There, in Carnapian theories, probability is a metalinguistic operator or function, everywhere defined on the sentences of a formal language. The laws of probability make no particular reference to quantifiers, so the relations between the probabilities of quantified sentences and the probabilities of their instances will be just those that are enforced by the invariance of probability for logical equivalence, and the consequent monotonicity of probability for logical implication: no sentence can have a higher probability than its logical consequence. Thus if $A(x)$ is an open sentence of one free variable, x, and A_i is the result of instantiating x with the individual constant a_i, then

$$P[(\forall x)A(x)] \leq P[A_1 \& \ldots \& A_k]$$

for every k. The differences from the theory of probability quantifiers are, first, that Carnapian probability is metalinguistic; secondly that it involves no parametrization (the operator "P" carries no variable with it) and thirdly that Carnapian probability is postulated to be everywhere defined: every sentence of the language is assigned a value by every probability P. There is thus no need here, as there was in the above discussion, to assume that the probabilities of all conjunctions of instances of $A(x)$ exist; that assumption is basic to the theory. It follows, then, that these probabilities converge to a greatest lower bound. The probability of $(\forall x)A(x)$ can consistently be any quantity which does not exceed this lower bound, even when

---

[28] See, for example, Ramsey's discussion at the beginning of "General Propositions and Causality".

every individual is presumed to have a name; that is to say, when the logic is augmented by an *omega rule* such as

R_ω: If a_1 . . . are all the individual constants of the language, then $\{A(a_1), A(a_2) . . .\} \vdash (\forall x)A(x)$

In 1964 H. Gaifman proposed augmenting Carnapian logical probability in the case of languages satisfying this rule to require that $P[(\forall x)A(x)]$ should be the greatest lower bound of $P[A_1 \& . . . \& A_k]$ as k increases without bound; that is to say, that in the case of languages satisfying R_ω, the Carnapian probability of a universal quantification should always be just the greatest lower bound of the probabilities of conjunctions of its instances.[29] This is clearly a consistent (and plausible) extension of the laws of logical probability. It is, however, not at all evident that it is properly a rule of general logic.

When appropriately formulated the Gaifman condition is a theorem of the logic of probability quantifiers. To see this, let us take the positive integers in their canonical ordering as the paradigm of a denumerable and well-ordered domain, and let us take each numeral as the canonical name of the corresponding integer. The restriction to models in which every individual has a name amounts to restricting models to those which satisfy the above rule R_ω, that is to say (writing "A_i" for the result of replacing each free x in A by the numeral i) to those models in which $\{A_1, A_2 . . .\}$ entails $(\forall x)A$ for every formula A.

Now let A(x,y) be a formula in which the variables x and y may be free. For each i let A(x,i) be the result of replacing each free y in A(x,y) by the numeral i, and for each k = 1, 2 . . . let $A_k(x)$ be the conjunction

A(x,1) & . . . & A(x,k)

Of course $(\forall y)A(x,y)$ implies each $A_k(x)$, so for every n and k, and every assignment s

(i) $F^n[(\forall y)A(x,y), s,x] \leq F^n[A_k(x), s,x]$

Further, for each n there is some k such that

(ii) $F^n[(\forall y)A(x,y), s,x] \geq F^n[A_k(x), s,x]$

(i) and (ii) support the following theorem:

---

[29] Gaifman, In "Concerning Measures on First-order Calculi".

5.5 Let $A(x,y)$ and $A_k(x)$ be as above. Let M be any model that satisfies the rule R_ω. Suppose further that for each $k = 1, 2 \ldots$ there is some quantity Q_k such that

$$M \vDash [Q_k x] A_k(x)$$

then the sequence $Q_1, Q_2 \ldots$ has a greatest lower bound, say P, and we have that

$$M \vDash [Px](\forall y) A(x,y)$$

5.5 has as an obvious corollary a dual form giving the probability of an existentially quantified formula as the least upper bound of its instances.

5
Probability Quantifiers: Multivariate and Conditional Quantifiers

5.1 *Conditional probability*

IN the classical theory of judgement sketched in chapter 1, hypothetical judgement has the epistemic function of guiding change in belief. Kant classed the hypothetical as a judgement in which "we consider two judgements" in the light not of their truth, but of their logical sequence. It was the category of cause that supported this sequence, in such a way that believing the hypothetical amounted to a readiness to come to believe its consequent upon believing its antecedent.[1] This view has more recently been put forward, by Ramsey and Ryle among others, as the "inference ticket" account of hypotheticals.[2] Ramsey, though not Kant or Ryle, allowed also that partial belief might have this function; partial hypothetical beliefs would then be represented as conditional probabilities, and belief change would follow the multiplication law

$$P(A \& B) = P(A)P(B/A)$$

Carnap, following Ramsey's suggestion,[3] thought of the probabilities as dated; P_i giving the probability or partial belief at the time t_i. Then belief in (A & B) following the observation of A should reasonably be what the belief in B conditional on A was before the observation:

(i) $P_{i+1}(A \& B) = P_i(B/A)$

given that A is observed between t_i and t_{i+1}. A considerable literature has thrived on this proposal and variants of it.[4]

---

[1] Kant, *Critique*, A 73 = B 98; B233 ff.

[2] See, for example, Ramsey, "General Propositions and Causality" and Ryle, *The Concept of Mind*, chapter 5.

[3] In Ramsey, "Truth and Probability". See Carnap, "Inductive Logic and Rational Decisions".

[4] See Jeffrey's discussion in the second edition of *The Logic of Decision* for references to some of this. See also the articles in *Ifs* (especially D. Lewis "Probabilities of

The structural changes described in section 1.4 above made it possible for propositions as the objects of belief or judgement to exist independently of the act of judgement. That was just not possible before Frege, when the structure of the proposition was always the structure of some judging act. Thus a conditional or hypothetical proposition could only be, as Kant had it, a proposition concerning judgements. Carnapian probability, for which all partiality is noetic or in the act, then naturally thought of conditional probability as a generalization of this: conditional probability was a partial or probabilistic relation between propositions or sentences: a metrical form of the hypothetical judgement. Given the liberation of propositional structure from the act of judgement, one could on the other hand also have probabilities or partial beliefs with conditional objects. It then became essential to distinguish the probability of the conditional $(A \rightarrow B)$ from the conditional probability of B given A.[5]

There are two orthogonal distinctions here: one structural and one functional. The structural distinction is that between conditional and non-conditional probability or judgement. The functional distinction is that between those probabilities or partial beliefs that serve as fixed points in probabilistic inference or in belief change from those probabilities or partial beliefs that may change in the face of evidence. The latter distinction is a generalization of the distinction between propositions based on laws and ordinary propositions: between *All the people in this room are safe from freezing*, which entails that anyone who enters the room will be safe from freezing; and *All the people in this room were born in February*, which supports no analogous inference. Before Frege these distinctions could not be separated, for the structural distinction depended on the functional one: hypothetical propositions were just those propositions that served as fixed points in belief change. That is no longer the case. For better or worse, in the present context logical form neither follows nor leads epistemic function: every conditional is also a disjunction, for example, and the distinction between these two sorts of judgement, which Kant took to reveal a distinction in the a priori conditions of experience, is now of no more than notational importance.

Conditionals and Conditional Probabilities" and Stalnaker, "Probability and Conditionals"), (ed.) Harper *et al.*

[5] See D. Lewis, "Probabilities of Conditionals" for a precise description of this difference.

This independence of form from function holds in the case of probability as well. On many accounts conditional and non-conditional probability are interdefinable (conditionals with antecedents of probability zero left to one side); conditional probability is uniquely determined by non-conditional probability and conversely. There is thus no support for making either of these epistemically primary: if conditional probabilities are the nomic or fixed points for belief change, then all probabilities are nomic or fixed. If certain conditional probabilities are to have this firmness or lawlikeness, then that cannot be based on their conditional form, but must depend on other, non-formal, characteristics of the epistemic structure in question. It will in many cases be theoretically simplest to give a certain, at least relative, a priori importance to equivalence relations or logical partitions and to those conditional probabilities which condition on members of the partition.[6] Symmetry conditions can work in this way: thus, in considering the classic case of coin tosses, it may be an a priori constraint that probability is invariant for permutations in the order in which heads and tails occur, being affected only by the relative frequency of heads. Conditioning on relative frequency then has the great advantage of conditioning on a disjunction of incompatible and equiprobable disjuncts. This gives great theoretical simplicity, but it should not on that ground be assigned any special epistemic importance: given the independence of logical form and epistemic function, that will require other arguments.

When change in belief or in probability is at issue, some free parameter, at least ranging over times, is required. In the Carnapian example above, the probability measures themselves are indexed for time. Then the expression (i), or some variant of it, assumes the status of an a priori synthetic principle governing change in belief or probability, for there is nothing in the laws of probability to constrain the ways in which distinct probability measures are related. Since the objects of Carnapian probability are sentences, it is not easy to accomplish the necessary parametrization internally; when Carnap wants, for example, to consider trials of an experiment, he does this by treating sentences which differ in including different individual constants naming the different trials.[7] The need for a free

---

[6] Cf. Skyrms's discussion in chapter 3 of *Pragmatics and Empiricism*.
[7] In *Logical Foundations of Probability*, section 94, for example.

parameter is particularly obvious in the case of conditional probability. It was no accident that Reichenbach generalized not the material conditional but formal implication—implication in which antecedent and consequent share a free variable—to arrive at probability conditionals. The most natural way to think of conditional probability is as a relation between properties or propositional functions. Carnapian probability is at a disadvantage in this regard, for it works on sentences. This means that structure is externally imposed; a c-function must see its objects as distinct and unrelated sentences, not as instances of the same open sentence. In sum, the logic and the probability are not integrated.

The integration of logic and probability is, on the other hand, essential in the system of probability quantifiers. It is natural to consider some or all of the objects in a model as discrete instants of time or as ordered trials. There is even a way, briefly explored in section 5.7 below, to recognize invariance or symmetry with respect to order in time. As concerns probability conditionals, they are defined by generalizing Reichenbach's account. We shall write

A –[Px]→ B

to express that the probability of B conditional on A is P. Here P is, as in the non-conditional probabilities of the preceding chapter, a reduced fraction between zero and one inclusive; and A and B are any formulas. This generalizes Reichenbach's account, first in making explicit the free variable x, and secondly in allowing arbitrarily complex finite embeddings of probability and standard quantifiers— including probability conditionals—and other logical operators within the formulas A and B. The interpretation provided below for these probability conditionals will leave standard first-order logic as well as the probability logic of chapter 4 completely undisturbed. There are also laws relating probability quantifiers and probability conditionals, resulting in a quite general theory of random variables and expectations.

5.2 *Probability conditionals*

Formal implication is redundant given the standard quantifiers and truth functions. The probabilistic analogue of formal implication is not, however, a redundant addition to the logic of probability quantifiers. Indeed, in general, as David Lewis has shown,[8] conditional probability cannot be considered as probability of any standard conditional. An interpretation of probability conditionals is thus required, and this should function as an integrated part of an expanded definition of satisfaction.

In section 3.4 above, three ways of introducing conditional probability were briefly discussed: conditional probability can be defined in terms of quotients of non-conditional probability; or, conversely, conditional probability can be taken as the basic notion and non-conditional probability then defined in terms of it; or, finally, conditional and non-conditional probability can be defined independently and the relations between them then derived as consequences of the ways in which they are interpreted. The last option is taken here.

The first step is notational. The syntax of probability quantifiers is modified by the addition of a formation rule for probability conditionals:

Rule of formation for probability conditionals. If A and B are formulas, x a variable, and P a rational number designator (of a number between zero and one inclusive), then A $-[Px]\to$ B is a formula.

The notational conventions introduced in the preceding chapter continue to apply, *mutatis mutandis*, to probability conditionals. Notice that the formulas A and B may include probability quantifiers, probability conditionals, and other logical structure, without finite limit.

As concerns semantics, the expanded definition of satisfaction of section 4.3 needs to be yet further expanded to apply recursively to the new formulas. There are two alternative ways to do this: either as the quotient of limits or as the limit of quotients. The first of these corresponds to the definition of conditional probability in terms of non-conditional probability (see section 3.4 above). It is to take the formula A $-[Px]\to$ B to be satisfied by an assignment s in an interpretation M when

(i) $\dfrac{\lim_{n\to\infty} F^n(A\,\&\,B, s, x)}{\lim_{n\to\infty} F^n(A, s, x)} = P$

---

[8] See "Probabilities of Conditionals".

Under this definition s satisfies A –[Px]↦ B in M just in case for some Q and R, P = Q/R and s satisfies both [Qx](A & B) and [Rx]A in M. So, if s satisfies [0x]A in M, then s can satisfy no probability conditional with A as antecedent. That is to say, the definition in terms of the quotient of limits rules out defining probability conditionals when the antecedent has zero probability (with respect to the same variable). There are several reasons to resist this. The most general of them is that, in the absence of regularity constraints (the equation of probability one and zero with necessity and impossibility, respectively), consistent conditions may have zero probability. That is indeed the case in the present development, as obvious modifications of the examples of section 3.6 above make evident. The limiting relative frequency of powers of ten in the natural numbers under the canonical ordering is zero. One wants to allow, however, that any consistent condition, no matter how implausible, can serve as a premiss in probabilistic argument. So, for example, the chance of a number being an even power of ten, given that it is a power of ten, is, in the canonical ordering, one-half. The above definition rules out such statements. This recommends defining the satisfaction of probability conditionals not in terms of the quotient of limits, but rather as the limit of quotients. And that is the option taken here.

The clause defining satisfaction of probability conditionals is as follows:

If P is a rational designator between zero and one inclusive, x a variable, and A and B formulas, then the assignment s satisfies the formula A –[Px]↦ B in the interpretation M if and only if

$$\text{(ii) } \lim_{n \to \infty} \left(\frac{F^n(A \& B, s, x)}{F^n(A, s, x)} \right) = P$$

This definition points up one disanalogy between conditional probability and formal implication: every formal implication with an inconsistent antecedent is true in every model. It is, however, not plausible that every probability conditional with an inconsistent antecedent should be true in every model; the above principle, in conjunction with the other clauses in the definition of satisfaction, has instead the consequence that *no* probability conditional with an inconsistent antecedent is true in *any* model. A similar consequence follows concerning consistent but empty conditions: if (∀x)¬ A is true in an interpretation M, then, since $F^n(A, s, x) = 0$ for every s and n, none of the terms in the above sequence of quotients is defined, and the limit of these quotients hence does not exist, so $(A -[Px] \to B)$ is false in M for every P. The definition does permit, however, that conditional probability be positive when the probability of the antecedent is zero, so long as the antecedent is non-null in the model in question. We have thus three stages or levels of the unlikely: logically impossible conditions, consistent but empty conditions, and non-null conditions of probability zero. The present approach allows that premises of the third sort may function in probabilistic argument and, as will become clear below, that they may combine with other probabilistic assertions in appropriate ways.

Before turning to consequences of the expanded definition, we recall some principles of the elementary arithmetic of limits. These are used in the sequel.

When $\lim_{n \to \infty} F^n(A,s,x)$ exists and is positive, then (i) above (the quotient of limits) is equal to (ii) (the limit of quotients) or both are undefined. The limit in (ii) may, however, be defined even when $\lim_{n \to \infty} F^n(A,s,x)$ does not exist. This may occur, first, when the numerator in (i) does not exist—when, for example, A and B are the same formula and $F^n(A,s,x)$ does not converge to a rational value as n increases without bound—but also, and less obviously, even when the numerator in (ii) does exist. An example, depending on fluctuating sequences like those of note 21 of chapter 4, will make this clear.

Consider an interpretation with the natural numbers in canonical order as domain. Let A hold of 1 of the first 10 numbers, of 90 of the first 100, of 100 of the first 1 000, and so on; for odd k, A holds of 1/10 of the numbers up to 10^k. For even k, A holds of 9/10 of the numbers up to 10^k. Thus $\lim_{n \to \infty} F^n(A,s,x)$ does not exist. Now let B hold of 9/10 of the numbers in A, evenly distributed. So $F^n(A \& B, s,x)$ is close to 1/n when n is a power of 10. Then the limit of (ii) is 1/10, the numerator of (i) is zero, and the denominator of (i) does not exist.

If $F^n(A,s,x)$ is zero for every n, then the limit in (ii) does not exist. If at some n' this quantity is positive, then this ratio remains positive for all $n > n'$, and all quotients beyond that point give rational numbers. In this case the limit in (ii) can be identified with the corresponding limit for $n > n'$, if the latter exists.

The above definition leaves theorem 3.1 of chapter 4 intact, and that theorem can also be extended to assert the uniqueness of P in (ii):

2.1 For each variable x and assignment s there is at most one P such that s satisfies A –[Px]↦ B in M.

Now here are some consequences of the definition and the results of chapter 4. The proofs are omitted and straightforward.

First, formal implication entails conditional probability one in the case of a non-null antecedent: if A formally implies B, and there are A's, then the probability of B conditional on A is 1.

2.2 $(\exists x)A, (\forall x)(A \rightarrow B) \vDash A$ –[1x]↦ B

Conditional probability is finitely additive,

2.3 (1) $(\forall x) \neg (A \& B \& C), A$ –[Px]↦ B, A –[Qx]↦ C $\vDash$ A –[(P + Q)x]↦ (B ∨ C)

Here, in 2.3 (1), we use "P + Q" in accordance with the conventions of section 4.3.

It is essential, in establishing principles governing probability conditionals, to assure that the hypotheses of a theorem like 2.3 (1) entail that the limits required in the conclusion exist. In view of this it is helpful to state a principle governing subtraction as a separate theorem:

2.3 (2) $(\forall x) \neg (A \& B \& C), (A$ –[Qx]↦ B), (A –[Px]↦ (B ∨ C)) $\vDash A$ –[(P – Q)x]↦ C

As remarked in the above discussion, if the limit of (ii) exists in a model, then the extension of A cannot be empty in the model. This holds even when [0x]A is true in the model:

2.4 A –[Px]↦ B $\vDash (\exists x)A$

The premiss $(\exists x)A$ is thus essential in 2.2, for $(\forall x)(A \rightarrow B)$ is consistent with $\neg (A$ –[1x]↦ B) in its absence. Indeed, if $\neg (\exists x)A$ holds in a model then for every P and B, A –[Px]↦ B is false in that model.

The multiplication law, and a contraposed form of it allowing division, also hold.

2.5 If Q is positive then [Px](A & B), [Qx]A $\vDash A$ –[(P/Q)x]↦ B
2.6 (1) (A –[Px]↦ B), [Qx]A $\vDash$ [(PQ)x](A & B)

Theorem 2.6 (1) holds for all values of P, including the case in which P = 0.

Theorems 2.5 and 2.6 yield a form of Bayes's theorem licensing a form of inverse inference.

2.6 (2) $[0x](B_1 \& \ldots \& B_k), [1x](B_1 \vee \ldots \vee B_k), [P_1 x]B_1, \ldots ,$
$[P_k x]B_k, B_1$ –[Q_1 x]↦ A, $\ldots , B_k$ –[Q_k x]↦ A, $\neg [0x]A \vDash A$ –[R_j x]↦ B_j

where, for each $j = 1 \ldots k$,

$$R_j = \frac{(P_j)(Q_j)}{\Sigma^k_{i=1}[(P_i)(Q_i)]}$$

Proof. By 2.6 (1) if s is any assignment satisfying the hypotheses in a model M, then s also satisfies, for each i,

$[(P_i)(Q_i)]x](A \,\&\, B_i)$

Now let $S = \Sigma(P_i)(Q_i)$. Then by 4.3.5 (4), and the additivity principle (4.3.4), it follows that S is positive and also that

$M \underset{s}{\vDash} [Sx]A$

so, by 2.5, the theorem follows.

Probability conditionals are invariant for extensional equivalence at both places; if all and only As are Bs in a model, then A and B are interchangeable as antecedents and consequents without affecting truth in that model.

2.7 (1) $(\forall x)(A \longleftrightarrow C), (A \,\text{-}[Px] \to B) \vDash C \,\text{-}[Px] \!\!\to\!\! B$
2.7 (2) $(\forall x)(B \longleftrightarrow C), (A \,\text{-}[Px] \to B) \vDash A \,\text{-}[Px] \!\!\to\!\! C$

Some particular properties of the zero and one quantifiers are given in the following theorems. First, conditional probability one entails that the corresponding material conditional has probability one.

2.8 $A \,\text{-}[1x] \!\!\to\!\! B \vDash [1x](A \to B)$

Proof. Suppose that s satisfies the hypothesis in a model M. Then, given any small positive ϵ, there is some n such that

$F^n(A,s,x) - F^n(A \,\&\, B, s,x) < F^n(A,s,x) - \epsilon$

from which it follows that

$F(A \,\&\, \neg B, s,x) = 0$

The general form of 2.8—with "P" in place of "1"—does not hold: probability of the material conditional is not conditional probability. Nor does the converse of 2.8 hold, even when $(\exists x)A$ is added as a premiss. This last is consistent with [0x]A. When A is interpreted in M as a non-empty set of probability zero (i.e., a "thin" set in the language of chapter 3 section 6) and when B is $\neg A$ we have that

$M \vDash [1x](A \to \neg A), M \vDash A \,\text{-}[0x] \!\!\to\!\! \neg A$

Though (∃x)A as an added premiss is not sufficient to assure the converse of 2.8, as this example shows, [Px]A with positive P is sufficient. Indeed, when P > 0 we have

$$[1x](A \rightarrow B), [Px]A \vDash A \text{ -}[1x] \mapsto B$$

which gives

2.9 If P is positive then $[1x](A \rightarrow B), [Px]A, \vDash A \text{ -}[1x] \mapsto B$.

Theorem 2.8 also yields a corollary,

2.10 $A \text{ -}[0x] \mapsto B \vDash [1x](A \rightarrow \neg B)$

and 2.1 has the following consequences relating the standard quantifiers and probability conditionals of strength one and zero:

2.11 (1) $(∃x)A, (∀x)B \vDash A \text{ -}[1x] \mapsto B$
2.11 (2) $(∃x)A, (∀x) \neg B \vDash A \text{ -}[0x] \mapsto B$.

The above counterexample to the converse of 2.8 shows that (∀x) cannot be replaced by [1x] in either of these.

If A is a formula of one free variable, x, then the sentence

$$C_j(A,y): (∃x_1) \ldots (∃x_j)\{D(x_1 \ldots x_j) \&$$
$$(∀y)[A(y) \longleftrightarrow (y = x_1) \vee \ldots \vee (y = x_j)]\}$$

(introduced in section 4.5 above) holds in just those models in which every assignment has exactly j y-variants that satisfy A(y). That is to say, intuitively, that $C_j(A,y)$ expresses that there are exactly j individuals in the extension of the (perhaps complex) predicate A(y). This led to theorems 5.1, 5.2, and 5.3 of chapter 4, which give reductions of prenex probability quantifiers to cardinality assertions in the case of finite models. This approach can be exploited to give a similar reduction of probability conditionals when finite extensions are involved, even when the models in question are infinite. If just j individuals satisfy A(x) & B(x) in M, and just k individuals (k > 0) satisfy A(x) in M, then $A \text{ -}[(j/k)x] \rightarrow B$ is true in M. We have thus the following theorem:

2.12 If A and B are open sentences of just one free variable, x, then

$$\vDash C_j(A \& B, x) \rightarrow [C_k(A,x) \rightarrow (A \text{ -}[(j/k)x] \mapsto B)$$

Notice that A and B may be complex formulas, including probability quantifiers and conditionals as well as other logical operators.

A few simple principles, easily established now, will serve in the treatment of symmetry conditions in the sequel.

Since only normal models for identity are in question, if x and y are distinct variables, and s any assignment, then there is just one x-variant of s that satisfies $x = y$ in a model M. Thus if A is any formula and s any assignment, the limit

$$\lim_{n \to \infty} \left(\frac{F^n(x = y \,\&\, A, s,x)}{F^n(x = y, s,x)} \right)$$

must be either zero (if the one x-variant of s that satisfies $x = y$ fails to satisfy A) or one (if that assignment satisfies A). No other values are possible, and the limit is always defined. This leads to the following theorem:

2.13 If x and y are distinct variables and A(x) and A(y) are alphabetic variants (i.e., x occurs free in A(x) at just those places where y occurs free in A(y)), then

(1) $\models (x = y - [1x] \!\!\mapsto A(x)) \longleftrightarrow A(y)$
(2) $\models (x = y - [0x] \!\!\mapsto A(x)) \longleftrightarrow \neg A(y)$
(3) With x, y, A(x), and A(y) as above, if E is any equivalence relation (indeed, if E is any reflexive relation) then

$\models (\forall y)[(\forall x)(E(x,y) \to A(x)) \to A(y)]$

2.13 (1) and (2) yield as a corollary that if x and y are distinct variables and P is neither zero nor one then

$\models (\forall y) \neg (x = y - [Px] \!\!\mapsto A(x))$

One general question for probability logic is how to formulate a property that holds of just those objects that have probability P of having a given property. If A(x) is a (perhaps complex) property, then what is the property $\phi[A(x)]$ such that $\phi[A(a)]$ if and only if the probability of A(a) is P? The answer to that question provided here is that there is in general no unique such property, that there are many alternative ways in which it may hold that the probability of A(a) is P. In any given model an object a either has or does not have the property A(x). If we are to express that a has A(x) with probability P, different from zero and one, then that must be done by reference to some condition or point of view. The essential conditions here are *symmetry* conditions or equivalence relations, which partition the domain of any model in which they are interpreted into exclusive and exhaustive equivalence classes. Let E be a relational predicate which is interpreted as an equivalence relation in a model M, and suppose that $|E|^M$ partitions the domain D_M into just k equivalence classes. Then an assignment s satisfies E(x,y) in M just in case s assigns members of the same equivalence class to x and to y. Let a_1 ... a_k be representative individual constants, so that $|a_1|^M$ ... $|a_k|^M$ are members of the k distinct equivalence classes that form a partition of D_M. Then an assignment s satisfies a formula E(x, a_i) just in case s(x) is a member of the ith equivalence class.

Under these conditions we say that E is a *symmetry condition for A(x) in the model M* if there are distinct P_1 ... P_k such that

$$M \vDash E(x, a_k) - [P_i x] \rightarrow A(x)$$

for each i = 1 ... k. The generalization of this definition to denumerably infinite partitions is obvious. If E is a symmetry condition for A(x) then E-equivalents, as such, are objects that have A(x) with the same probability. Different symmetry conditions will give different probabilities for the same property. Identity is the strictest equivalence relation, the one that partitions any domain into a maximum number of distinct cells. When discriminations are this fine then, as 2.13 shows, probability attributions of zero and one are the only ones possible. The universal relation (according to which all objects in the domain are equivalent to each other) is the weakest equivalence relation, from this point of view, the probability of an object having A is just the probability of A in the domain, if that exists:

2.13 (4) $(\forall x)(\forall y)E(x,y) \vDash \{(\exists y)[E(x,y) - [Px] \rightarrow A(x)] \longleftrightarrow [Px]A(x)\}$

Between these two extremes are the interesting and genuine probability attributions, those that depend on substantive symmetry conditions, the paradigms of which are provided by symmetrical gambling devices such as fair coins and dice and well-shuffled cards.

Probability logic based on probability quantifiers and probability conditionals is extensional in the straightforward sense of theorems 4.3.6 and 5.2.7. The use of symmetry conditions makes it possible to express in extensional terms of some of the ways in which probability can depend on aspects or points of view. Since the antecedent and consequent of a probability conditional can share a free variable, the aspect or condition can be tied to the property in question. This gives a good account of how the assertion that an object a has a property A can be consistent with a having A with probability less than one. If E is a symmetry condition for A(x) then

A(a) & [E(x, a) -[Px]↦ A(x)]

expresses just this. At the same time, bivalence is unaffected and the logic is completely extensional.

We return to this subject in section 5.6 in the treatment of expectations, following the introduction of multivariate probability quantifiers and the application of the de Finetti hierarchy in probability quantifiers.

5.3 *Multiplication and weighted averages*

The multiplication theorem (2.6) supports certain relations between prenex probability quantifiers and probability conditionals. If the antecedent of a conditional has probability one, then the probability of the conditional is equal to the conditional probability:

3.1 (1) [1x]A ⊨ [Px](A → B) ⟷ (A -[Px]↦ B)

We have also a rule for combining conditionals and probability conditionals:

3.1 (2) [1x](A → B), (A -[Px]↦ C) ⊨ A -[Px]↦ (B & C)

In view of 4.3.2 (in chapter 4) the first premiss of 3.1 (2) can be replaced by its universally quantified analogue. The antecedents of probability conditionals can also be extended to include formulas in which the quantified variable is not free:

3.2 If x is not free in C then ⊨ [C & (A -[Px]↦ B)] ⟷ [(A & C) -[Px]↦ B]

The following consequence of 3.1 and the additivity principle (2.3) will be used in the treatment of conditionals with zero antecedents in the next section:

3.3 (A ∨ B) -[0x]↦ A ⊨ (A ∨ B) -[1x]↦ B

3.1 and 3.2 support certain further transformations of conditionals involving formulas in which the quantified variable is not free. 3.1 (1) entails that if T is any logically valid formula and B and formula then (since T entails [1x]T)

⊨ [Px]B ⟷ (T -[Px]↦ B)

By 3.2 and the redundancy of logically valid formulas in conjunctions we have that if T is logically valid and x is not free in the formula C then

$$\vDash \{C \,\&\, (T -[Px]\!\!\rightarrow B)\} \longleftrightarrow (C -[Px]\!\!\rightarrow B)$$

Thus, by the consequence of 3.1 mentioned above, we have

3.4 (1) If x is not free in C, then $\vDash C \,\&\, [Px]B \longleftrightarrow (C -[Px]\!\!\rightarrow B)$

In view of 3.3.8 of chapter 3, which asserts that when P is positive and x is not free in C then

$$\vDash [Px](C \,\&\, B) \longleftrightarrow C \,\&\, [Px]B$$

we have also that

3.4 (2) If x is not free in C and P is positive then $\vDash [Px](C \,\&\, B) \longleftrightarrow (C -[Px]\!\!\rightarrow B)$

One interesting consequence of this is

3.5 $\vDash [Px]A \longleftrightarrow ([Px]A -[Px]\!\!\rightarrow A)$

The right side of 3.5

$$([Px]A -[Px]\!\!\rightarrow A)$$

is a form of Miller's principle (see chapter 3, section 8, above). This form is hence not valid. It says that the conditional probability of A with respect to x, given that the probability of A with respect to x is P, is P. This form of the principle is pretty uninteresting; by 3.4 (1) it is equivalent to [Px]A & [Px]A, and it thus fails to express the intuition that motivates Miller's principle; that probabilistic conditionalization should preserve probability (the probability of A, given that the probability of A is P, should be P). 3.5 depends only on the way in which probability in the present system relates always to a parameter. Some other and more interesting forms of the principle are discussed below in connection with symmetry conditions.

How do probability quantifiers combine? What is the logic of weighted averages, for example? The addition and multiplication laws are the foundation of a simple and fairly comprehensive treatment of this, given in section 5.6 below. That treatment depends on multivariate probabilistic quantification. There are, however, a few principles about averages that can be formulated with single-variable quantifiers. There is first a form of the finite conglomerative condition (see section 5 of chapter 3, above). That condition states that the probability of a property B is the weighted average of its probabilities conditional on the members of a logical partition, the weights being the probabilities of those members. Hence, for example, we should have that

(i) $A -[P_1x] \mapsto B$, $\neg A -[P_2x] \mapsto B$, $[Qx]A \models [Rx]B$

where $R = (P_1)Q + (P_2)(1 - Q)$. Indeed (i) is a valid principle of probability logic. To see this notice first that by the addition law (3.4 of chapter 4) and the multiplication principle (2.6 (1)) its premises entail $[R_1x](A \& B)$ and $[R_2x](\neg A \& B)$, where

$$R_1 = (P_1)Q \qquad\qquad R_2 = (P_2)(1 - Q)$$

Principle (i) follows then from the invariance of probability for logical equivalence and the principle of finite additivity (2.3 (1)). This argument generalizes to yield the following theorem.

3.6 Let $A_1 \ldots A_k$ be formulas. Let X include all formulas

$$(\forall x)(A_i \to \neg A_j)$$

for i and j distinct indices between 1 and k, and also the formula

$$(\forall x)(A_1 \lor \ldots \lor A_k)$$

Then, where $R = (P_1)(Q_1) + \ldots + (P_k)(Q_k)$,

X, $[Q_1x]A_1 \ldots [Q_kx]A_k$, $(A_1 -[P_1x] \mapsto B) \ldots (A_k -[P_kx] \mapsto B)$
$\models [Rx]B$

A variation of 3.6 drops the constraint that the A_i are disjunctively exhaustive. In place of this the conditional probabilities must all be equal, and not all the Q_i can be zero. Here the conclusion is also a conditional. Briefly put, if the probability of B is P conditional on each of several incompatible hypotheses, not all of which have zero probability, then the probability of B conditional on the disjunction of these hypotheses is also P.

3.7 Let $A_1 \ldots A_k$ be formulas and let Y include all formulas $(\forall x)(A_i \to \neg A_j)$ for i and j distinct indices between 1 and k. Then if not all of $Q_1 \ldots Q_k$ are zero

Y, $[Q_1x]A_1 \ldots [Q_kx]A_k$, $(A_1 -[Px] \mapsto B) \ldots (A_k -[Px] \mapsto B) \models$
$(A_1 \lor \ldots \lor A_k) -[Px] \mapsto B$

Corollary. If Y includes also the formula $(\forall x)(A_1 \lor \ldots \lor A_k)$ then, where G is the premises of the theorem,

$$G \models [Px]B$$

It is again important to remark that 3.6 and 3.7 are properly logical principles. They hold in all models of the sort in question here, with no additional assumptions about probability. This provides a part of an answer to the general question of this book: to what extent is probability properly a logical concept?

3.6 and 3.7 are principles of finite disintegrability or conglomerability. Probability quantifiers are not however denumerably disintegrable. To see this, consider the denumerable analogue of 3.6. Now there may be denumerably many formulas A_i and in place of the formula $(\forall x)(A_1 \lor \ldots \lor A_k)$ the models in question must be constrained by the requirement that in each case the extensions $|A_i|^M$ form a partition of the domain D_M. A model in which the denumerable analogue of 3.6 does not hold is then the following: let the formulas in question consist of distinct one-place predicates, all applied to the same individual variable, x. Take the domain of M to be just the natural numbers in their standard ordering. For each i = 1 . . . let $|A_i|^M = \{i\}$ and let $B = N = D_M$. Then the Q_i are all zero and the P_i are all one. The sum of the products $(P_i)(Q_i) = R$ is thus zero, but we have that in this model $M \vDash [1x]B$.

For a counterexample to the denumerable form of 3.7, de Finetti's example discussed in section 3.8 of chapter 3 can be slightly modified. Let the formulas be as above, and again take the domain of the model to be just the natural numbers. Let $|B|^M$ be the even numbers, and let $|A_1|^M = \{1, 2, 4\}$, $|A_2|^M = \{3, 6, 8\}$, and so on. So $|A_i|^M = \{(2i - 1), (2^{(i+1)} - 2), 2^{(i+1)}\}$. Then for each i, we have that

$$A_i -[(2/3)x]\rightarrow B$$

holds in M, but $M \vDash [(1/2)x]B$.

Although the logic of probabilities is not denumerably conglomerative, it does display a denumerable super-additive property which is expressed as follows:

3.8. Let $A_1 \ldots$, B be formulas, M a model, and suppose that

(i) For some Q, $M \vDash [Qx]B$
(ii) For each i, there is some P such that $M \vDash [P_ix](A_i \,\&\, B)$
(iii) $M \vDash (\forall x)[(A_i \,\&\, B) \rightarrow \neg A_j]$ whenever $i \neq j$
   then $\Sigma_1^\infty P_i \leq Q$

Proof. It must also be shown that the infinite sum

$$\Sigma_1^\infty P_i = \lim_{n \to \infty} \Sigma_1^n P_i$$

exists. For each n let $P^n = \Sigma_1^n P_i$. Then for each n we have that

$$M \vDash [P^n x](A_1 \& B \vee \ldots \vee A_n \& B)$$

and since for each n

$$\vDash (\forall x)[(A_1 \& B \vee \ldots \vee A_n \& B) \to B]$$

we have (by an obvious application of the monotonicity established in 4.6 of chapter 4, above) that for each n, $P^n \leq Q$. Hence the limit of the sequence P^n of partial sums exists and cannot exceed Q.

That probability quantifiers are super-additive follows as an immediate

Corollary. Let $A_1 \ldots$ be formulas, M a model, and suppose that

(i) For each i there is some P_i such that $M \vDash [P_i x]A_i$
(ii) $M \vDash (\forall x)(A_i \to \neg A_j)$ when $i \neq j$.

Then $\Sigma_1^\infty P_i \leq 1$

Proof. Take the formula B of the theorem to be $A_1 \vee \neg A_1$. Then by 1.2 and 1.1 the corollary follows.

5.4 *Conditionals with zero antecedents: the de Finetti hierarchy*

The definition of probability conditionals as limits of quotients rather than as quotients of limits enables the treatment of conditionals with zero antecedents. That definition neither depends upon nor is essential to probability quantifiers—any account of probability based upon limiting relative frequencies could make use of it—and the theory of probability quantifiers could, as Reichenbach's theory did, use the other definition. Although the limits of quotients definition is not essential to probability quantifiers, it is the definition in effect here, and it opens the way to the treatment of zero probabilities. The semantics of these is at hand in the de Finetti hierarchy of thin sets developed in chapter 3, section 6.

Some definitions will help to make use of this. When A and B are formulas, M an interpretation, and x a variable, we define (suppressing reference to M and x in the notation):

$$A < A \leftrightarrow (A \vee B) -[0x] \!\!\to B$$
$$A \lesssim B \leftrightarrow \text{for some positive P, } M \vDash (A \vee B) -[Px] \!\!\to B$$
$$A \sim B \leftrightarrow A \lesssim B \text{ and } B \lesssim A$$

Following the terminology introduced earlier, we say respectively that A is *strictly thinner than*, *thinner than*, or *comparable to* B *in* M *at* x. These relations order formulas with respect to a model and a variable. The discussions of chapter 3, section 6 and the present chapter lead to the following theorems.

4.1 Let M be a structure and x a variable. Then

(1) < is transitive, irreflexive, and asymmetric. $\leq$ is transitive, and, though it is not totally reflexive, we do have that A $\leq$ A when (∃x)A is true in M.

(2) ~ is transitive and symmetric and, again, if (∃x)A is true in M then A ~ A.

(3) Comparable formulas (in M at x) may be replaced at either argument of $\leq$ and at either argument of <. If A is strictly thinner than B then A is thinner than B.

(4) If there are P and Q such that M ⊨ (A ∨ B) –[Px]↦ A and M ⊨ (A ∨ B) –[Qx]↦ B then either (i) A is strictly thinner than B or (ii) B is strictly thinner than A or (iii) A and B are comparable (in M at x). These conditions are also pairwise exclusive.

(5) If A is strictly thinner than B in M at x then M ⊨ (A ∨ B) –[1x]↦ B.

One good reason for introducing the hierarchy of thin sets and the order imposed by this hierarchy on formulas in a model is to make possible a general treatment of independence, sufficiently general to make distinctions among formulas of zero probability. The treatment here follows that of chapter 3, section 6. The central idea is that of *conditional independence*. This amounts to taking some condition as a framework and putting it in the place of the space or truths of logic in the standard definition. In the standard case we should say that A and B are independent in M at x if for some P and Q all of the following are true in M

[Px]A, (B –[Px]↦ A), [Qx]B, (A –[Qx]↦ B)

There are, however, cases in which A and B seem independent, where one has positive probability conditional upon the other and where one or both have probability zero. The example given in chapter 3, section 6—the set of odd numbers is independent of 1,2 but not of 1,2,3—is an instance of this. Questions of the independence of predicates with finite or thin extensions in infinite domains provide further examples.

In some cases conditional independence can be a conceptual help. The present definition follows that of chapter 3, section 6. Let A and B be formulas, M a model and x a variable. Suppose that A is thinner than B (in M at x). Now let C be a formula which is (i) comparable to B, and (ii) such that

$$(\forall x)[(A \lor B) \rightarrow C]$$

so C is the condition that will play the role of an assumed framework. (In the important case in which A is strictly thinner than B and B itself is thin, all the formulas concerned will have probability zero.) With A, B, and C as above, we say that B is *independent* of A *conditional on* C in M at x, and we write

Ind(B,A/C,M,x)

if and only if for some P,

$$(A -[Px] \rightarrow B) \text{ and } (C -[Px] \rightarrow B)$$

are true in M. So, informally put, this says that given the condition the chance of B is the same, independently of whether or not A holds.

The point of introducing conditional independence is this: in the absence of a regularity axiom, formulas that are not false in a model may have zero probability in that model. If a formula of one free variable is taken to express a concept then this means that a concept that is true of some objects may nevertheless be false of almost every object. For such a concept the hypothesis that an object falls under the concept is thus consistent, though highly unlikely. It is an invidious confusion to take this implausibility of the hypothesis as undermining or even affecting its legitimacy as a premiss in argument. Two among the many reasons why this is a confusion may be mentioned here. First, having zero probability is, as far as consistent propositions are concerned, not an absolute feature of them. What has zero probability today may have positive and even high probability tomorrow, while the structural features of its logical and evidential relations with other propositions remain unchanged. It might be objected that from the point of view of applied logic the detailed consideration of these relations is, in view of the unlikelihood that they will assume any genuine relevance, not worth the trouble. When this argument is taken seriously, however, it is obvious that this depends on the importance of being right about the relations in question. Further, and this leads to the second reason, what the logical and evidential relations are in a specific case of zero probability can often have consequences of a more general sort (when infinite additivity is restricted or denied) for cases of positive probability. This is clearly so when conditions of symmetry, which permit the collection of hypotheses, obtain: in the absence of denumerable additivity, a denumerable collection of hypotheses of zero probability may have positive probability when disjunctively considered.

These considerations have traditionally been advanced in favour of reasoning with arbitrarily low positive probabilities. Then logical and evidential relationships should be invariant with changes in the magnitude of their probabilities so long as those magnitudes are positive. In the present development the theoretical treatment of logical relations is extended to comprehend consistent propositions of zero probability as well.

Conditional independence—and the conditionalizing of probabilistic relations that it supports—deals with these issues in the following way. Given consistent formulas of zero probability, some formula entailed by them is introduced as a hypothesis. This is the C of the definition. It follows from 4.1 and the first condition of the definition that if the B of that condition has zero probability then C cannot have positive probability. Thus whatever hypothesis is assumed as condition must, if its probability is defined, have zero probability. The sort of reasoning in question is thus conducted in a framework of the unlikely. What is essential to the present development is that the reasoning is structurally unaffected by this feature of its premisses. The logical relations are invariant with changes in the magnitudes of probabilities of consistent formulas, even when these are zero.

The discussion of chapter 3, section 6 shows that

4.2 (1) If A and B are comparable in M at x then Ind(B,A/C,M,x) if and only if Ind(A,B/C,M,x)

So conditional independence among comparable formulas—which may have probability zero—is symmetrical. It is of course important to certify that conditional independence is a genuine generalization of independence in the usual sense; that when some truth is taken as condition, conditional independence is just independence. Accordingly we have:

4.2 (2) If C is true in M then Ind(B,A/C,M,x) if and only if

(i) A $\lesssim$ B and B $\sim$ C

(ii) For some P, M $\vDash$ [Px]B and M $\vDash$ (A $-$[Px]$\rightarrow$ B)

In view of 2.7 (1) the choice of C in the above condition is immaterial.

Theorem 4.2 (2) shows that conditioning on a consistent proposition of zero probability amounts to a reduction of the class of probability models or an extension of the theory. When the improbable but consistent condition C is presumed, then independence conditional upon C becomes independence in the standard and non-conditional sense. It is an advantage of the present account that no constraints are placed on the form of C. In particular C may—and normally will—include free occurrences of the variable x. So the presumption of C may be the presumption that objects of a certain sort are in question. Further, this sort may be characterized in probabilistic terms. The formula C may itself include probability quantifiers. This represents a considerable generalization over an approach to conditioning that thinks of probability as a measure over sets of worlds, models, or maximal consistent theories, for such an approach normally thinks of conditioning in terms of non-probabilistic constraints restricting the sets measured. From the logical point of view the distinction is between taking probability to be a concept that applies to logically structured objects, and taking it to figure in the logical structure of objects. The theory of the present chapter does the latter. This corresponds to the epistemic distinction between taking probability to be noetic or illocutionary—part of the force of judgement—and taking it to be noematic or part of the content of judgement.

Further special cases give some standard features of independence and show how non-conditional independence is defined. Application of the multiplication law (2.6 (1)) gives

4.3 (1) If M $\vDash$ [Qx]A, then Ind(B,A/C,M,x) entails that M $\vDash$ [(PQ)x](A & B)

and 2.5 permits strengthening 4.3 when A has positive probability:

4.3 (2) If

(i) A $\lesssim$ B and B $\sim$ C

(ii) M $\vDash$ (∀x)(A ∨ B $\rightarrow$ C)

(iii) M $\vDash$ C $-$[Px]$\rightarrow$ B

(iv) For some positive Q, M $\models$ [Qx]A
(v) M $\models$ [(PQ)x](A & B)

then Ind(B,A/C,M,x)

These lead to the definition of non-conditional independence: if A and B are formulas, M an interpretation, and x a variable, then we say that B is *independent* of A in M at x, and write

Ind(B,A/M,x)

if for some C that is true in M, Ind(B,A/C,M,x). Now two essential properties of (non-conditional) independence follow from 4.3:

4.4 (1) If both M $\models$ [Px]B and M $\models$ [Qx]A and Ind(B,A/M,x) then M $\models$ [(PQ)x](A & B)
(2) Under the same assumptions, if in addition P > 0 then Ind(A,B/M,x)
(3) Ind(B,A/M,x) if and only if Ind($\neg$ B,A/M,x)
(4) If M $\models$ [Qx]A and Q < 1 then Ind(B,A/M,x) entails that Ind(B, $\neg$ A/M,x)

We have thus a quite general theory of independence, which functions within the hierarchy of thin sets and the theory of conditionals with zero antecedents.

5.5 *Multivariate probability quantifiers*

The theory of probability quantifiers analyses probability in terms of the variation of a propositional function at a free variable or parameter. The association with the standard, non-probabilistic, logic of quantifiers passes by way of a generalization of the concepts of model and satisfaction on which the semantics of predicate logic is based. The Tarskian definitions of universality and particularity equate these with the satisfaction by all and some respectively of the x-variants of an assignment of objects to variables. The semantics of probability quantifiers introduces in addition the limiting relative frequency of x-variants that satisfy a formula and in this way permits the natural generalization of the standard quantifiers, while preserving the recursive structure of the properties or formulas to which they are applied; there is no finite limit to the internal complexity of the quantified matrix.

One of the great insights that opened the way for the resolution of the problems of generality and relations was that these are at bottom the same problem, at least as far as extensional contexts are concerned. Without relations quantification requires only a single variable, and there is in this case no need for nested or embedded quantifiers. Single-variable quantification theory is thus little stronger than class or syllogistic logic. Reciprocally, when relations are considered without generality, a dyadic relational property is just a monadic property of one of the relata. Great logicians worked at the problems of generality and relations for two millennia before these were identified and solved. Quantifier logic is in fact the quantified logic of relations, not only in the sense that relational expressions may be quantified, but also in the strict sense that it is only in the multivariate quantification of relations that the theory is fully developed. That this is so may not be immediately obvious on the surface of the theory. The definition of satisfaction treats quantifiers one at a time, and it is only in proving its justifying theorems that its essentially relational character becomes clear. Indeed, one could define multivariate quantifiers: "For all x_1 . . . x_k"; "For every x there is a y", and the like, and no strengthening or ramification of the basic definitions would be required by this addition. Multivariate universal and existential quantifiers are reducible without remainder to sequences of single-variable quantifiers.

The introduction of probability quantifiers changes this. First, it should be emphasized that the simultaneous variation of distinct parameters is at the heart of probability. Random variables are just functions, and the ways in which their variations are interrelated—whether they vary independently or not, the nature of conditional variation, and so on—constitute the subject matter of the theory of random variables. So relational probability is not at all a peripheral sort of probability, it is probability properly speaking. What is in question is the probability with which random variables take on certain values, and in some cases these random variables may themselves be probability measures or functions. The theory of random variables is thus in important part the theory of embedded probabilities. The analogy with generality is striking here: so long as generality was considered a property of judgements, the logic of embedded generality was a mystery. Only when generality became the quantification of a concept, propositional function, or open formula did multiple and embedded generality become clear at a theoretical level. In the same way, so long as probability is considered a property of judgements, the logic of embedded probability will remain unclear. One virtue of probability quantifiers is to enable arbitrarily complex embeddings of probability. The definition of satisfaction shows how this works. In distinction from the situation of non-probabilistic quantifiers, however, multivariate quantification is not reducible to the single variable case. Thus, for example, we have in first-order logic that $(\forall x,y)A$ is equivalent to $(\forall x)(\forall y)A$, but, speaking intuitively in anticipation of a precise definition,

$$[Px,y]A$$

has no equivalent in terms of single-variable probability quantifiers. Think, for example, of a proposition such as "The chance that the product of two numbers is odd is 1/4".

We are thus led to introduce a generalized form of multivariate probability quantifiers, writing

$$[Px_1 \ldots x_m]A \qquad A - [Px_1 \ldots x_m] \rightarrow B$$

where $x_1 \ldots x_m$ are distinct variables, P a designator between zero and one inclusive, and A and B are formulas. These formulas express that the probability of A is P, or that the probability of B conditional upon A is P, when variation is restricted to the parameters or free variables $x_1 \ldots x_m$. The truth conditions for these are to be given in terms of the limiting relative frequency of A or the limiting relative frequency of B in A in an interpretation. We turn now to the ramification of the definition of satisfaction to accommodate these. Let us start for simplicity with the understanding of multivariate probabilities in the case of finite interpretations. And for simplicity of notation let us write

$$\hat{x}_m \text{ for } x_1 \ldots x_m$$

For each $m \geq 1$, and distinct variables $x_1 \ldots x_m$, let $D(\hat{x}_m)$ be the conjunction of all formulas $\neg(x_i = x_j)$ for distinct indices i and j. Then an assignment satisfies $D(\hat{x}_m)$ in an interpretation M just in case it assigns distinct members of M to the variables $x_1 \ldots x_m$. We recall that interpretations are always presumed to be normal for identity. Next, for each $m \geq 1$, let C_m be the sentence:

$$(\exists \hat{x}_m)[D(\hat{x}_m) \& (\forall y)(y = x_1 \lor \ldots \lor y = x_m)]$$

So C_m holds in M just in case M includes in its domain exactly m distinct individuals. In this case there are m^2 distinct ordered pairs of members of M, and in general there are m^k k-tuples of members of M. We write M^k for this set of k-tuples. Now, given an interpretation M and distinct variables $x_1 \ldots x_k$, we say that assignments to M are $\hat{x}_k$-*variants* if they agree for all variables except (perhaps) $x_1 \ldots x_k$. If M is finite, then we say that s satisfies $[P\hat{x}_k]A$ in M if the proportion P of $\hat{x}_k$-variants of s satisfy A. So, for example, where $P = (k - 1)/k$, we have:

$$C_k \vDash [Px,y]D(x,y)$$

If there are just k objects in M then an r-tuple ($r \le k$) of members of M is an ordered sample with replacement of size r drawn from M. Each such sample gives an $\hat{x}_r$ variant of a given assignment s. There are just k^r of these samples all told; k^r $\hat{x}_r$ variant of a given assignment s. The class of r-tuples of *distinct* members of M is the class of ordered samples without replacement. There are

$$(k)_r = k(k - 1) \ldots (k - r + 1) = k!/(k - r)!$$

of these, so there are just this many $\hat{x}_r$-variants of a given assignment that satisfy $D(\hat{x}_r)$. The proportion of $\hat{x}_r$-variants of a given assignment s that satisfy $D(\hat{x}_r)$ is thus

$$\frac{\text{number of } \hat{x}_r\text{-variants of s that satisfy } D(\hat{x}_r)}{\text{number of } \hat{x}_r\text{-variants of s all told}} = (k)_r / k^r$$

Thus we have that when $r \le k$, with

$$P = (k)_r / k^r$$

(i) $C_k \vDash [P\hat{x}_r]D(\hat{x}_r)$.

For $r > k$,

$$C_k \vDash [0\hat{x}_r](D(\hat{x}_r),$$

and when $r = k$,

$$C_k \vDash [1\hat{x}_r]D(\hat{x}_r)$$

Notice that for a given finite r, as k increases without bound, $(k)_r$ approaches k^r. Hence:

(ii) Given r, for any $\epsilon > 0$, there is some k such that

$$C_k \vDash [P\hat{x}_r]D(\hat{x}_r);$$

where $(1 - \epsilon) < P < 1$. This gives the status of a truth of logic to the obvious principle that it is highly likely that members of a very large collection are distinct.

We turn now to some laws relating single-variable and multivariate probabilistic quantification. In measure-theoretic developments of probability this is usually put as the question of the determination of a product measure by the measures of which it is a product. If, for example, p_1 and p_2 are probabilities on sigma-algebras Ω_1 and Ω_2, then (under appropriate restrictions) the function on the product algebra $\Omega_1 \times \Omega_2$

$$p(A \times B) = p_1(A) \times p_2(B)$$

is also a probability. In measure-theoretic developments the relation is established by the Fubini theorem. A form of the Fubini theorem, adapted to the well-ordered and denumerable models in use here, relates single and multivariate probability quantifiers. We begin this exposition by looking at the case of finite models.

At the base of this is a finite form of the product relation. This principle can be simply put: we call it the *finite product principle*. It asserts that if the relative frequencies of sets A and B in a finite set M are a and b respectively, then the relative frequency of the set $A \times B$ of couples in M^2 is (ab). In general, if the relative frequencies of $A_1 \ldots A_k$ in a finite set M are $a_1 \ldots a_k$ respectively, then the relative frequency of the set of k-tuples, $A_1 \times \ldots \times A_k$ in M^k is $(a_1)(a_2) \ldots (a_k)$.

Consider a formula A(x) where x does not occur free within the scope of a y quantifier and y is a variable distinct from x. Let A(y) be the result of replacing all free occurrences of x in A(x) by occurrences of y—so A(x) and A(y) are what are sometimes called *alphabetic variants*. Now let M be a finite model of size k with domain $D_M = \{1, \ldots, k\}$. For a given assignment s let $s_1, \ldots, s_k$ be the x-variants of s, and let $s^1, \ldots, s^k$ be the y-variants of s, where

$$s_1(x) = 1 = s^1(y)$$

and similarly for the other indices. Further, let

$$s_1^1, \ldots, s_k^k$$

be the x-y variants of s, where the subscript gives the value assigned to x and the superscript that assigned to y: there are k^2 of these. Now with A(x) and A(y) as above, if just m of $s_1, \ldots, s_k$ satisfy A(x), then by Theorem 3.1 (3) of chapter 4 just m of $s^1, \ldots, s^k$ will satisfy A(y).

Hence m^2 of the k^2 x-y variants of s will satisfy $(A(x) \& A(y))$. This leads to the following entailment, where x, y, $A(x)$ and $A(y)$ are as above:

$$C_k, [Px]A(x) \vDash [P^2x,y](A(x) \& A(y))$$

Generalization of this reasoning supports a principle relating single and multivariate probability quantifiers:

5.1 Let $x_1 \ldots x_r$ be variables, $A_1 \ldots A_r$ be formulas, and for each distinct i and j suppose that x_i is not free in A_j. Then where $Q = \pi_{i=1}^r P_i$

$$C_k, [P_1x_1]A_1 \ldots [P_rx_r]A_r \vDash [Q\hat{x}_r](A_1 \& \ldots \& A_r)$$

Notice that in consequence of 3.5 (1) of chapter 4 if x_i is not free in A_i and $[P_ix_i]A_i$ is true in M, P_i is zero or one.

Theorem 5.1 shows that in the finite case (the general and infinite case is considered below) when just one variable per formula is quantified, the multivariate quantification of a conjunction is determined by the single-variable quantifications of the conjuncts. This determination has the simple form of draws with replacement from a finite population: if $A_1 \ldots A_r$ occur in the proportions $P_1 \ldots P_r$ respectively in a finite population, then when r draws are made with replacement after each draw, the chance is $\pi_i(P_i)$ that the first draw will give an A_1, the second draw an $A_2, \ldots$ the r'th draw an A_r. As a special case of 5.1 we have the standard formula for success and failure of independent trials:

5.2 Let $A(y)$ be a formula in which none of the distinct variables $x_1 \ldots x_r \ldots x_s$ occurs, and for each i from 1 to s let A_i be the result of replacing every free y in $A(y)$ by x_i. Then where

$$Q = (P^r)(1 - P)^{s-r},$$
$$C_k, [Py]A \vDash [Q\hat{x}_s](A_1 \& \ldots \& A_r \& \neg A_{(r+1)} \& \ldots \& \neg A_s)$$

Theorem 5.2 gives the probability of r successes and s-r failures in a given order. The case in which order is irrelevant follows from 5.2 in the light of two logical considerations and the additivity principle: first notice that permuting the variables in a multivariate quantifier yields a logically equivalent formula:

$$[Px,y,z]A \text{ is equivalent to } [Py,z,x]A$$

and, of course, permuting the A_i within the conjunctive matrix yields a logically equivalent formula. The *different* ways in which r successes and s-r failures may come about are thus given by the different ways of negating s-r of $A_1 \ldots A_s$. The order of the variables in the quantifier is immaterial, as is the order of the conjuncts, negated or not. So, given formulas as in 5.2 above, keeping the order of the conjuncts and that of the variables unchanged, there are $\binom{s}{r} = (k)_r/r!$ distinct formulas

$$[Q\hat{x}_s](A_1' \& \ldots \& A_r' \ldots \& A_s')$$

where A_i' is either A_i or $\neg A_i$. Let us call these formulas

$$K_1(r,s), \ldots, K_m(r,s)$$

where $m = \binom{s}{r}$. These conjunctions are pairwise logically incompatible —every two of them differ in the negation of some conjunct—and it follows from 5.2 and the above remark about permutations that for each formula $K_i(r,s)$, where

$$Q = (P^r)(1 - P)^{s-r}$$

$$[Py]A(y) \vDash [Q\hat{x}_s]K_i(r,s)$$

Now let us write simply $K(r,s)$ for the disjunction

$$K_1(r,s) \vee \ldots \vee K_m(r,s)$$

Additivity then yields the following theorem which gives the probability of r successes and s-r failures in any order:

5.3 With the formulas and variables as above, for each k, where

$$R = \binom{s}{r}(P^r)(1 - P)^{s-r}$$

we have

$$C_k, [Py]A(y) \vDash [R\hat{x}_s]K(r,s)$$

Notice that this result is independent of the size of k.

As far as draws without replacement are concerned, the general formula—which is simple enough—will not be given here. One special case is of interest, however: if the proportion of As in a model of size k is P, then k draws without replacement must yield exactly kP As in some order or other. Or, to put this in semantical terms: suppose the formulas and variables are as above, and let M be a model, s an assignment, and let $P = r/k$. Suppose further that C_k is true in M, and that s satisfies both

$$[Py]A(y) \text{ and } D(\hat{x}_k)$$

then every $\hat{x}_k$-variant of s must satisfy

$$K(r,k) = K_1(r,k) \vee \ldots \vee K_m(r,k)$$

This leads to the following theorem governing exhaustive draws without replacement:

5.4 With the formulas and variables as above, for each k, when $P = r/k$,

$$C_k, [Py]A(y) \vDash D(\hat{x}_k) - [1\hat{x}_k] \mapsto K(r,k)$$

Multivariate formulas express probabilities for ordered k-tuples of objects: $[P\hat{x}_k]A$ is satisfied by an assignment s in an interpretation M if the proportion P of $\hat{x}_k$ variants of s satisfy A in M, where an $\hat{x}_k$ variant of s is an assignment of s that agrees with s for all variables other than $x_1 \ldots x_k$. If the interpretation M is infinite, then this proportion depends upon the way in which the k-tuples of members of the domain are ordered, and this is not determined by the ordering of the domain itself. The general definition of satisfaction for multivariate formulas thus depends upon fixing an ordering of k-tuples.

To discuss this we take the positive integers as the paradigm of a denumerable and well-ordered set. One simple and standard ordering of the k-tuples of positive integers, for given finite k, is the *lexicographic* ordering, so called because it gives the structure of the ordering of words in a dictionary on the basis of the alphabetic ordering of letters. The lexicographic ordering of the k-tuples of positive integers is defined as follows:

(i) If $(x_1 + \ldots + x_k) < (y_1 + \ldots + y_k)$ then $\hat{x}_k$ precedes $\hat{y}_k$.

(ii) If $(x_1 + \ldots + x_k) = (y_1 + \ldots + y_k)$ then $\hat{x}_k$ precedes $\hat{y}_k$ if and only if for some $j < k, x_1 = y_1, \ldots, x_j = y_j$, and $x_{(j+1)} < y_{(j+1)}$.

It is easy to see that the lexicographic ordering is complete and unambiguous. It is the usual way to establish the denumerability of k-tuples of positive integers. For present purposes a slight modification of it will serve better. We call this modified ordering the *Fubini* ordering, and define it as follows for given finite k:

(i) If the greatest of $x_1 \ldots x_k$ is less than the greatest of $y_1 \ldots y_k$ then $\hat{x}_k$ precedes $\hat{y}_k$.

(ii) If the greatest of $x_1 \ldots x_k$ is equal to the greatest of $y_1 \ldots y_k$, then $\hat{x}_k$ precedes $\hat{y}_k$ if and only if for some $j < k, x_1 = y_1, \ldots, x_j = y_j$, and $x_{(j+1)} < y_{(j+1)}$.

This modification leaves the completeness and unambiguity of the ordering unaffected. An important feature of the Fubini ordering is the following: let $Sn = 1 \ldots n$ for each n. Then every k-tuple in $(Sn)^k$ precedes every k-tuple in $(S(n + 1))^k$. This feature supports a useful lemma, which is the main step in generalizing some of the above theorems to the infinite case.

Lemma. Let $X_1 \ldots X_k$ be sets of positive integers. Let πX_i be their cartesian product, and, where "C" gives the (finite) cardinality of its argument, let

$$F^n(\pi X_i) = 1/k^n \, C[\pi X_i \cap (Sn)^k]$$

give the relative frequency of πX_i in $(Sn)^k$. Then if

$$F(\pi X_i) = \lim_{n \to \infty} F^n(\pi X_i)$$

when the limit exists, we have that this limit does in fact exist, and is equal to $\pi_i \lim_{n \to \infty} F^n(X_i)$ when these limits exist. (Notice that the product in the conclusion is an arithmetical, not a cartesian, product.)

Proof. By the finite product principle

$$F^n(\pi X_i) = \pi_i F^n X_i$$

where the left product is cartesian and the right is arithmetical. Hence, assuming the limits $F(X_i)$ to exist, we have that

$$F(\pi X_i) = \lim_{n \to \infty} \pi F^n(X_i)$$

The lemma follows from this. It is essential that k be finite.

We can now establish the generalized form of 5.1. Given an ordering of a domain $D_M = D$, the set of k-tuples D^k is assumed to be ordered by the Fubini ordering determined by the ordering of D. The limits in question are to be taken with respect to this ordering.

5.6 Let $A_1 \ldots A_r$ be formulas, $x_1 \ldots x_r$ variables, and suppose that for each distinct i and j x_i is not free in A_j. Then

$$[P_1 x_1]A_1 \ldots [P_r x_r]A_r \vDash [Q \hat{x}_r](A_1 \& \ldots \& A_r)$$

where $Q = \pi_i P_i$.

Proof. Given an assignment s in an interpretation M, let X_1 be the subset of D_M such that for each x_1-variant of s, s_i,

$$M \vDash A_1 \text{ if and only if } s_i(x_1) \in X_1$$

and in general, for $j = 1 \ldots k$, let X_j be the subset of D_M such that if s_i is an x_j-variant of s

$$M \models A_j \text{ if and only if } s_i(x_j) \in X_j$$

Then the hypothesis of the theorem entails that for $j = 1 \ldots k$,

$$F(A_j, s, x_j) = F(X_j) = \lim_{n \to \infty} F^n(X_j \cap Sn)$$

Further, reasoning as in the finite case, we see that for each n,

$$F^n(A_1 \& \ldots \& A_k, s, \hat{x}_k)$$

is just the relative frequency of πX_i in $(Sn)^k$. That is to say, it is the quantity

$$F^n(\pi X_i)$$

of the lemma. Hence, applying the lemma, we have that

$$F(A_1 \& \ldots \& A_k, s, \hat{x}_k) = F(\pi X_i) = \pi_i \lim_{n \to \infty} F^n(X_i) = \pi_i P_i,$$

which proves the theorem.

Before investigating the consequences of this theorem, it should be emphasized that it depends upon selecting an appropriate ordering of the k-tuples of the elements of the model. Where infinite domains are concerned, the existence and magnitude of limiting relative frequency vary with order. And this order—in the instance of the Fubini ordering—is not determined by the ordering of the domain. How the k-tuples are ordered changes with different orderings of the domain. The ordering of the domain conforms to the Fubini ordering, in the sense that this is just the Fubini ordering of the singletons of the domain, but the imposition of the Fubini ordering in general is a synthetic principle. Since the nature and foundation of the principles of probability logic are at the centre of the concerns of the present work, something should be said about this.

From one point of view, 5.6 could be taken as an axiom, and its proof is then a proof of its consistency, and a description, if not of the precise class of orderings that it defines, at least of a simply described class of orderings—the Fubini orderings—in which the axiom is valid. From this point of view the plausibility of the axiom rests on the way in which it is the infinite generalization of the principle 5.1 that holds in all finite cases with no additional presumptions about ordering. Here, as always in probability logic, the passage to infinity is delicate and quite unilluminated by intuition. From the standpoint of non-probabilistic logic compactness is just the precise formulation of the classical intuitive requirement that inference should always be a finite process with access to an infinite collection of possible premises. From the point of view of probability, as we have seen, the issues of denumerable additivity, the denumerable conglomerative condition, and regularity bring into play the use of limits, where the reduction of the infinite to the finite case cannot be maintained. The present question is a good example of this; the logical connections created by the introduction of infinite models, which may be conceived as a contraction of the corpus of logical principles, in which those that do not hold in infinite models are bracketed, are supervenient to those that hold when only finite models are in question. Because of the central role of limits in the present development this supervenience takes the form of principles and constraints governing the orderings in terms of which the limits are defined.

As concerns the justification of these principles and constraints, in general one wants to find natural ways of extending and generalizing those methods that are justified on purely logical grounds in the finite case. Theorem 5.1, for example, is a metatheorem of classical pure or general logic, when this logic is understood in terms of well-ordered models. In this light the justification of the Fubini ordering is that it supports what can plausibly be viewed (namely theorem 5.6) as the translation of this classical principle to apply in infinite domains. It is in particular worth emphasizing that this amounts to preserving the classical probabilistic structure of the binomial distribution and of the quite fundamental intuitions about draws with replacement which the binomial distribution elaborates. Draws with replacement is the instantiation in experience of the abstract description of the binomial distribution. From this point of view the phenomenon of draws with replacement gives the schema—in the Kantian sense—of this distribution in the case of infinite probability models. The issue is too complex to be settled here, and, given the sketchy state of the present research, it would be rash not to be indecisive. Throughout this chapter the Fubini ordering is presumed. This presumption should be understood as hypothetical, as a proposal for the treatment of multivariate quantifiers in the case of infinite models.

Theorem 5.6, along with some consequences of it to which we

now turn, shows how, so long as just one variable is quantified in each conjunct, the multivariate quantification of a conjunction is determined by the single-variable quantifications of the conjuncts. This will not hold when the matrix quantified is a relation. In this way 5.6 reveals a distinction that is analogous to that between the quantification of monadic and that of relational formulas in non-probabilistic logic. The first consequence generalizes 5.2. No new principles are needed in its proof:

5.7 As in 5.2 above, let $A(y)$ be a formula in which none of the distinct variables $x_1 \ldots x_r \ldots x_s$ occurs free. Let A_i be $A(x_i)$ for each $i = 1 \ldots s$. Then

$$[Py]A(y) \vDash [Q\hat{x}_s](A_1 \& \ldots \& A_r \& \neg A_{(r+1)} \& \ldots \& \neg A_s),$$

where $Q = P^r(1 - P)^{s-r}$.

A second consequence generalizes 5.3 to give the probability of r successes and s − r failures in any order. Again, no new principles are needed.

5.8 With the formulas and variables as above in 5.3, where

$$R = \binom{s}{r} P^r(1 - P)^{s-r}$$

we have

$$[Py]A(y) \vDash [R\hat{x}_s]K(r,s)$$

Multivariate quantifiers can be thought of as single-variable quantifiers that range over vectors or k-tuples. When this is done— under the presumption of the Fubini ordering—all the theorems of the previous and succeeding sections remain in force for them.

5.6. *Expectations and Miller's principle*

Theorem 3.5, above, shows that a certain form of Miller's principle is not valid. That theorem is

$$\vDash [Px]A \longleftrightarrow ([Px]A - [Px] \!\!\mapsto A)$$

It asserts that the form in question (the right side of the above equivalence) is just a complicated way to express a simple probability assertion (namely that $[Px]A$). As remarked there, this theorem says more about the involvement in the present development of probability with variables and scope than it does about the semantics of conditioning. From this point of view the principle on which 3.5 depends, namely 4.3.8 of chapter four:

4.3.8 If x is not free in C then $\models$ [Px](C & B) $\longleftrightarrow$ C & [Px]B

should be thought of as analogous to the corresponding equivalences for the universal and existential quantifiers: if x is not free in C then

$$\models (\forall x)(C \ \& \ B) \longleftrightarrow C \ \& \ [\forall x]B$$

The antecedent of the right side of 3.5 does not function as a probabilistic condition of the consequent in any non-trivial sense. The genuine employment of probability quantifiers depends always on association with a variable bound by the quantifier. There are, strictly speaking, no objects to which probability attaches or is applied, there are only models and ways of ordering their domains. Embedded probabilities are nested quantifications, and the parameters they bind or govern show how the nestings are structured and what the probabilistic dependencies are.

In section 5.2 above the question of how to formulate probabilistic properties was briefly discussed. The suggestion there was that the probabilistic property

(i) x has A with probability P

be expressed with the aid of *symmetry conditions for A*. Such a condition is an equivalence relation which enforces a partition on a domain in such a way that each cell of the partition (each equivalence class in the domain) is distributed in the property A with a known probability. Given such a condition, the property (i) can then be expressed as

(ii) Exy –[Py]$\rightarrow$ Ay

If E is a symmetry condition for A, then (ii) will hold of just those members of the domain which are in that cell of the partition which is distributed in A with probability P.

This way of looking at probabilistic properties supports a formulation of Miller's principle as a genuine truth about probability logic: namely as the assertion that when E is a symmetry condition for A then the probability that an object has A, given that it has the property (ii), is P. This will be formulated as

(iii) (Exy –[Py]$\rightarrow$ Ay) –[Px]$\rightarrow$ Ax.

(iii) allows the detachment of probabilistic conclusions from probabilistic hypotheses in a non-trivial way, and is thus an interesting principle of probability logic. It will, in particular, be used in the calculation of expectations. In this case we shall have a symmetry condition for a property A, giving rise to a finite collection of assertions of the form (ii), for different values of P. These divide the domain into cells, members of the same cell having A with the same probability. These cells will then have also a known distribution in the domain, so there will be a collection of conditions

$$[P_i x_i](Exy -[Q_i y] \mapsto Ay)$$

giving the distribution of the probabilistic properties of form (ii). It will then be a question of detaching the conclusion that the expectation of the property A is $\Sigma_i(P_i)(Q_i)$. The way in which this is done is described in theorem 6.2 below. Miller's principle is an important part of the proof of that theorem. It is again worth remarking that in all these discussions the property A may itself have a complex probabilistic and logical structure: In syntactical terms, A may include standard and probability quantifiers and other logical operators and also include free variables.

The proof of Miller's principle depends first on formulating the requirement that the equivalence relation E is a symmetry condition for the property A. To say this is to say that whatever has the property (ii) is symmetrical or equivalent to all and only things that have (ii). That is to say that for all objects y and z,

(iv) $(Exz -[Px] \mapsto Ax) \rightarrow [(Exy -[Px] \mapsto Ax) \longleftrightarrow Eyz]$

In addition to (iv), it will also be required that the equivalence class for P is not empty.

Theorem 6.1. (Miller's principle) Let E be an equivalence relation, Ax and Ay alphabetic variants (so these formulas differ only in that x occurs free in Ax just where y occurs free in Ay) then

$(\exists z)(Exz -[Px] \mapsto Ax),$

$(\forall y)(\forall z)\{(Exz -[Px] \mapsto Ax) \rightarrow [(Exy -[Px] \mapsto Ax) \longleftrightarrow Eyz])\}$

$\vDash (Exy -[Px] \mapsto Ax) -[Py] \mapsto Ay$

Proof. To see first that the premisses are consistent for each rational P, let P = m/n. Let M be a model with $D_M = Sn = \{1 \ldots n\}$ and let $|A|^M = S_m = \{1 \ldots m\}$, or ϕ if P = 0. Take $|E|^M$ to be just the universal 2-place relation in D_M, i.e., $|E|^M = [D_M]^2$. Then both premisses are true in M. Now let M be any model in which both premisses hold for a given fixed quantity P. On the basis of the first premiss we can assume without loss of generality that there is an individual constant a such that

(i) $M \models Exa -[Px] \rightarrow Ax$

Then, since Ax and Ay are alphabetic variants, we have also,

(ii) $M \models Eya -[Py] \rightarrow Ay$

From (i) and the second premiss,

(iii) $M \models (Exy -[Px] \rightarrow Ax) \longleftrightarrow Eya$

So, by (ii) and (iii)

$$M \models (Exy -[Px] \rightarrow Ax) -[Py] \rightarrow Ay$$

which proves the theorem.

We turn now to the logic of the calculation of expectations of random variables. Recall that theorem 3.6, above, governs the calculation of simple weighted averages:

3.6 Let $A_1 \ldots A_k$ be formulas. Let X include all formulas

$$(\forall x)(A_i \rightarrow \neg A_j)$$

for i and j distinct indices between 1 and k, and also the formula

$$(\forall x)(A_1 \vee \ldots \vee A_k)$$

Then, where $R = (P_1)(Q_1) + \ldots + (P_k)(Q_k)$,

$X, [Q_1 x]A_1 \ldots [Q_k x]A_k, (A_1 -[P_1 x] \rightarrow B) \ldots (A_k -[P_k x] \rightarrow B)$
$\models [Rx]B$

In the present context expectations have a multivariate logic, informally described above in terms of the distribution of the cells of a symmetry condition. Symmetry conditions allow also a simple description of random variables. Miller's principle will then be the essential bridge connecting the simple averaging method of theorem 3.6 with the general theory of random variables and their expectations.

A random variable is a way to quantify data so as to make them accessible to general probabilistic and stochastic treatment. From a logical point of view a random variable is just a (single-valued) function that assigns a numerical value to each individual in its domain. So a function that gives the height of each person in New

York City is a random variable, as is a function that gives the relative frequency of heads in each finite sequence of coin tosses. In keeping with the general restrictions of the present work, we consider only rational-valued random values. The *distribution* of a random variable gives, for each numerical value in its range, the probability that the random variable will take on that value. If there are only finitely many distinct possible values, then the random variable is said to be *simple*. In the present section only simple random variables are in question. For present purposes, then, a random variable is a function that assigns some one of a finite collection of rational numbers to each object in its domain. The domain of such a function can be partitioned into a finite number of cells in such a way that objects in the same cell are assigned the same numerical value. Such a partition—a *k-fold* partition—for given finite k can always be effected by an equivalence relation. When this is done there will be k distinct objects in the domain of the relation, none of which is equivalent to any other, and such that every object in the domain is equivalent to one or the other or them. If a simple random variable, f, takes on each of its possible values P_i with a known probability Q_i, then its *expected value* or *expectation* is the probabilistically weighted average

$$Ex(f) = \Sigma_i(P_i)(Q_i)$$

The concept of random variable is a quite general one—any numerical function can be looked at in this way—and the expectation of such a function has a clear meaning so long as the probability assignments have a clear meaning. Thus probability itself may sometimes have the structure of a random variable. This will be the case when various probability values are possible and where these values occur with certain probabilities. A standard example is that of biased coins: if one coin is biased 2 : 1 in favour of heads and another is biased 2 : 1 in favour of tails, and if the chances are equal that a coin to be tossed is one or the other, then the expectation of the probability of heads is $(1/2)(2/3) + (1/2)(1/3) = 1/2$. The theoretical development of such expectations in a general way is straightforward in the framework of probability quantifiers.

The enabling theorem is simple and simply stated. Its proof turns on an obvious application of Miller's principle which reveals that principle's import. If B is the property in question and E the equivalence relation that partitions the domain into symmetry classes for

B, symmetric things having B with the same probability, then, where $Q_1 \ldots Q_k$ are distinct quantities,

$$(Exy -[Q_1y] \mapsto By) \ldots (Exy -[Q_ky] \mapsto By)$$

give different values of the random variable. As x takes on values in the different cells of the partition, the value Q_i gives the probability that x has B. Since the (finite) distribution of this random variable is in question, we express that the random variable takes on the values $Q_1 \ldots Q_k$ with probabilities $P_1 \ldots P_k$ in the k formulas

$$[P_1x](Exy -[Q_1y] \mapsto By) \ldots [P_kx](Exy -[Q_ky] \mapsto By)$$

When these conditions are satisfied, then the expectation of B is

$$(P_1)(Q_1) + \ldots + (P_k)(Q_k)$$

This is the standard case of the expectation of a simple random variable. It is shown here to be a logical consequence of the description of the random variable.

Theorem 6.2. (Expectation theorem) Let By be a formula in which the variable x does not occur, let $Q_1 \ldots Q_k$ be distinct quantities, and let Ax(E) include first the assertion that E is an equivalence relation, and further for each i, from 1 to k, the formula

(i) $(Exy -[Q_iy] \mapsto By) \to \{Ezy -[Q_iy] \mapsto By) \to Exz\}$

Then if $P_1 \ldots P_k$ are positive quantities that sum to one, and

$R = \Sigma_{i=1}^{k}(P_i)(Q_i)$,
Ax(E), $(\forall x)\{(Exy -[Q_1y] \mapsto By) \lor \ldots \lor (Exy -[Q_ky] \mapsto By)\}$,
$[P_1x](Exy -[Q_1y] \mapsto By), \ldots, [P_kx](Exy -[Q_ky] \mapsto By) \vDash$
[Ry]By

Proof. Since the quantities P_i are all positive, the premisses imply, for each i,

(ii) $(\exists z)(Eyz -[Q_iy] \mapsto By)$

Since E is an equivalence relation, by extensionality (theorem 2.7) the premisses (i) imply for each i

(iii) $(Eyz -[Q_iy] \mapsto By) \to \{(Eyx -[Q_iy] \mapsto By) \longleftrightarrow Exz\}$

Since x does not occur in the formula By, Bx and By are alphabetic variants. Hence by the preceding theorem Miller's principle applies, and we have that the premisses entail, for each i

(iv) $(Eyz -[Q_iy] \mapsto y) -[Q_ix] \mapsto Bx$

Finally, applying 3.6, cited above, the theorem follows.

The universal quantifier in the second premise can be replaced by [1x]. The proof is then slightly complicated, but involves no essentially new principles or methods. It is worth emphasizing that the conditions and properties involved in the theorem can themselves be probabilistic. There is in fact no finite limit to the depth of logical, including probabilistic, structure in E and B, so long as the premises are satisfied. In this way the account of expectation in terms of probability quantifiers is more general than the usual account where conditionalization relates non-probabilistic conditions.

The theorems of the preceding section show that and how a conjunction of expressions in each of which just one variable is quantified entails the multivariate quantification of a conjunction of expressions. The semantics of this entailment are based on the finite and infinite product principles and, in the infinite case, the method of ordering k-tuples there introduced: the Fubini ordering. These principles are the finite and denumerable forms of the structure underlying the Fubini theorem in the continuous case. Perhaps the simplest way to describe this structure is to say that distinct single-variable probabilities are independent and that they give always the schema of independent trials or draws with replacement.

Although the situation is more complicated when the multivariate quantification of relations is in question, there are nevertheless a few fundamental principles at work which can be seen to govern the quite rich case of expectations involving probabilities of relations. There are, in the first place, applications of the above theorems with vectors or k-tuples of variables in place of the individual variables in the probability quantifiers. This amounts, essentially, to single-variable quantification over k-tuples thought of as objects, and the complications of the preceding theorems to allow for this are no more than clerical. When we turn, however, to combinations of single and multivariate quantifications of genuine relations, the situation is conceptually richer and more interesting. The structure of simple independence no longer obtains. To see what structures do obtain, let us look first at some consequences of the Fubini ordering.

Under the Fubini ordering, the first n^2 couples of members of a given set are just those couples formed from the first n members of the set. One consequence of this can be illustrated in the positive integers. If $S_n = \{1 \ldots n\}$, then

$$(S_n)^2 = \text{the first } n^2 \text{ members of } N^2 = \cup_{i=1}^{n} \{\langle i,y \rangle : y \leq n\}$$

Hence if $B \subseteq N^2$ is a set of couples, the relative frequency of B in $(Vn)^2$ approaches the relative frequency of B in $(Vn \times N)$ as n increases without bound.

This feature of the Fubini ordering supports a semantical principle of multivariate probabilistic quantification. Consider a model with the positive integers as domain. Let s be an assignment and t_1 . . .be the x–variants of s. Then if B is a formula in which x and y may be free (abusing the distinction of use from mention for the moment)

$$(1/n)\Sigma_{i=1}^n F^n(B, t_i, y)$$

is the relative frequency of B in $(S_n)^2$, while

$$(1/n)\Sigma_{i=1}^n F(B, t_i, y)$$

is the relative frequency of B in $(S_n \times N)$. The above reasoning shows that these are equivalent in the limit, i.e. that

$PF \lim_{n \to \infty}(1/n)\Sigma_{i=1}^n F^n(B, t_i, y) = \lim_{n \to \infty}(1/n)\Sigma_{i=1}^n F(B, t_i, y)$

This principle leads to a lemma which is central to the semantics of multivariate quantification. Let M be any model, s an assignment, and t_1 . . . . be the x–variants of s. Take f to index the couples of elements in M according to the Fubini ordering. Then

$$F^f(B, s, xy)$$

is the relative frequency of the first f x-y variants of s that satisfy B, and at $f = n^2$,

$$F^f(B, s, xy) = (1/n)\Sigma_{i=1}^n F^n(B, t_i, y)$$

Which, by the above principle *PF*, entails,

(i) $\begin{aligned} F(B, s, xy) &= \lim_{f \to \infty} F^f(B, s, xy) \\ &= \lim_{n \to \infty}(1/n)\Sigma_{i=1}^n F^n(B, t_i, y) \\ &= \lim_{n \to \infty}(1/n)\Sigma_{i=1}^n F(B, t_i, y) \end{aligned}$

The central lemma can now be formulated and proved.

Lemma. Let Q_1 . . . Q_k be distinct quantities, M a model, and s an assignment. Then if

$$F[([Q_1y]B \vee . . . \vee [Q_ky]B), s, x] = 1$$

then

$$F(B, s, xy) = (Q_1)F([Q_1y]B, s, x) + . . . + (Q_k)F([Q_ky]B, s, x)$$

Proof. We argue for the case $k = 2$. The general finite case differs only inessentially from this. Again, let $t_1 \ldots$. be the x-variants of s. Then, since y is not free in $[Q_1 y]B$,

$F([Q_1 y]B, t_i, y)$

is one if t_i satisfies $[Q_1 y]B$ and zero otherwise. Hence

$F([Q_1 y]B, t_i, y)$

gives just the number of $t_1 \ldots t_n$ that satisfy $[Q_1 y]B$. So

(ii) $F^n([Q_1 y]B, s, x) = (1/n)\Sigma_{i=1}^n F([Q_1 y]B, t_i, y)$

and similarly for Q_2.

The hypothesis of the lemma entails that

$F(\neg [Q_1 y]B \,\&\, \neg [Q_2 y]B, s, x) = 0$

and hence that

$F_3 = \lim_{n\to\infty}\Sigma_{i=1}^n (1/n)\{F(\neg [Q_1 y]B \,\&\, \neg [Q_2 y]B, t_i, y)F(B, t_i, y)\} = 0$

Since

$\Sigma_{i=1}^n F([Q_1 y]B, t_i, y)$

is the number of $t_1 \ldots t_n$ that satisfy $[Q_1 y]B$,

$\Sigma_{i=1}^n F(B, t_i, y) =$
$(Q_1)\Sigma_{i=1}^n F([Q_1 y]B, t_i, y) +$
$(Q_2)\Sigma_{i=1}^n F([Q_2 y]B, t_i, y) +$
$\Sigma_{i=1}^n \{F(\neg [Q_1 y]B \,\&\, \neg [Q_2 y]B, t_i, y)F(B, t_i, y)\}$

Taking averages and limits, we have

$\lim_{n\to\infty}(1/n)\Sigma_{i=1}^n F(B, t_i, y) =$
$(Q_1)\lim_{n\to\infty}(1/n)\Sigma_{i=1}^n F([Q_1 y]B, t_i, y) +$
$(Q_2)\lim_{n\to\infty}(1/n)\Sigma_{i=1}^n F([Q_2 y]B, t_i, y) + F_3$

Applying (i) and (ii),

$F(B, s, xy) = (Q_1)\lim_{n\to\infty}F^n([Q_1 y]B, s, x) +$
$(Q_2)\lim_{n\to\infty}F^n([Q_2 y]B, s, x)$
$= (Q_1)F([Q_1 y]B, s, x) + (Q_2)F([Q_2 y]B, s, x)$

which proves the lemma.

The first theorem gives the expectation of a simple random variable as the weighted average of the values it takes on as it varies over the cells of its partition, the weights being the probabilities of those values. In terms of probability logic, this is the amalgamation of a finite number of pairs of single-variable quantifiers into one quantifier of two variables. This is a genuine instance of relational quantification. The theorem follows easily from the above lemma.

Theorem 6.3. If $Q_1 \ldots Q_k$ are distinct quantities and $P_1 \ldots P_k$ sum to one, then where $R = \Sigma_{i=1}^k (P_i)(Q_i)$

$$[P_1x][Q_1y]B, \ldots, [P_kx][Q_ky]B \vDash [Rxy]B$$

Proof. If s satisfies the premisses in a model M then

$$F([Q_1y]B, s, x) = P_1$$

and similarly for $P_2 \ldots P_k$. Since the Q_i are distinct and the P_i sum to one the premiss of the lemma holds. The theorem follows immediately.

The multivariate quantification of conditionals involves some ramification of these principles. It is of some interest to remark a certain proposition that does *not* hold: we do not have (with P_i, Q_i, and R as above) that

C_1 $[P_1x](A-[Q_1y]\rightarrow B), \ldots, [P_kx](A-[Q_ky]\rightarrow B) \vDash$
$(A -[Rxy]\rightarrow B)$

A simple counterexample shows this. Take the domain of M to be $\{1, 2\}$. Let

$$A = \{\langle 1, 2 \rangle, \langle 2, 1 \rangle, \langle 2, 2 \rangle\}$$
$$B = \{\langle 1, 2 \rangle, \langle 2, 1 \rangle\}$$

Then the premisses with $k = 2$ are satisfied for $P_1 = P_2 = 1/2$; $Q_1 = 1$; $Q_2 = 1/2$. But

$$M \vDash (A -[2/3\ xy]\rightarrow B)$$

C_1 does hold when y is not free in the formula A. To prove this and other theorems involving conditionals, we first assert without proof a conditional form of the above lemma. The proof, though more complex, involves the same principles. (The simple form of the lemma is a special case of the conditional form with a logical truth in place of the formula A.)

Lemma (Conditional form). We write $F(B/A, s, xy)$ for

$$\lim_{f \to \infty} \left(\frac{F^f(A\&B, s, xy)}{F^f(A, s, xy)} \right)$$

and similarly for similar quotients. If y is not free in A, $Q_1 \ldots Q_k$ are distinct quantities and

$$F([Q_1y]B/A, s, x) + \ldots + F([Q_ky]B/A, s, x) = 1$$

then

$$F(B/A, s, xy) = (Q_1)F([Q_1y]B/A, s, x) + \ldots$$
$$+ (Q_k)F(Q_ky]B/A, s, x)$$

The proof of this form of the lemma depends upon the fact that, since y is not free in A,

$$(1/n)\Sigma_{i=1}^{n}F^n(A, t_i, y) = (1/n)\Sigma_{i=1}^{n}F(A, t_i, y) = F^n(A, s, x)$$

where $t_1 \ldots$ are the x-variants of the assignment s.

The main theorem combining single and multivariate quantification follows from the conditional form of the lemma.

Theorem 6.4. If $Q_1 \ldots Q_k$ are distinct quantities, $P_1 \ldots P_k$ sum to one, and y is not free in A, then where $R = \Sigma_{i=1}^{k}(P_i)(Q_i)$

$$(A-[P_1x]\!\mapsto [Q_1y]B), \ldots, (A-[P_kx]\!\mapsto [Q_ky]B) \vDash$$
$$A-[Rxy]\!\mapsto B$$

Proof. If an assignment s satisfies the premisses in a model M, then

$$F([Q_iy]B/A, s, x) = P_i$$

for each i from 1 to k. Since the Q_i are distinct and the P_i sum to one, the premiss of the lemma holds and the theorem follows immediately.

Theorem 6.4 yields a series of corollaries.

Theorem 6.5. Under the conditions of theorem 6.4,

6.5 (1) $A-[1x]\!\mapsto [Qy]B \vDash A-[Qxy]\!\mapsto B$

6.5 (2) $(\exists x)A, (\forall x)(A-[Qy]\!\mapsto B) \vDash A-[Qxy]\!\mapsto B$

6.5 (3) If y is free in neither A nor C and if $Q_1 \ldots Q_k$ are all positive, then

$$(A-[P_1x]\!\mapsto (C-[Q_1y]\!\mapsto B)), \ldots, (A-[P_kx]\!\mapsto (C-[Q_ky]\!\mapsto B))$$
$$\vDash A-[Rxy]\!\mapsto (C \& B)$$

Proof. By Theorem 3.4 (2), C –[Q_iy]↦ B is in each case equivalent to [Q_iy](C & B). The theorem then yields the corollary.

Theorem 6.3 is also a corollary of theorem 6.4. Indeed, it follows as a special case when A is a logical truth. The same method leads to further corollaries.

Theorem 6.6. Under the conditions of theorem 6.3;

6.6 (1) [1x][Qy]B ⊨ [Qxy]B
6.6 (2) ($\forall$x)[Qy]B ⊨ [Qxy]B
6.6 (3) If y is not free in C and Q_1 . . . Q_k are all positive, then
[P_1x](C –[Q_1y]↦ B), . . . , [P_kx](C –[Q_ky]↦ B) ⊨ [Rxy](C & B)

Again, as in the case of expectations involving just one quantified variable, the conditions and properties may themselves be probabilistically complex. It should again be recalled that the models in question are the same well-ordered standard models introduced at the beginning of the chapter, here ramified only by the presumption of the Fubini ordering. The addition of a finiteness premiss, that is to say of a sentence C_n, for given n, renders this presumption unnecessary.

We recall some cardinality results from section 5 of chapter three:

3.5.1 C_k ⊨ ($\forall$x)[(1/k)y](x = y)
3.5.4 (2) Inf ⊨ ($\forall$x)[0y](x = y)
3.5.4 (3) Inf ⊨ ($\forall$x)[1y] ¬ (x = y)

Applying theorem 6.6 to these yields the following multivariate forms:

6.7 (1) C_k ⊨ [(1/k)xy] x = y
6.7 (2) Inf ⊨ [Oxy] x = y
6.7 (3) Inf ⊨ [1xy] ¬ (x = y)
6.8 (1) M is infinite ⇔ M ⊨ [0xy] x = y
6.8 (2) M is finite ⇔ M ⊨ ¬ [0xy] x = y

5.7 *Modal probability logic: ordered models and symmetry conditions*

Standard predicate logic can be enriched by the addition of modal operators for necessity and possibility.[9] The truth conditions for

---

[9] See, for example, Hughes and Cresswell, *An Introduction to Modal Logic*, for an elementary and thorough exposition of these matters.

formulas involving these operators are given in terms of classes of model or interpretation. Given a model M, R(M) is a class of models—those *accessible* to M. Necessity is interpreted as truth in all accessible models:

$$M \vDash \Box A \text{ if and only if } K \vDash A \text{ for all K in } R(M)$$

and possibility as truth in some accessible model:

$$M \vDash \Diamond A \text{ if and only if } K \vDash A \text{ for some K in } R(M)$$

It can be shown that the usual axiom schemata for the modal system S5:

M1: $\Box A \rightarrow A$

M2: $\Box(A \rightarrow B) \rightarrow (\Box A \rightarrow \Box B)$

M3: $\Box A \rightarrow \Box\Box A$

M4: $\Diamond A \rightarrow \Box\Diamond A$

in company with the rule of *necessitation*:

From A infer $\Box A$

amount conjunctively to the constraint that the classes R(M) of accessible models should be equivalence classes—that accessibility be an equivalence relation.[10]

The logic of probability quantifiers also permits a modal expansion. The addition of the above axiom schemata and rule, interpreted in terms of classes of accessible model, goes quite as in the non-probabilistic case. Further, in view of the ordering relation present in probability models, there is a natural interpretation of accessibility, namely that models that differ only by permuting the domain are mutually accessible. These are just those ordered models that are not distinguished in non-probabilistic logic. Interpreting accessibility in this way thus provides a means for formulating, and, as we shall see, goes some way towards answering, two related logical questions: how much probability logic remains when different orderings of the same model are not distinguished, and how can the dependence upon ordering be marked off within formulas in some perspicuous way? One illuminating principle is this: when every infinite extension has a finite complement in the domain then the satisfaction and truth of formulas in probability logic is

---

[10] See Kripke, "Semantical Considerations on Modal Logic".

unaffected by order. The introduction of modalities enables the precise formulation of this and helps to chart its effects. To pave the way for this introduction we first discuss this special case in a little more detail.

Let us say that a set of natural numbers is *essentially finite* if it is either finite or has a finite complement. An algebraic structure is said to be essentially finite if each of its member sets is essentially finite. Since the complement of an essentially finite set is always essentially finite, and the intersection of finitely many essentially finite sets is always essentially finite, a Boolean algebra the atoms of which are essentially finite and each member of which is the union of finitely many atoms is always essentially finite. This does not hold in general for sigma algebras: for the union of infinitely many finite sets may be an infinite set with an infinite complement; the collection $\{\{0\}, \{2\}, \{4\}, \ldots\}$ is an obvious instance.

The relative frequency measure on an essentially finite Boolean algebra is always two-valued: it assigns zero to each finite set and one to each infinite set. Conditional relative frequencies, $P(B/A)$, in such an algebra can take on values different from zero and one only when both $A \cap B$ and A are finite: if both these are infinite, then $P(B/A) = 1$. If A is infinite and $A \cap B$ is finite then $P(B/A) = 0$ or is undefined.

Let us say that a model M is *essentially finite* if for each k and each k-place predicate F^k, at least one of $|F^k|^M$, $D^k - |F^k|^M$ is finite. And let us say that a model M' is a *permutation* of a model M if (i) the domain of M' is a simple permutation of type ω of the domain of M, and (ii) for each predicate F, and individual constant a, $|F|^M = |F|^{M'}$ and $|a|^M = |a|^{M'}$. Now the theorem concerning permutations of essentially finite models is the following:

Theorem 7.1. If M is an essentially finite model and M' is a permutation of M, then for each sentence A, $M \models A$ if and only if $M' \models A$.

The main step in the proof of 7.1 is a lemma:

Lemma. Given a model M, for each formula A let $\hat{x}$ be the variables free in A. For each assignment s let $N(A, s)$ be the set of $\hat{x}$-variants of s that satisfy A, and let N_s be the set of $\hat{x}$-variants of s. If M is essentially finite then for every A and s, not both $N(A, s)$ and N_s are infinite.

The proof of the lemma is by induction on the structure of the formula A. The lemma obviously holds if D_M is finite, so suppose D_M to be infinite. The main points of the argument are as follows, other details and special cases are straightforward when they are not obvious.

If A is an atomic formula, $F^k(x_1 \ldots x_k)$, then an $\langle x_1 \ldots x_k \rangle$-variant of an assignment s satisfies A if and only if

$$\langle s(x_1) \ldots s(x_k) \rangle \, \epsilon \, |F^k|^M;$$

so, given s, the members of N(A, s) are in biunique correspondence with the members of $|F^k|^M$. Since this latter set is essentially finite, so is N(A, s).

$N(\neg A, s) = N_s - N(A, s)$ and $N(A \,\&\, B, s) = N(A, s) \cap N(B, s)$. Recalling the remarks of chapter 3, section 2 (with respect to example (ii)) about essential finiteness in Boolean algebras, we see that this character is inherited in truth-functional combination. Again, $N[(\forall x)A, s] \subseteq N(A, s)$, so if the latter is finite, so is the former. On the other hand, if $N(\neg A, s)$ is finite, then so is $N[(\exists x)\neg A, s] = N_s - N[(\forall x)A, s]$, so essential finiteness is inherited in (non-probabilistic) quantification.

Since D_M is infinite, for each formula B, assignment s, and variable x, if $M \vDash_s [Px]B$, then P is zero or one. Hence if P is positive and less than one, $N([Px]B, s)$ is null. If N(B, s) is finite, then $N([0x]B, s)$ is finite and $N([1x]B, s]$ is null. If, on the other hand, $N_s - N(B, s)$ is finite, then $N_s - N([1x]B, s)$ is finite, and $N([0x]B, s)$ is null.

If N(A, s) is infinite and $M \vDash_s A -[Px]\!\!\rightarrow B$, then P is zero (if N(B, s) is finite) or one (if N(B, s) is infinite) and an argument similar to the preceding shows that $N(A -[Px]\!\!\rightarrow B, s)$ is finite or has a finite complement. If N(A, s) is finite and $M \vDash_s A -[Px]\!\!\rightarrow B$, then $N(A \,\&\, B, s)$ is finite, and this entails that $N(A -[Px]\!\!\rightarrow B, s)$ is finite as well.

Theorem 7.1 is now proved as follows: suppose M to be essentially finite and let M' be a permutation of M. The argument is by induction on the structure of a formula A. Since the non-probabilistic fragment of the logic of probability quantifiers is unaffected by order and permutation, the basis and those steps involving truth-functions and non-probabilistic quantifiers are trivial. It remains to be shown that if $M \vDash A$ if and only if $M' \vDash A$, then $M \vDash [Px]A$ if and only if $M' \vDash [Px]A$, and similarly for probability conditionals. The permutation of an essentially finite set is always essentially finite, so if N(A, s), N'(A, s) are defined (for the same assignment s) in the models M and M' respectively, then these are always essentially finite, and both are finite or both infinite. Thus M ⊨ [0x]A if and only if M' ⊨ [0x]A; and M ⊨ [1x]A if and only if M' ⊨ [1x] A. Again—since the permutation of a finite set is finite—the ratio F(A,s,x) is the same in M and M' for all formulas A, assignments s, and variables x. In particular the satisfaction of formulas A –[Px]→ B with P distinct from zero and one is invariant when M is permuted to M'. This completes the sketch of the proof of 7.1.

Accessibility between models fixes the meanings of necessity and possibility. For each model M we take *every* simple permutation of the domain of M, leaving unchanged extensions of predicates, function symbols, and individual constants, to give a model accessible to M. It is important to emphasize, first that a class of mutually accessible models is closed under permutations—that is the force of the above italicized "every"—and secondly that accessible models are indistinguishable in the non-probabilistic fragment of the logic. In view of this indistinguishability it will be simpler to work not with a class of models but with a class of orderings or permutations of a model in the ordinary, unordered, sense. By a (*modal probability*) *structure* we mean such a model with its orderings. If the model is finite, this distinction of orderings is irrelevant. If the model is (denumerably) infinite there are non-denumerably many distinct orderings of its domain. For certain purposes it is convenient to introduce a denumerable partition of orderings—in particular with respect to conditions of symmetry and exchangeability—but this issue is not broached here, where the main motivation is a clean and general exposition of the theory.

We write "S" for the structure as a whole. S determines the domain D(S) of individuals and the extensions $|A|^S$, $|f|^S$, $|a|^S$ of predicates, function-symbols, and individual constants. We write "Γ", "Δ", . . . for the different orderings of D(S). Given an assignment s and a variable x, each ordering Γ also orders the x-variants of s. It should be kept in mind that the identity of assignments—what values an assignment gives to what variables—does not change from one ordering to another. It is only the order in which variants are taken for the calculation of limits that changes. We write

$$S:\Gamma \underset{s}{\vDash} A$$

to mean that the formula A is satisfied by the assignment s in the ordering Γ (i.e., when limits are taken according to Γ) in the structure S. The definition of satisfaction of sections 1 and 2 is expanded to include:

$S{:}\Gamma \underset{s}{\vDash} \Box A$ if and only if $S{:}\Delta \underset{s}{\vDash} A$ for every ordering Δ of $D(S)$

$S{:}\Gamma \underset{s}{\vDash} \Diamond A$ if and only if $S{:}\Delta \underset{s}{\vDash} A$ for some ordering Δ of $D(S)$

Here "Γ" takes the place of "M" in the original definition. Since the orderings are varied, it will be convenient to write:

$F_\Gamma(A,s,x)$

for the limiting relative frequency, calculated according to Γ, of the x-variants of s that satisfy A. This is merely a notational change; reference to a model M is implicit in the notation introduced in section 3 of chapter 4, and it could be suppressed there since it was not varied.

We say that A is *true* in Γ in S, and write:

$S{:}\Gamma \vDash A$

if every assignment satisfies A in the ordering Γ of $D(S)$. A is *valid* in S, written:

$S \vDash A$

if true in every Γ in S, and A is *universally valid*, written:

$\vDash A$

if valid in every structure S. All valid formulas of probability logic are universally valid in this extended sense, as are all instances of the schemata M1–M4 and all instances of

$\Diamond A \longleftrightarrow \neg \Box \neg A$

The rule of necessitation when applied to a premiss valid in S always yields a conclusion valid in S, but does not preserve truth in an ordering. Formulas are *equivalent* that are satisfied by the same assignments in every ordering in every structure. One formula *entails* another if every assignment that satisfies the first in an ordering in a structure, also satisfies the second in that ordering in that structure.

Since the non-probabilistic fragment of the logic is insensitive to difference of order, we have:

7.2 If A includes no probability quantifiers, then A, $\Box A$, and $\Diamond A$ are equivalent.

Theorem 7.1 leads immediately to a theorem on essentially finite models.

7.3 If (every model in) the structure S is essentially finite then for each formula A,

$$A \rightarrow \Box A \text{ and } \Diamond A \rightarrow A$$

are valid in S.

Corollary. If D_k expresses that there are at most k individuals, then for each formula A,

$$D_k \vDash A \rightarrow \Box A$$
$$D_k \vDash \Diamond A \rightarrow A$$

The modern logic of modalities makes a clear distinction between $(\forall x)\Box A$ and $\Box(\forall x)A$, as it does between their duals $\Diamond(\exists x)A$ and $(\exists x)\Diamond A$. This distinction follows from the possibility that predicates may have different extensions in different worlds: $(\forall x)\Box A$ says that everything in the present world has A in every world. This is consistent with there being, in some other world, something that does not have A in that world. That is to say,

(i) $(\forall x)\Box A$

is consistent with:

(ii) $\Diamond(\exists x)\neg A$

and hence (i) does not entail:

(iii) $\Box(\forall x)A$

which is the contradictory of (ii). Nor does (iii) entail (i), since it may be true in every world that all the objects that exist in that world have A in that world, while there is nevertheless an object in some world that fails to have A in some world in which it does not exist. That is just to say that (iii) is consistent with:

(iv) $(\exists x)\Diamond\neg A$

which is the contradictory of (i).

The restrictions of the present interpretation change this. We have that:

$$S{:}\Gamma \vDash_s (\forall x)\Box A \text{ if and only if } S{:}\Gamma \vDash_s \Box(\forall x)A$$

so,

7.4 (1) $\vDash \Box(\forall x)A \rightarrow (\forall x)\Box A$
     (2) $\vDash (\exists x)\Diamond A \rightarrow \Diamond(\exists x)A$
7.5 (1) $\vDash (\forall x)\Box A \rightarrow \Box(\forall x)A$
     (2) $\vDash \Diamond(\exists x)A \rightarrow (\exists x)\Diamond A.$

Although necessity and possibility commute with the universal and existential quantifier respectively, we do not have:

(v) $\Box(\exists x)A \rightarrow (\exists x)\Box A$; $\qquad$ $(\forall x)\Box A \rightarrow \Diamond(\forall x)A$,

for some x-variant of an assignment may satisfy A in an ordering without doing so in all orderings. To see this notice that

$(\forall x)\Diamond(\forall y)(x \leq y)$

holds in the positive integers (i.e., every positive integer is first in some ordering) but

$\Diamond(\forall x)(\forall y)(x \leq y)$

is false in this interpretation. We turn now to the more complex question of the interactions between modalities and probability quantifiers.

The introduction of the modal operators permits the distinction of three classes of truth in a model: those that are logically valid—the theses of probability logic; those that are true in all orderings of the domain; and those that are true in some orderings but not in others. Whatever restriction there is in the requirement of ordered models is thus neutralized and precisely described by the modal semantics of the present section. To see how this works, consider a model M with the positive integers as domain and in which the predicate E is true of the even numbers. Then—since E(x) includes no probability quantifiers—

(vi) $M \vDash E(x) \longleftrightarrow \Box E(x)$.

Now let Γ give the standard ordering of the positive integers: $\Gamma_1 = 1$, $\Gamma_2 = 2$. . . Then:

$F_\Gamma(E(x),s,x) = 1/2$

so

$S:\Gamma \vDash [(1/2)x]E(x)$

and, by (vi)—

(vii) $S:\Gamma \vDash [(1/2)x]\Box E(x)$.

But there are other orderings, Δ, of the integers (see, for example, chapter 2, section 5) such that it is not the case that $S:\Delta \vDash [(1/2)x]E(x)$. So it is not the case that $S:\Delta \vDash \Box[(1/2)x]E(x)$. Hence—referring to (vii)—

(viii) $[Px]\Box A \rightarrow \Box[Px]A$

is not universally valid.

This shows that the probabilistic analogue of 7.4 does not hold. Nor does the analogue of 7.3. To see this let

$$H = \{H_1 \ldots\}$$

be a denumerably infinite partition of the positive integers, each member, H_i, of which is infinite. Now define the relation G to include all pairs $\langle i,y \rangle$ where $y \in H_i$, for $i = 1, 2 \ldots$ So G is a relation which holds between 1 and every member of H_1, between 2 and every member of H_2, and so on. Call this structure I.

Each H_i is infinite and there is thus for each i some ordering, call it Γ_i, in which the limiting relative frequency of H_i in N is one. (Just let Γ_i put $N - H_i$ in correspondence with the powers of ten, and H_i in correspondence with the other integers.) Hence, for each integer n there is some ordering Γ (namely Γ_n) such that:

(ix) $I{:}\Gamma \vDash [1y]G(n,y)$

Or, to put this in more precise semantical terms: if s is any assignment, then for every x-variant, t, of s there is some Γ such that:

$$I{:}\Gamma \underset{t}{\vDash} [1y]G(x,y)$$

so every s satisfies $\Diamond[1y]G(x,y)\}$ in every Γ, and

$$I \vDash (\forall x)\Diamond[1y]G(x,y)$$

Thus,

(x) $I \vDash \neg(\exists x)\Box \neg [1y]G(x,y).$

Hence, by the laws of the previous chapter governing entailments between standard and probabilistic quantifiers:

$$I \vDash [0x] \neg [1y]G(x,y)$$

and,

(xi) $I \vDash [1x]\Box \neg [1y]G(x,y).$

For each ordering Γ there is, on the other hand, at most one integer n for which (ix) holds. Thus by any ordering the limiting relative frequency of integers that satisfy (ix) in that ordering is zero. That is to say, for each Γ, if s is any assignment, then the limiting relative frequency in Γ of x-variants of s that satisfy $[1y]G(x,y)$ is zero. Hence for each Γ and each s, the limiting relative frequency of x-variants of s that satisfy $\neg [1y]G(x,y)$ in Γ is one. So for each Γ,

$$I{:}\Gamma \vDash [1x] \neg [1y]G(x,y)$$

(xii) $I \vDash \Box[1x] \neg [1y]G(x,y).$

(xii) and (xi) entail that

(xiii) $\Box[Px]A \rightarrow [Px]\Box A$

is not universally valid. That is to say, neither the probabilistic analogue of 7.4 nor that of 7.5 is valid.

Although (xiii) is not universally valid, two special cases in which it holds should be remarked: if A includes no probability quantifiers, then A and $\Box A$ are equivalent (7.2). Hence

7.6 If A includes no probability quantifiers, then $\vDash [Px]A \rightarrow [Px]\Box A$.

Next, by 7.3,

7.7 If the extension of every predicate in A is essentially finite in S then $S \vDash [Px]A \longleftrightarrow [Px]\Box A$.

In view of axiom schema M2, referring also to 3.6 of chapter 4,

4.3.6 (1) $[1x](A \rightarrow B) \vDash [Px]A \rightarrow [Px](A \& B)$

we have

7.8 $\vDash \Box[1x](A \rightarrow B) \rightarrow \{\Box[Px]A \rightarrow \Box[Px](A \& B)\}$

which, since $(\forall x)A \vDash [1x]A$, by 7.4 gives the further result:

7.9 $\vDash (\forall x)\Box(A \rightarrow B) \rightarrow \{\Box[Px]A \rightarrow \Box[Px](A \& B)\}$

and we have the following principle of extensionality:

7.10 $\vDash \Box(A \longleftrightarrow B) \rightarrow (\Box[Px]A \longleftrightarrow \Box[Px]B)$.

As regards probability conditionals, we can distinguish *necessitation of the conditional*:[11]

(i) $\Box(A \text{ -}[Px] \rightarrow B)$

from *conditional necessitation*:

(ii) $\Box A \text{ -}[Px] \rightarrow \Box B$.

That neither of these implies the other may be seen by reference to the special case in which A is logically valid. Then A is equivalent to [lx]A, so, in consequence of

3.1 (1) $[1x]A \vDash [Px](A \rightarrow B) \longleftrightarrow (A \text{ -}[Px] \rightarrow B)$

(i) and (ii) are equivalent to

(ia) $\Box[Px]B$
(iia) $[Px]\Box B$

respectively. The above counterinstances to (viii) and its converse show that these are logically independent.

---

11 See the articles by D. Lewis and Stalnaker referred to in note 4, above.

Afterword

THIS book began with a brief sketch of a classical view of knowledge and probability: according to that view, probability and the uncertainty it measures are not objects of experience, but products of our experience of objects; not things to which knowledge can correspond, but points at which the correspondence of knowledge to things fails. Certain Kantian principles and certain forms of atomism were said, in the Introduction, to motivate this view. To appreciate this classical position one must take care to distinguish noumenal independence and objectivity from phenomenal independence and objectivity. Whether probability and uncertainty are noumenal sources of our experience or not, we can never know. Whether they are objective phenomena, and not merely subjective, is at least arguable. Kant and his classical sympathizers insisted, in this argument, that uncertainty is not an objective character of phenomena. The principle of complete determination is an important part of the support for that proposition.

In the absence of the distinction of noumenal from phenomenal objectivity, or something like it, arguments about the objectivity of probability and uncertainty threaten to move by equivocation from the radical inaccessibility of noumenal uncertainty to the denial that uncertainty is or can be objective. Subjectivism, in particular, runs this risk, as section 3 of chapter 2 makes clear. That can be understood, at least vaguely, as consequent on the dedicated anti-Kantianism of the positivists. The positivists themselves avoided the fallacy by being as resolutely anti-psychologistic as they were anti-Kantian. Their successors have often forfeited this protection.

The book began with a brief sketch of a classical view of knowledge and probability; and work on the book began, some years ago, with reflection on that view. Kantianism, and critical philosophy in general, provides one answer to the question of the nature and possibility of probable knowledge: whatever seems to be knowledge of probabilities is always in part ignorance. To the extent that ignorance is replaced by genuine knowledge, what is known cannot be probable. It is not easy to retrace and to criticize the critical route to this answer without making use of Kantian vocabulary and principles. But, for reasons briefly rehearsed in the Introduction, that vocabulary and those principles should no longer be presumed. Some alternative way of examining the question is thus needed. Subjectivism, which is from the point of view of philosophical principle a sort of pre-Kantian subjective and empirical idealism, is less a genuine alternative than an anachronism. It just does not answer the question. The positivistic options of empirical frequentism and logicism fare little better: both are in fact firmly rooted in the Kantianism they so firmly disavow. Again, both join subjectivism in refusing to question certain anachronistic, strong, and inadequate presumptions about the nature and form of judgement. Indeed, as far as the question of the nature of probable knowledge is concerned, much of the epistemological discussion of this century—having to do with the form of judgement, with the relation of judgement to truth, with the role of reflection in knowledge—might never have taken place. If there has been recent progress in philosophy, the development of a general and recursive theory of propositional structure and the concomitant translation of features of the act of judgement into recurring and embedded parts of the object of judgement is certainly an instance of it. Frege's account of generality and relations is the corner-stone of this development. Analytic philosophy from Frege to Quine has been vitally concerned with it, and phenomenology and its heirs have been no less so. As concerns probability, however, only empirical frequentism and propensity interpretations have made any effort to shift probability from the act to the object of probable judgement, and neither of these has provided or could easily provide a thorough account of embedded probabilities. Carnapian logicism and subjectivism are hostile or indifferent to the question of embedded probabilities. That is to say, to repeat, that these positions have been bypassed by much of the epistemological discussion of this century.

The theory of probability quantifiers of chapters 4 and 5 takes up the discussion at this point. It starts with the question of logicism, in the form: to what extent is probability properly a part of pure or general logic? Two criteria of adequacy are presumed: first that pure or general logic must be quite a weak extension of standard first-order logic. Secondly that embedded probabilities must be smoothly and recursively accounted for. These are of course far from sufficient, but they are necessary, and their contribution to sufficiency is not negligible. A third principle is less a criterion than an aim or an end: the resulting theory should account for a fair amount of simple and elementary probabilistic inference with few extra or synthetic assumptions.

The reader should keep those criteria and that aim in mind in judging the theory.

Bibliography

ADAMS, ERNEST, "The Logic of Almost All", *Journal of Philosophical Logic* 3 (1974), 3–17.

AMER, MOHAMED A., "Classification of Boolean Algebras of Logic and Probabilities Defined on them by Classical Models", *Zeitschrift für mathematische Logik und Grundlagen der Mathematik* 32 (1985), 509–15.

AMER, MOHAMED A., "Extension of Relatively ς-additive Probabilities on Boolean Algebras of Logic", *The Journal of Symbolic Logic* 50 (1985), 589–96.

ARNAULD, ANTOINE, *The Art of Thinking: Port-Royal Logic*, trans. and ed. James Dickoff and Patricia James, New York: The Bobbs-Merrill Company, Inc. 1964.

AUROUX, SYLVAIN, *La sémiotique des encyclopédistes: Essai d'épistémologie historique des sciences du langage*, Paris: Payot, 1979.

BERNSTEIN, ALLEN R., and FRANK WATTENBERG, "Nonstandard Measure Theory", in W. A. J. Luxemburg, (ed.), *Applications of Model Theory to Algebra, Analysis, and Probability*.

CARNAP, RUDOLF, "A Basic System of Inductive Logic", in R. Carnap and R. Jeffrey (eds.), *Studies in Inductive Logic and Probability* vols I, II.

CARNAP, RUDOLF, "The Elimination of Metaphysics Through Logical Analysis of Language", trans. Arthur Pap, in A. J. Ayer (ed.), *Logical Positivism*, Glencoe, Ill.: The Free Press, 1959.

CARNAP, RUDOLF, "Empiricism, Semantics and Ontology", *Revue Internationale de Philosophie* 4 (1950), 208–28.

CARNAP, RUDOLF, "Inductive Logic and Rational Decisions", in R. Carnap and R. Jeffrey (eds.), *Studies in Inductive Logic and Probability* vol. I.

CARNAP, RUDOLF, *Introduction to Semantics*, Cambridge, Mass.: Harvard University Press, 1942.

CARNAP, RUDOLF, *Logical Foundations of Probability*, Chicago: University of Chicago Press, 1950.

CARNAP, RUDOLF, *The Logical Syntax of Language*, London: Routledge and Kegan Paul, Ltd. and New York: Harcourt Brace, 1937.

CARNAP, RUDOLF, and RICHARD JEFFREY, (eds.), *Studies in Inductive Logic and Probability*, vol. I, Berkeley: University of California Press, 1971.

CHURCH, ALONZO, "Review of Carnap's *Introduction to Semantics*", *The Philosophical Review* 52 (1943), 298–304.

DAVIDSON, DONALD, *Essays on Actions and Events*, Oxford: Clarendon Press, 1980.

DAVIDSON, DONALD, *Inquiries into Truth and Interpretation*, Oxford: Clarendon Press, 1984.

DIACONIS, PERSI, "Finite Forms of de Finetti's Theorem", *Synthese* 36 (1977), 271–81.

DUBINS, LESTER E., "Finitely Additive Conditional Probabilities, Conglomerability and Disintegrations", *The Annals of Probability* 3 (1975), 89–99.

FELLER, WILLIAM, *An Introduction to Probability Theory and Its Applications*, (2 vols.; 2nd edn.), New York: John Wiley and Sons, 1971.

FENSTAD, JENS ERIK, "The Structure of Logical Probabilities", *Synthese* 18 (1968), 1–23.

FINETTI, BRUNO DE, "Foresight: Its Logical Laws, its Subjective Sources", trans. Henry E. Kyburg Jr., in Henry E. Kyburg Jr. and Howard Smokler (eds.) *Studies in Subjective Probability*.

FINETTI, BRUNO DE, "Les probabilités nulles", *Bulletin des sciences mathématiques* 1936.

FINETTI, BRUNO DE, *Probability, Induction and Statistics: The Art of Guessing*, London: John Wiley and Sons, 1972.

FINETTI, BRUNO DE, *Theory of Probability: A Critical Introductory Treatment*, (2 vols.), London: John Wiley and Sons, 1974.

FRAASSEN, BAS VAN, "Belief and the Will", *The Journal of Philosophy* 81 (May 1984), 235–56.

FREGE, GOTTLOB, *Begriffschrift, eine der arithmetischen nachgebiltete Formelsprache des reinen Denkens*, Halle, 1879.

FREGE, GOTTLOB, *The Foundations of Arithmetic: A logico-mathematical Enquiry into the Concept of Number*, trans. J. L. Austin, (2nd revised edn.), New York: Harper and Brothers, 1953.

FREGE, GOTTLOB, "The Thought", trans. A. Quinton and M. Quinton, *Mind* 65 (1956) 289–311.

FREGE, GOTTLOB, *Translations from the Philosophical Writings of Gottlob Frege*, ed. Peter Geach and Max Black, Oxford: Basil Blackwell, 1952.

FREGE, GOTTLOB, "What is a Function?", in P. Geach and M. Black, (eds.), *Translations from the Philosophical Writings of Gottlob Frege*.

GAIFMAN, H., "Concerning Measures on First-order Calculi", *Israel Journal of Mathematics*, 2 (1964), 1–18.

GOODMAN, NELSON, *Fact, Fiction, and Forecast*, (2nd edn.), New York: The Bobbs-Merrill Company Inc., 1965.

HALMOS, PAUL R., *Lectures on Boolean Algebras*, Princeton: D. Van Nostrand Company, Inc., 1963.

HARPER, WILLIAM L., ROBERT STALNAKER, and GLENN PEARCE (eds.), *Ifs*. Dordrecht, Boston, and London: D. Reidel Publishing Co., 1981.

HENRICH, DIETER, "The Proof-Structure of Kant's Transcendental Deduction", *Review of Metaphysics* 22 (1969), 640–59.

HOOVER, DOUGLAS, "A Normal Form for $L(\omega 1P)$, with Applications", *Journal of Symbolic Logic* 47 (Sept. 1982), 605–24.

HOOVER, DOUGLAS, "Probability Logic", *Annals of Mathematical Logic* 14 (1978), 287–313.

HUGHES, G. E., and M. J. CRESSWELL, *An Introduction to Modal Logic*, London: Methuen, 1968.

HUME, DAVID, *A Treatise of Human Nature*, ed. L. A. Selby-Bigge, (2nd edn. revised by P. H. Nidditch), Oxford: Clarendon Press, 1978.

JANIK, ALLAN, and STEPHEN TOULMIN, *Wittgenstein's Vienna*, New York: Simon and Schuster, 1973.

JEFFREY, RICHARD, *The Logic of Decision* (2nd edn.), Chicago and London: University of Chicago Press, 1983.

JEFFREY, RICHARD, Review of David Miller, "A Paradox of Information" and other papers on the question, *The Journal of Symbolic Logic* Vol. 35, no. 124 (1970), 124–7.

JEFFREY, RICHARD, "Probability Integrals", in R. Carnap and R. Jeffrey, (eds.), *Studies in Inductive Logic and Probability* vol. I.

JEFFREY, RICHARD, (ed.), *Studies in Inductive Logic and Probability* vol. II, Berkeley: University of California Press, 1980. Kant, Immanuel, *Immanuel Kant's Critique of Pure Reason*, trans. Norman Kemp Smith, New York: St. Martin's Press, 1965.

KADANE, JOSEPH B. See Schervish.

KANT, IMMANUEL, *Immanuel Kant's Critique of Pure Reason*, trans. Norman Kemp Smith, New York: St. Martin's Press, 1965.

KANT, IMMANUEL, *Logic*, trans. Robert S. Hartman and Wolfgang Schwarz, New York: The Bobbs-Merrill Company, Inc., 1974.

KEISLER, H. JEROME, *Elementary Calculus*, Boston: Prindle, Weber & Schmidt, Inc., 1976.

KEISLER, H. JEROME, "Hyperfinite Model Theory", in R. Gandy and M. Hyland (eds.), *Logic Colloquium 76*, Amsterdam: North Holland Publishing Co., 1977. 5–110.

KOLMOGOROV, A. N., *Foundations of the Theory of Probability*, trans. and ed. Nathan Morrison, (2nd English edn.), New York: Chelsea Press, 1956.

KRAUSS, PETER. See Scott, Dana.

KRIPKE, SAUL, "Outline of a Theory of Truth", *The Journal of Philosophy*, vol. 52, no. 19 (Nov. 1975), 690–715.

KRIPKE, SAUL, "Semantical Considerations on Modal Logic", *Acta Philosophica Fennica* 16 (1963), 83–94.

KYBURG, HENRY, *The Logical Foundations of Statistical Inference*, Dordrecht and Boston: D. Reidel Publishing Co., 1974.

KYBURG, HENRY E. Jr., and Howard Smokler (eds.), *Studies in Subjective Probability*, New York: John Wiley and Sons, 1964.

LAPLACE, PIERRE SIMON, *A Philosophical Essay on Probabilities*, trans. Frederick Wilson Truscott and Frederick Lincoln Emory, New York: Dover Publications, 1951.

LEIBNIZ, GOTTFRIED WILHELM, *Philosophical Papers and Letters*, ed. Leroy E. Loemker, (2nd edn.), Dordrecht: D. Reidel Publishing Co., 1969.

LEWIS, C. I., *A Survey of Symbolic Logic*, New York: Dover Publications Inc., 1960.

LEWIS, DAVID, "Probabilities of Conditionals and Conditional Probabilities", in William L. Harper *et al.* (eds.), *Ifs*.

LEWIS, DAVID, "A Subjectivist's Guide to Objective Chance", in Rudolf Carnap and Richard Jeffrey (eds.), *Studies in Inductive Logic and Probability*.

LOCKE, JOHN, *An Essay Concerning Human Understanding*, ed. Alexander Campbell Fraser. (2 vols.), New York: Dover Publications Inc., 1959.

LOEB, P., "Conversion from Nonstandard to Standard Measure Space and Applications to Probability Theory", *Transactions of the American Mathematical Society* 211 (1975), 113–22.

LOÈVE, MICHEL, *Probability Theory*, (2nd edn.), Princeton: D. Van Nostrand Publishing Co., 1960.

ŁOS, J., "Remarks on Foundations of Probability", *Proceedings of the International Congress of Mathematicians*, Stockholm, 1962, 225–9.

ŁUKASIEWICZ, JAN, "The Logical Foundations of Probability", in *Selected Works*. ed. L. Borowski, trans. O. Wojtasiewicz, Amsterdam: North-Holland Publishing Co., 1970.

LUXEMBURG, W. A. J., (ed.) *Applications of Model Theory to Algebra, Analysis, and Probability*, New York: Holt, Rinehart and Winston, 1969.

MAZURKIEWICZ, STEFAN, "Über die Grundlagen der Wahrscheinlich-keitsrechnung I", *Monatshefte für Mathematik und Physik* 40 (1934), 343–52.

MELLOR, D. H., *Prospects for Pragmatism*, New York: Cambridge University Press, 1980.

MILLER, DAVID, "A Paradox of Information", *The British Journal for the Philosophy of Science* vol. 17, no. 1 (1966).

MONTAGUE, RICHARD, *Formal Philosophy*, ed. Richmond H. Thomason, New Haven and London: Yale University Press, 1974.

NAGEL, ERNEST, with P. Suppes and A. Tarski (eds.), *Logic, Methodology and Philosophy of Science: Proceedings of the 1960 International Logic Congress*, Stanford: Stanford University Press, 1962.

NEURATH, OTTO, RUDOLF CARNAP, and HANS HAHN, "The Scientific Conception of the World", trans. R. S. Cohen, in R. S. Cohen and M. Neurath (eds.) *Empiricism and Sociology*, Dordrecht, Boston, and London: D. Reidel Publishing Co., 1973.

PEANO, GIUSEPPE, *Selected Works of Giuseppe Peano*, trans. and ed. Hubert C. Kennedy, Toronto: University of Toronto Press, 1973.

PEARCE, GLENN. See Harper, William L.

PEIRCE, CHARLES S., "On the Doctrine of Chances, with Later Reflections", in Justus Buchler (ed.), *Philosophical Writings of Peirce*, New York: Dover Publications, Inc., 1955.

PEIRCE, CHARLES S., *The Collected Works of Charles Saunders Peirce*, vols. I–VI, ed. Charles Hartshorne and Paul Weiss, Cambridge, Mass.: Harvard University Press, 1931–5; vols. VII–VIII, ed. Arthur Burks, Cambridge, Mass.: Harvard University Press, 1958.

QUINE, W. V., "Three Grades of Modal Involvement", in W.V., Quine, *The Ways of Paradox and Other Essays*, New York: Random House, 1966.

QUINE, W. V., *Word and Object*, New York and London: The Technology Press of The Massachusetts Institute of Technology and John Wiley and Sons, Inc., 1960.

RAMSEY, FRANK PLUMPTON, "General Propositions and Causality", in R. B. Braithwaite (ed.) *The Foundations of Mathematics and Other Logical Essays*, London: Routledge and Kegan Paul Ltd., 1931.

RAMSEY, FRANK PLUMPTON, "Truth and Probability", in R. B. Braithwaite (ed.) *The Foundations of Mathematics and Other Logical Essays*, London: Routledge and Kegan Paul Ltd., 1931.

REICHENBACH, HANS, *The Theory of Probability: An Inquiry into the Logical and Mathematical Foundations of the Calculus of Probability*, trans. Ernest H. Hutten and Maria Reichenbach, (2nd edn.) Berkeley: University of California Press, 1971.

RENYI, ALFRED, *Foundations of Probability*, San Francisco: Holden-Day, Inc., 1970.

ROBINSON, ABRAHAM, *Non-standard Analysis*, Amsterdam: North-Holland Publishing Co., 1966.

ROSENBLOOM, PAUL C., *The Elements of Mathematical Logic*, New York: Dover Publications, Inc., 1950.

RUSSELL, BERTRAND, "The Philosophy of Logical Atomism", in *Logic and Knowledge*, ed. Robert Charles Marsh, London: George Allen & Unwin Ltd. and New York: The Macmillan Company, 1956.

RYLE, GILBERT, *The Concept of Mind*, London: Hutchinson Publishing Co., 1949.

SCHERVISH, MARK J., TEDDY SEIDENFELD, and JOSEPH B. KADANE, "The Extent of Non-Conglomerability of Finitely Additive Probabilities", *Zeitschrift für Wahrscheinlichkeitstheorie und verwandte Gebiete* 66 (1984), 205–26.

SCHILLP, PAUL ARTHUR, (ed.). *The Philosophy of Rudolf Carnap*, La Salle Illinois: Open Court, and London: Cambridge University Press, 1963.

SCHLICK, MORITZ, *The Problems of Ethics*, New York: Prentice-Hall, 1939.

SCOTT, DANA, and PETER KRAUSS, "Assigning Probabilities to Logical

238   BIBLIOGRAPHY

Formulas", in J. Hintikka and P. Suppes, (eds.) *Aspects of Inductive Logic*, Amsterdam: North-Holland Publishing Co., 1966.

SEIDENFELD, TEDDY. See Schervish, Mark J.

SHOENFIELD, JOSEPH R., *Mathematical Logic*, Reading, Mass.: Addison-Wesley Publishing Co., 1967.

SIKORSKI, ROMAN, *Boolean Algebras* (2nd edn.), New York: Academic Press Inc., Publishers, and Berlin–Göttingen–Heidelberg: Springer-Verlag, 1964.

SKYRMS, BRIAN, "Higher Order Coherence", unpublished typescript.

SKYRMS, BRIAN, "Higher Order Degrees of Belief", in D. H. Mellor (ed.), *Prospects for Pragmatism—Essays in Honor of F. P. Ramsey*.

SKYRMS, BRIAN, *Pragmatics and Empiricism*, New Haven and London: Yale University Press, 1984.

SMOKLER, HOWARD. See Kyburg, Henry.

STALNAKER, ROBERT, "Probability and Conditionals", in William Harper *et al.* (eds.), *Ifs*.

STEVENSON, C. L., *Ethics and Language*, New Haven: Yale University Press, 1945.

SUPPES, PATRICK, *A Probabilistic Theory of Causality*, Amsterdam: North-Holland Publishing Co., 1970.

SUPPES, PATRICK. See Nagel, Ernest.

TARSKI, ALFRED, *Logic, Semantics, Metamathematics: Papers from 1923 to 1928*, trans. J. H. Woodger, Oxford: Clarendon Press, 1956.

TARSKI, ALFRED. See Nagel, Ernest.

TARSKI, ALFRED, "The Concept of Truth in Formalised Languages", trans. J. H. Woodger, in A. Tarski, *Logic, Semantics, Metamathematics*.

VICKERS, J., *Belief and Probability*, Dordrecht: D. Reidel Publishing Co., 1976.

VICKERS, J., "Definability and Logical Structure in Frege", *Journal of the History of Philosophy* 17 (July 1979).

VICKERS, J., "Phenomenology of Partial Belief", *Grazer Philosophische Studien* 2, (1976).

VICKERS, J., "On the Phenomenology of Partial Judgment", *Grazer Philosophische Studien* vol. 2 (1976), 105–32.

VICKERS, J., "On the Reality of Chance", *PSA 1978*, 2.

VICKERS, J., "Truth, Consensus and Probability: On Peirce's Definition of Scientific Truth", *Pacific Philosophical Quarterly* 61 (1980), 183–203.

VICKERS, J., "On the Reality of Chance", in Peter D. Asquith and Ian Hacking (eds.), *PSA 1978* East Lansing, Michigan: Philosophy of Science Association (1978) vol. 2.

WATTENBERG, FRANK. See Bernstein, Allen R.

WITTGENSTEIN, LUDWIG, *Tractatus Logico-Philosophicus* (7th impression), London: Routledge and Kegan Paul Ltd., 1958.

Index